Muslim Women Speak

Muslim Women Speak

A TAPESTRY OF LIVES AND DREAMS

AMANI HAMDAN

Women's Press

Toronto

Muslim Women Speak: A Tapestry of Lives and Dreams
Amani Hamdan

First published in 2009 by
Women's Press, an imprint of Canadian Scholars' Press Inc.
180 Bloor Street West, Suite 801
Toronto, Ontario
M5S 2V6

www.womenspress.ca

Every reasonable effort has been made to identify copyright holders. Canadian Scholars' Press Inc. would be pleased to have any errors or omissions brought to its attention.

Canadian Scholars' Press Inc./Women's Press gratefully acknowledges financial support for our publishing activities from the Ontario Arts Council, the Canada Council for the Arts, the Government of Canada through the Book Publishing Industry Development Program (BPIDP), and the Government of Ontario through the Ontario Book Publishing Tax Credit Program.

Library and Archives Canada Cataloguing in Publication

Hamdan, Amani, 1973-
   Muslim women speak : a tapestry of lives and dreams / Amani Hamdan.

Includes bibliographical references.
ISBN 978-0-88961-468-0

   1. Muslim women—Canada. 2. Sex role—Religious aspects—Islam.
I. Title.
HQ1170.H248 2009   305.48'6970971   C2009-901196-4

Book design: Aldo Fierro
Cover photo by enviromantic/iStockphoto

09 10 11 12 13   5 4 3 2 1

Printed and bound in Canada by Marquis Book Printing Inc.

Contents

Prologue

There is no one right path to empowerment; there is not one right way
to enact resistance against oppressive power relations. The terms of
resistance and bids for empowerment emerge out of the specific circumstances of a particular life, and who is to say what terms and which bids
are more efficacious? What matters is the challenging of power relations. (Chaudhry, 1997, p. 449)

This passage speaks for me ...
for my resistance and empowerment....
My journey started when I was 10 years old
sitting in the first row of my Grade 4 classroom....
My teacher ignored my question ...
silenced me....

When I asked, "Why does a boy get to choose which parent
he goes with in a divorce while the girl must go with father?" ...
The teacher hushed me....

Then I knew the difference between boys and girls.
Right then I knew what it meant to be born a girl.
I knew it again when my cousin and best friends were taken out of school
to get married and start a family and raise children at the age of 16....

I know that there are others like myself.
Like JoAnne Deak's (2003) example of a girl who would stand up
for what she believed in, who would not lose her voice ...
did not grow up as a pleaser, like so many girls who silence themselves,
marginalize their own needs, or measure their worth
by their ability to win the approval of parents, teachers, friends, or
others (p. 64).

At various times I have sought the freedom.
"The freedom to spread my wings brought with it the thrill
of discovery and self-discovery" (El-Solh, 1988, p. 92).
That was the beginning of a long journey,
a journey that started one afternoon in a Grade 4 classroom....
At that moment my journey began and there was a hope....

I continue my journey.

Chapter One

ARABIAN NIGHTS: ONE MORE NIGHT

Over the past three decades, a substantial body of literature has been written about Muslim women. Yet "in many Western writings, including some scholarly writings, Muslim women have typically been constructed as one of the most oppressed groups of women in the world" (Cayer, 1996, p. 2).

This fixed, pervasive Western misconception of Muslim women appalled me as a young graduate student in Canada. Soon after my arrival in 1998, I began to question my sense of self as a Muslim woman. Although I believe that Islam, through the Holy *Quran* and the teaching of the Prophet Mohammed (Peace Be upon Him[1]) forwarded the liberation of women as early as the 7th century, I cannot deny the second-class status of women in most Muslim societies today. Yet how accurate are the prevalent representations of Muslim culture in general, and Muslim women in particular, in mainstream Western media and opinion? While scrutinizing Western academic and popular culture[2] stereotypes and their various dynamics, I identified a binary of contradiction within the ways Muslim women are portrayed:

> The prevailing images of Arab Muslim women in the occidental world seem to shift between dual paradigms, between either the image of salient beast of burden, or that of a capricious princess, the half naked ... or the shapeless figure of woman behind the veil. (Mehdid, 1993, p. 21)

Through reading a plethora of books about Islam and the West—such as Edward Said's *Orientalism* (1978), *Covering Islam: How the Media and the Experts Determine How We See the Rest of the World* (1997), and *Culture and Imperialism* (1993) and a counterpoint perspective found in Bernard Lewis's *The Middle East* (1997), *Islam and the West* (1994), and *Islam in History: Ideas, People, and Events in the Middle East* (2001)—I concluded that, historically, the status of Muslim women was used by imperialist and colonialist powers (as in Egypt and Algeria, for instance) to refer mainly to the inferiority of Islam as the dominant faith of the colonized countries.

In the Western hegemonic discourses, not only was Muslim women's status used to target Islam, but these discourses also used other images of Arabs and Muslims that commonly characterized them as anti-Western, uncivilized, backward, uneducated, illiterate, violent, and rife with men who subordinate women (L. Ahmed, 1999; Basarudin, 2002; Cayer, 1996, p. 46; Said, 1978). Such images of Arabs, Muslims, "and particularly Arab Muslim women are considered Common Knowledge," and are found in approximately 60,000 books on the Arab Orient that were published in the West between 1800 and 1950 (Nader, as cited in Hoodfar, 1993, p. 8). In other words, these images were accumulated over periods of historical eras. Moreover, much of the Western feminists' work about Muslim women either oversimplifies, mistakenly confuses cultural practices with religious doctrine, or refers to a sole interpretation of Islam and its demonization of women. Leila Ahmed[3] (1992) and John Esposito (1998) concur with Read and Bartkowski (2000) that "caricatures that portray Muslim women as submissive and backward have become more pervasive within recent years" (p. 396). Even when studied in some Western feminist discourses, Arab Muslim women are portrayed as victims of their cultural traditions and/or religion without further investigation into the patriarchal cultural practices that oppress them or the differences between cultural practices and religious teachings (Mohanty, 1991b).

Muslim women are not only negatively and constantly stereotyped but also regarded as a homogenized entity. Discourses that generalize all women based on their cultural and religious backgrounds or that isolate any one facet of identity while ignoring others (Cayer, 1996) fail to grasp the complexity of women's lives. At an academic scholarly level, most of the Western feminist discourses, and many scholarly productions in disciplines such as women's studies, anthropology, and sociology, have situated and perpetuated the views of Muslim women in a homogeneous group context that follows a monolithic culture (Alghamdi, 2002). The uniqueness of the Arab Muslim women's cultural context is often overlooked (Mohanty, 1991a, 1991b; Tsing, 1993).

Accordingly, Cayer (1996) states that,

> Muslim women's identities and positionalities are multiple, shifting, and produced within various configurations and contexts of power and meanings. Therefore, any attempt to define them within confined and bounded notions of "community," "culture" or gender, whether constructed within

the group and the wider Canadian society or with academic [sic], only serve
to undermine the complexity of their lives. (p. 188)

Another example is provided by Chandra Talpade Mohanty (1991a), who states
that "Feminist writings [on Muslim women] discursively colonize the material and historical heterogeneities of the lives of women in the 'Third World,'
thereby producing a composite, singular 'third world woman'" (p. 53).[4] Indeed,
the mere categorization of "Third World Women" denies the heterogeneity of
various lifestyles and perspectives. Within a "Third World Women" category,
Muslim women have rarely been studied as subjects having their own voices,
agency, choices, and critical perspectives (Cayer, 1996; Mohanty, 1991b). However, many do not have the opportunity to "encounter the dominant discourses
that speak to their lives" (Toress, 1991, p. 285). Like Mani (1992), Cayer (1996),
and other Muslim feminists, I disagree with the homogeneity attributed to
Muslims, particularly Muslim women. I argue that such a view is an unfair
limitation of a complex and intriguing group of people.

Therefore, this homogeneity needs to be deconstructed and the cultural
historical specificities of Muslim women's lives must be considered (Cayer,
1996). The heterogeneity of Muslims, and thus Muslim women, needs to be
unveiled as they are geographically, historically, politically, economically,
and ideologically diverse.

Some Eurocentric feminist scholars who have study Muslim women have
focused primarily on issues of gender when trying to understand Muslim
women. By focusing solely on the issue of gender, they have largely excluded
the contexts, experiences, and perspectives of women from Arab Muslim backgrounds and all women from non-European and non-Christian
backgrounds (Cayer, 1996, p. 180). According to Cayer (1996) and Abdo
(2002), some books on Muslim women's gender construction carried out
by Western scholars have often overlooked these women's specific contexts,
experiences, and perspectives.

Tsing's (1993) assertion that women are cross-cultural commentators
(p. 221) is a viable framework in ending the "homogeneity of classical
understanding" (p. 223) of Muslim women—the very motivation for my
exploration of Arab Muslim women's narratives. Cayer (1996) encourages my endeavour by emphasizing that "any analyses that seek to break
homogenous notions of Muslim women, so called 'Third World Women'
must begin with the *narratives of women* [italics added], situated within the
social, political, material, and historical contexts that inform their lives,
in whatever way that these contexts may apply" (pp. 5–6). In a vigilant account, Eleanor Doumato (1996) asserts that "negative perceptions of Mus-

lim women stemmed from the fact that all of the literature about Muslim women was written by Western women and men who did not understand or did not want to understand Muslim societies" (p. 12). This requires the persistent efforts of Arab Muslim women to oppose the "uncritical" perpetuation of stereotypes in many Western discourses. In saying this, Cayer (1996) argues that through minority discourses (i.e., narratives) the diverse gender issues challenged by Muslim women in a variety of social sites will be revealed. In concurring with Said (1978) that it is the responsibility of indigenous people to provide their narratives to counter the vision of outsiders, the following nine narratives will allow me to offer Muslim women's various perceptions. These narratives by Arab Muslim women will also explore how gender issues intersect and profoundly influence the Arab Muslim women's social realities, as well as their educational experiences in Arab Muslim Middle Eastern societies and within Canada.

Focusing on various Arab Muslim women's narratives, I juxtapose these with Western assumptions of the homogeneity of Muslim women. I argue that the discussions and difference in viewpoints among the women interviewed will provide evidence of the heterogeneity of Muslim women: "The differences among Muslim women are surfacing, thus the imagined homogeneity of the Muslim community is falling apart" (Cayer, 1996, p. 26). The narratives will propose how Muslim women's experiences are diversified by their class, gender perceptions, life experiences, and education.

The abundance of studies by Muslim scholars about Muslim women focuses on traditional perceptions of women within Muslim communities and in Arab Muslim societies, neglecting to consider the increasing figures of Muslim immigrants to Western societies (Camarota, 2002). Only in the past decade have some studies by insider Muslim scholars (males and females) directed attention to the experiences of young Arab Muslims in the United States and in Canada (as in Abu-Laban, 1980; Sarroub, 2005). Because relatively few studies have been conducted about Arab Muslim communities in North America, little has been discovered about individual struggles, achievements, and adaptations to life in the West.

In this book, the disentanglement of cultural traditions and societal norms from religious gender discourses is critically examined in terms of its relevance to Arab Muslim women's experience. My analysis incorporates women's knowledge of the way in which their gender is constructed in the Arab culture, and how this differs from the way their gender is constructed by Islamic teachings.

This book will also assist Muslim and Western scholars interested in studying Arab Muslim women by providing a necessary alternative to the stereotypical images of Arab Muslim women as shadowy figures in exotic *harems*.[5] Through providing an alternative perception of Muslim women, these narratives will be particularly empowering to young Muslim women in the diaspora. As Zine's (2003) book about Muslim female youth within a Canadian context indicates, "Muslim girls need to have more empowering narratives available to them" (p. 448).

The narratives will not only foster new and deeper understandings of Arab Muslim women, they may also "create bridges of appreciation between Western women and Arab Muslim women" (Ali, 2000, p. 6). Readers can appreciate and admire the creativity and complexity within Arab Muslim women's lives. The mini-autobiographies of the participants will contribute to a fuller understanding of the issues relating to gender discourse in the Arab Muslim societies where these women were raised (i.e., Egypt, Libya, Lebanon, Saudi Arabia, Abu Dhabi, and Sudan).[6] This study will also help form new understandings of how Arab Muslim women perceive women's education, what education means to them, and whether education, in their opinion, helps to improve their positions in society. Following Bateson (1990), this type of book will have implications in how members of the next generation of Arab Muslim women are educated and in how they raise their children.

Educators can also draw from this work to learn more about Arab Muslim women's lives through hearing individual voices and perspectives. While care must be taken not to make generalizations from this study of all Arabs, all Muslims, or all Arab Muslims, the stories these women share of their experiences in their native societies and in Canada may be applicable to other contexts, such as in planning strategies to assist immigrant students.

This work will help provide a balance in the way Muslim women are presented in Western scholarly literature: "We need to hear the life stories from those who are underrepresented [or misrepresented] to help establish a balance in the literature and expand the options for us all on the cultural level" (Atkinson, 1998, p. 19). My venture to "re-write these scripts in more positive and empowering ways involves re-mapping the discursive boundaries through which Muslim women identities are circumscribed and defined" (Zine, 2003, p. 448), something I hope to achieve through this book.

SETTING THE STAGE

This endeavour is an exploration of how Arab Muslim women perceive themselves, and how they view their gender roles after having attended Canadian academic institutions. This book takes a different stand from the underlying assumptions of some of the current literature on Arab Muslim women's lives. Some of this literature (Bardach, 1993; Lewis, 1994; Mabro, 1991) indicates that women from "Third World" societies (e.g., Arab Muslim and Middle Eastern societies) will be "emancipated and liberated" through Westernization and experiencing Canadian education and living. In my view, Arab Muslim women who have immigrated to live and study in Canada have moved from one form of "patriarchy" to another—only the context differs. Like many feminist scholars (e.g., Gaskell & McLaren, 1991; D. Smith, 1987a, 1987b; L. Smith, 1999), I argue that Western women—Canadian women, in this context—are not necessarily "emancipated and liberated." Indeed, I will explore the extent to which aspects of living and studying in Canada may have led Arab Muslim women participants to think differently about themselves and their lives.

More importantly, the narratives debunk various myths surrounding Arab Muslim women's realities. The Arab Muslim women's narratives presented here highlight the heterogeneity of their perceptions, their abilities to create diverse models of reality, and their competency to make decisions. What is particularly fascinating is the participants' strong commitment to their faith and their abilities to distinguish between Islamic teachings and traditional cultural practices.

These stories from Arab Muslim women create a rich and textured sort of artwork, much like a tapestry. While "quilting" these colourful narratives, I revisited a few personal and insightful experiences, not as an author or researcher, but as a woman listening to other women with whom I share a religious background, language, cultural traditions, and life experiences. Although the intersection of Arabic culture with political, historical, social, economic, and patriarchal forces generated a more conflicting platform for women than those presented by Islam, nearly all of the women interviewed were more inclined to challenge and resist, rather than to live passively in a ready-made world. Not only have I sought the narratives of Arab Muslim women, but I have also included fragments of my own story. As hooks (1988) argues, sharing one's past and one's memories through a narrative allows others to view these experiences from a different perspective, not as singular isolated events, but as part of a continuum.

This project has been, by far, one of the most enriching of my life, informing me of what it means to "engage with a more open notion of Muslim, [a notion] that is informed not only by religion" (Khan, 2000, p. 130), but also by the experiences of indigenous people. I learned a great deal from these women, who are subjects of their history. Some aspects of my experience differed from theirs, while some of my long-standing uncertainties were assuaged. Listening to these women gave me a better understanding of issues that even I, an Arab Muslim woman raised in an Arab Muslim society, could not fully appreciate. These women's stories, which I perceive as a platform for empowerment, had a profound impact on my personal perspective. I will fondly remember the looks in their eyes, their gestures, and their words—not only what has been documented in this book, but their enlightening viewpoints, compelling stories, and uniqueness as people to whom I feel connected on a personal level.

THE BOOK'S CONTRIBUTION

The importance of this book is twofold. First, it contributes to a better understanding of Arab Muslim women as significant members of Canadian society by exploring their views and perceptions about their lives. Such understandings not only broaden the knowledge about Arab Muslim women's lives and their social positions, but also provide an impetus for improvement in the way Canadian society views Arab Muslim communities in Canada. Second, after reviewing pertinent literature, I found that, thus far, there have been no other attempts to write a book narrated by an Arab Muslim woman that studies Arab Muslim women's lives in Canada. " Feminist scholars who have been concerned to document and analyze the ways that *women* [italics in original] have shaped discourses on gender through their intellectual production as well as through their everyday lives" (Booth, 2001, p. 174) will also benefit from my book. This book will also shed light on the controversial debate about women and gender in Islam by looking beyond Western writing and outsiders' assumptions about Islamic tenets of women's issues. It also reveals the various standpoints of some Arab Muslim women within gender discourses regarding their rights, roles, and responsibilities as Muslim women.

This book is among the first contributions in a growing body of literature on Arab Muslim women in Canada, offering a glimpse into their lives. Subsequently, this book will make an important contribution to Canadian literature on immigrant Arab Muslim women, and to literature on Muslim women as a whole.

NOTES

1.   As a Muslim, the phrase "Peace Be upon Him" should be said and written after the mention of the Prophet Mohammed (PBUH).

2. It is interesting to note that even Western scholarly literature that studies Muslim women of Arabic origin often wrongly accepts that all Arabs are Muslims, or that all Muslims are of Arabic origin. This generalization is based on two false assumptions. One assumption is that the majority of Muslims live in Arab countries when, in fact, the majority live in Indonesia and Pakistan, which have the two largest Muslim populations. The second assumption is that all Arab-speaking countries are followers of Islam. In fact, there are Christians and Jews among Arab-speaking populations. Muslims are diverse in their language, culture, ethnicity, and their approach to faith (Sunni, Shii, Sufi, and Ismaili). For a detailed discussion on Sunni and Shii, see Esposito (1988). These oversights may have come about as a result of White domination (i.e., colonial discourses) in the fields of anthropology and colonial studies, and of their narrow perceptions of the Arab Muslim world (Esposito, 1988). In fact, Arabness represents a set of values and traditions that are common to people in the Arab world and that have been passed down through generations. It also signifies a particular world view marked by attachment to family, for instance (Nagel, 2002, p. 271). An Arab entity is like a Muslim entity in that both should not be seen as fixed categories.

3. Leila Ahmed is among the first Arab Muslim feminist scholar to analyze the ignorance of Western feminists regarding Arab Muslim women's struggles (L. Ahmed, 1989, 1992, 1999).

4. This term has been used to identify women in the West with origins in the geopolitical definition of the so-called "Third World" (Cayer, 1996). "Third World Women" and "Third World" are used to contrast and contest the term "Western" women and feminists (Mohanty, 1991a). The term is limiting as it overlooks the focus of feminists in the "Third World," which is "gender in relation to race and/or class as part of a broader liberation struggle" (Mohanty, 1991a, p. 54). Further, Mohanty argues that by insisting on using the phrase "Third World Women," non-Western and non-White women are frozen in time, space, and history. Women are being judged based on the criteria of a White, Western hierarchy. I add that the term "Third World" neglects the varieties of location and struggles related to these women in what is referred as the "Third World." The phrase is often associated with "underdevelopment, oppressive value systems, high illiteracy, rural and urban poverty, religious fanaticism, and overpopulation of particular and highly diverse backgrounds: such as African, Middle Eastern, Asian, and Latin American" (Mohanty, 1991a, p. 47).

5. White male scholars who are referred to by Edward Said as "Orientalist" contributed to the concept of *harem* and the exotic images of Arab Muslim women.

6. Morooj, Nora, and Fadwa expressed their enthusiasm for taking part in this book and constantly referred to it as an enriching experience.

8

Chapter Two

MUSLIM WOMEN IN NORTH AMERICA

LOCATING MYSELF IN THE DISCOURSE[1]

My interest in exploring Arab Muslim women's lives and dreams stems from the fact that I am a Muslim woman who lived in Saudi Arabia during my undergraduate years and moved to Canada to pursue graduate studies. My years in Canada as a graduate student have provided me with incredible opportunities to develop a critical sense of self. Throughout my schooling in both countries, my gender identity as a woman was shaped and reshaped. Patriarchy and racism are inherent in the construction of my identity as a Muslim woman. My multifaceted and rich experiences enabled me to contest dominant perceptions of gender discourse both in my native society and in Canada. I emphasize that as much as these experiences have been personally challenging, they have also been enriching and ultimately exciting. I also maintain that it is a privilege to be a member of both worlds—Saudi and Canadian—which are equally rich and have greatly contributed toward my personal growth.

Understanding my life experiences, as well as those of Arab Muslim women, is imperative because "they allow us to examine prior ways of being and present ways of becoming. These experiences also allow us to reflect on the social and cultural context that influences these processes of being and becoming" (Qin, 2000, p. 75).

WHY ARAB MUSLIM WOMEN?

Although the number of immigrants coming to Canada from Arab Muslim nations is increasing, I found that the literature focusing on

Arab[2] Muslim women living in Canada and their gender perceptions is limited. Studies focusing exclusively on the connection between Arab Muslim women's educational pursuits and their gender perceptions, and how their gender perceptions may have changed as a result of living in two different cultures, are rarely conducted. Additionally, the factors that may influence an Arab Muslim woman's educational pursuits are seldom investigated.

Through women's narratives I explore possible common themes, similarities, and differences in gender perceptions of educated Arab Muslim women from diverse Middle Eastern societies. In particular, I explore how Arab Muslim women studying in Canada perceive the impact of their experiences in Canadian educational institutions, considering their perceptions in relation to their role as women.

ARAB MUSLIMS IN CANADA: HISTORICAL PERSPECTIVE

According to Statistics Canada in 2005, the number of immigrants from Arab Muslim countries is steadily increasing. The Canadian population in 1996 included 188,430 Arab Muslims, and this number is on the rise (as cited in Smick, 2006). Since 1999, Islam has been among the top 10 religious denominations in Canada.

The first wave of Muslims immigrated to Canada in the early 20th century, and continued during World War II. Numbers were small, and most came from Lebanon, Syria, Palestine, Jordan, and Turkey (B. Abu-Laban, 1980; S.M. Abu-Laban, 1991). The second wave of Muslim immigrants arrived following World War II as a result of political strife and upheaval in their native countries, and continued until 1967. The majority were from Lebanon, Syria, Palestine, Jordan, and Iraq, and the remainder from India and Pakistan (Haddad, 1978). Most of these early immigrants settled in Ontario; in fact, Ontario has the largest Muslim population of all the Canadian provinces.

Immigration dynamics and Canada's immigration policies during these periods are worth noting. During the second wave of immigration, between 1950 and 1967, immigration policy was based on the quota system, which encouraged immigrants from the upper-middle class with professional backgrounds, such as lawyers, doctors, and skilled technicians (Awan, 1989; Azmi, 2001), and was based on how closely the prospective immigrants ranked in racial, cultural, and linguistic similarities to the British Protestant ideal (Haddad, 1978; Hamdani, 1991).

Two points warrant emphasis. First, up until the second wave of immigration, Muslim immigrants were predominantly Arabs from Lebanon,

Syria, Palestine, and Jordan who could "pass," due to their light skin, as members of other Mediterranean groups such as Italians and Greeks. Second, emphasizing the socio-economic status of the early Arab immigrants who were upper-middle-class professionals, the third wave of Muslim immigrants arrived after 1967 following the replacement of the quota system within the points system. Within the point system, fewer requirements were necessary to be accepted as an immigrant (B. Abu-Laban, 1980).

Research indicates that in 1997, of all immigrants coming to Canada, 18 percent were from Africa and the Middle East (Agnew, 2002). Since 2001 there has been a 25 percent increase in the Muslim population and, according to Statistics Canada (2005), between 1990 and 2001 the number of immigrants from Muslim countries increased by 128 percent (as cited in Smick, 2006). In addition, "two percent of Canada's 31 million are Muslims" (Nimer, 2002, p. 21) and two-thirds of the entire Canadian Muslim population reside in Ontario. The Muslim population comprises South Asians (37 percent), Arabs (21 percent), and West Indians (14 percent), with the remainder from Africa, China, and other countries. Also, in the past 20 years there has been a 400 percent increase in the number of Canadians who say that they are members of the Islamic faith. In fact, since the 1991 census, there has been a 122 percent increase in those of the Islamic faith.

The impact of such large numbers of a particular immigrant group on Canadian society cannot be underestimated. Further, given the way in which women are positioned in Arab Muslim societies, and in Canadian society, it is important to examine the perceptions of Arab Muslim women of their role within this new context.

ISLAMIC ESSENCE ON GENDER

What stand do authentic Islamic resources, the *Quran* and *Hadith*, take on gender issues? Can one study gender issues from the perspectives of the *Quran* and the authentic *Hadith*? According to Ahmed (1992), "Islam and *Quran* insistently stressed the importance of the spiritual and ethical dimensions of being and the equality of all individuals" (p. 66). I will briefly explore the representations of women in early Islamic history[3] and highlight the extent to which Islamic religious beliefs promote gender biases. To what extent do Islamic teachings about women value their educational, social, and political participation? Note that "religious text (or any text for that matter) implies an interpretation and, hence, the possibility of various and diverse readings" (al-Faruqi, 2000, p. 76).

As a practising Muslim woman, I note a difference between the Islamic essence as taught in the Holy *Quran* and the Prophet's (PBUH) *Sunna*, and the misogynistic interpretations of these texts, which have long been predominant in Arab Muslim societies. Therefore, I agree that,

> Islamic theology has stressed that gender roles should be fair and more egalitarian than is seen in most Muslim nations today. In the early days of Islam, gender roles were more egalitarian in nature. Women were encouraged to attain an education in both religious and social domains. Preference was not given to men over women in educational pursuits and both sexes were equally encouraged to acquire an education. (Jawad, 1998, as cited in Schvaneveldt, Kerpelman & Schvaneveldt, 2005, p. 80)

I argue that gender inequality and the subordination of women in many Muslim societies have no basis in the foundational essence of Islam. Women's confinement within the private sphere was not a part of early Islamic ideology and/or practices. Nancy Shilling (1980) compares the status of women in the *Quran* to the current status of women in Muslim societies, which she sees as being poles apart. Shilling (1980) argues that the Prophet Mohammed (PBUH) was the first teacher for women and men, in early Islamic days, did not restrict women's lives to narrow domesticity, a practice that is common in some Muslim societies today (p. 127).

Many scholars do not dispute that the Prophet Mohammed (PBUH) encouraged women to participate in building a new Islamic society. One of many examples in early Islam is Khadija,[4] the first wife of the Prophet Mohammed (PBUH) and also his first believer. She was an independent entrepreneur who had employed the Prophet Mohammed (PBUH) during one of her merchant trips prior to his prophecy. She was impressed with his honesty and made him a marriage proposal. Following their marriage, Khadija continued her business (Arebi, 1994, p. 17).

A wealth of historical incidents in the early days of Islam involving wives and daughters of the Prophet (PBUH) and his companions serves as a great example of women's participation and presence in the public spheres. Both the Holy *Quran* and *Sunna* mention women as active participants in public life:

> Islam did not intend to exclude women from collective social activities. It is reported that during the Prophet's [PBUH] lifetime, women not only nursed the wounded but also fought in battles. During the Prophet's [PBUH] lifetime, women left their homes frequently to satisfy their economic, intellectual, and religious needs. (Dangor, 2001, p. 122)

Nowadays, many Muslim women are inspired by the Prophet's wives and daughters (Peace Be upon Them). Recent examples of women in the Muslim world who have achieved political influence and powerful political positions (e.g., Indonesia and Pakistan) indicate there is an immense breadth of interpretation of Islamic teachings to women, of Islamic sources, and of Islamic law (Marcotte, 2003; Roald, 2001).

Moreover, it is significant to note that the Prophet Mohammed (PBUH) was a father to four daughters at a time when having daughters was shameful and infanticide was common. Monogamy and the prohibition of female infanticide are two of the often-cited innovations of Islam (Leo, 2005, p. 130). Many argue that Islam was introduced to eradicate traditions that violated respect for human beings. For instance, the tradition of burying girls alive was common before the advent of Islam. Under Islam and during the Prophet Mohammed's (PBUH) time, however, this practice was prohibited by a divine order. Arab Muslim societies, like many others, inherited complex power structures that reflect inequalities in gender, race, and social class. The Prophet Mohammed (PBUH), however, always advised his companions to respect women and grant them the right to be active in both public and private spheres.

In 1989 Mohammed Al-Ghazali published a book that focuses on verses from the Holy *Quran*, *Sunna*, and narratives in the Islamic history that traditional interpreters used to argue women's exclusion from any public roles. Al-Ghazali's book concluded that there were "several authentic juristic interpretations of Islamic law which allowed women to serve in any public role—as judges, ambassadors, cabinet members, and rulers" (as cited in Mooney, 1998, p. 98).

Another decree that caused disturbance for many traditional scholars came from a well-known, contemporary, progressive Muslim[5] scholar, Yusuf Al-Qaradwai. He issued a religious decree in which he suggested that women could seek out parliamentary offices, be judges, and issue religious decrees. Al-Qaradwai relied on the Holy *Quran*'s many verses regarding this, which are well known to Muslims (Ghadbian, 1997; Mooney, 1998). In the *Quran* many female leaders such as Bilqis, the Queen of Sheba, Merriam, Jesus's mother (Peace Be Upon Them), and many others were represented as astute and competent women. Moreover, Al-Qaradwai criticized those Muslim scholars who tend to exclude women from public spheres and endorse negativity against women in the name of Islam. In his book, *The Voice of a Woman in Islam*, Al-Qaradwai cites several of the misogynistic *Hadith*, claiming them to be false or weak (Mooney, 1998).

Al-Ghazali, Abdu, Qaradwai, Kazim, and many other progressive Muslim thinkers, both male and female, believe that women and men in

Islam are crucial members of society. Progressive Muslim gender ideology, unlike secular or traditional Muslim ideology, acknowledges the need for progressive gender discourse and the need for women's presence and active involvement in public spheres. Obtaining education, participating in all fields of knowledge, and finding employment are all within the framework of Islamic teachings to women.

Although the Holy *Quran* and the *Hadith* are foundational resources of the Islamic tenets, there is no single definitive interpretation of each, or of both. Muslims do not have a single, divine interpretation of the Holy *Quran* or *Sunna*, and I argue that the lack of a sole divine interpretation is a testament to the flexibility of Islam as a faith. In other words, the absence of a definite interpretation of the Islamic divine text means that Muslims are encouraged to interpret the Holy *Quran*[6] in light of contemporary contexts. Many Muslim scholars argue that "the *Quran* and *Hadith* are translated [interpreted] within the textual and historical contexts" (Nimer, 2002, p. 3). Therefore, the interpretations provided by progressive Muslim scholars in this century are valid because they are inclusive of the historical and contextual aspects that were not present in the life of the Prophet (PBUH) and his companions (Ali, 2000; Al-Qaradawi, 2005; Nimer, 2002).

STATUS OF MUSLIM WOMEN

Today, Muslim women are not accorded the elevated status enjoyed by their predecessors. The status of Muslim women in most societies today, unfortunately, carries certain negative connotations. A girl's parents decide if she will be educated—and for how long—and whom she will marry and at what age. After marriage, her husband and often her mother-in-law (in many Arab Muslim rural cultures) make almost all decisions; her husband decides whether or not she may work, as well as the type of employment she may undertake (Dangor, 2001).

Many historians relate the decline of women's status in Muslim societies to a certain period of Islamic history, particularly the Abbasid Empire (846–1740), which is indeed known as "the dark period of Islamic History" (Afifi, 1993, p. 78, as cited in Al-Manea, 1984, p. 51). Historians have indicated that many *Hadiths* that expressed women's social inferiority were fabricated in the "Abbasid Ruling Period":

> The high status granted to women by the *Quranic* reforms which prevailed during the early Islamic period did not last long. Firstly, certain

14

pre Islamic customs reappeared, especially during the Abbasid period;
secondly, various social attitudes infiltrated Islamic culture from con-
quered peoples and were assimilated as norms and identified with
Islam. Hence, the status of Muslim women started to deteriorate. This
was accelerated by catastrophic historical events such as the Mongol
and Turkish invasions and the ensuing decline of the Islamic civilization. The ambience generated by these conditions served to undermine
the position of Muslim women who became less and less a part of general
social life.... (Jawad, 1998, p. 24)

Thus, denying women's education, limiting the role of women to that of
obedient wives, and banning them from public spheres originated from
cultures in the post-Islamic era, and did not originate in the Holy *Quran*
or authentic *Sunna*. Islamic sacred texts have been interpreted[7] to fit tribal
traditions that existed both in the pre-Islamic and post-Islamic periods.

    While both the Holy *Quran* and *Hadith* give distinct instruction concern-
ing a woman's role and position, there is diversity when implementing this
teaching inside and outside Arab Muslim societies. According to some
interpretations, men are superior to women because they have more knowledge and power (Siddiqi, 1991; Stowasser, 1994). Although interpreters
accept the notion of radically distinct physical and emotional differences
between the sexes, "this implies no superiority or advantage before the
law ..." (Badawi, 1995). Even minority traditionalist Muslim interpreters
would advocate that women work alongside men "as educators, scholars,
and experts" (Ibn-Hisham, 1978, as cited in Al-Manea, 1984, p. 39).

    This assumption of a higher status for men over women originates from
narrow interpretations of the *Quranic* verses, Prophetic (PBUH) narrations,
and Islamic philosophical and theological literature, texts from which pas-
sages have been taken out of context (Altorki, 1988): For instance, "Women
have been taught that the law of God orders them to stay close to their homes
and unreservedly to obey their husbands" (Al-Manea, 1984, p. 25).

    While the Holy *Quran* generally advocates that men provide for women,
this does not give men unconditional authority over women (Barlas, 2002;
Al-Hibri, 1982; Wadud, 1992), nor does it mean that women cannot provide
for themselves (Naseef, 1999). The Holy *Quran* does not prohibit women's
political participation, the right to vote, or the right to attain leadership.
The explanation presented in Wadud's[8] interpretation of *Quwama*[9] and in
the *Quranic* teachings to women brings new perspectives that are different
from those long offered by Muslim men. For example, *Quwama* is mentioned
once in the following verse:

> Men have *Quwama* over women, [on the basis] of what Allah has [pre-
> ferred] some of them over others, and [on the basis] of what they spend of
> their property (for the support of women). So good women are [*qanitat*],
> guarding in secret that which Allah has guarded. (The Holy *Quran*, 4:34)

Many Muslims perceive that this is the most important verse regarding
the relationship between men and women (Wadud, 1999, p. 70; Ali, 2000,
pp. 66–67). Traditional interpretation suggests that Allah preferred men
over women. It also suggests superiority, authority, guardianship, and an
"unconditional indication of the preference" of men over women (Wadud,
1999, p. 71; Barlas, 2002, p. 186). However, progressive interpreters argue
that "the [traditional] interpretation of the verse is unwarranted and incon-
sistent with other Islamic teachings ... the interpretation is unwarranted
because there is no reference in the passage to male physical or intellectual superiority" (Al-Hibri, 1982, pp. 217–218; Hassan, 1999; Wadud, 1992,
1999; Barlas, 2002). Ali (2000) adds that "The major concern for *Quran*, in
the early Islamic era, was the betterment of woman's position by establish-
ing her legal capacity, granting her economic rights (dower, inheritance,
etc.) and thus raising her social status" (p. 67).

Despite these teachings in the Holy *Quran*, Doumato (1991) suggests that
pre-existing Christian customs and Roman laws, as well as pre-Islamic
customary practices in Arabia, influenced early Muslim views of women
and family. When family laws were codified and modernized across the
Muslim world[10] much later,[11] they were based on a combination of the
Islamic legal schools (Hanafi, Maleki, Hanbali, and Shafii), pre-Islamic or
tribal customs, and Western (French, Swiss, Belgian) legal systems, which
are related to the colonization of some Arab Muslim countries (i.e., Egypt
and Lebanon). Muslim family law gave male family members extensive
control over key decisions affecting "their" women's lives.

For instance, Muslim women's legal and religious right to inherit, own,
and dispose of property has often been circumvented by male relatives, including brothers, uncles, or husbands (Moghadam, 2003, 2004). Another
traditional view of women's roles held by many Muslim religious scholars,
based on rigid interpretations, is that a woman's main and only role is that
of a mother and wife. This view prescribes that a woman holding any public
role is a threat to the social order. Therefore, Muslim women are encouraged
to value traditional roles such as that of homemaker and mother, and careers outside of the home have traditionally been considered a male domain
(Al-Smadoni, 1991; Jawad, 1998; Mernissi, 1987; Schvaneveldt, Kerpelman
& Schvaneveldt, 2005; Walther, 1993).

Most of the customs surrounding the current status of Arab women are not the direct result of *Quranic* prescription or Islamic legal practice. The *Quran* actually improved the status of women over what it was in Pre-Islamic times.... But popular Islam has come to view women as unfit for public responsibility. This view, rather than the *Quranic* one, has come to be the operative concept that circumscribes women's role in the male dominant tradition of the contemporary Arab world. (Shilling, 1980, p. 127)

If women are granted rights, roles, and responsibilities in the *Quran* and *Sunna* (in *Hadith* and *Seera*), and if they are highly valued and given positions of respect, why are women today, in most Arab Muslim societies, subordinated by men?

Moreover, many male Muslim religious scholars view encouragement of women to move beyond the prevailing physical and mental seclusion to participate in public life, and therefore interacting with men, as destructive to Muslim society (Al-Manea, 1984). It is important to note that for some male and female Muslims, the similarities of societal functions or roles may lead to competition between the two sexes, which may destabilize and disturb the relations between men and women (Hessini, 1994). According to Paul Schvaneveldt, Jennifer Kerpelman, and Jayd Schvaneveldt (2005),

Islamic fundamentalists[12] argue that women's liberation and the education of women will create immorality through corrupting their thinking and diverting their attention away from the essential role as good wives and mothers. In essence, the traditional view is that female liberation will create instability in both the home and society. (p. 81)

Progressive Muslim scholars argue that both the practice of women's veiling, which is regarded as an Islamic practice to subordinate women, as well as their seclusion, were adopted by upper-class Arabs from previous civilizations as a sign of social status and prestige (Lerner, 1986; Shabaan, 1995). Indeed, Keddie (1991) asserts that "veiling and seclusion were known in the Greco-Roman world, pre-Islamic Iran and Byzantine empire" (p. 3). This implies that women's seclusion from public life, which is prevalent in some Muslim societies, is a pre-Islamic custom. However, I argue that "women's public visibility during the Prophet Mohammed's [PBUH] own lifetime undermines the arguments for seclusion" (Hashim, 1999, p. 10). Islamic conservative, misogynistic, and narrow interpretations that involve the seclusion of women are rooted more in tribal culture than in religion (Engineer, 1992).

17

Progressive Muslim male and female scholars argue for the need to adapt to the changing world in light of new interpretations of the *Quran* and the *Hadith*, particularly in relation to gender and women as these areas seem to be major areas of controversy within Muslim communities worldwide. Historically, cultural traditional practices that discriminate against women have been accepted as religious beliefs, while Islamic teachings and practices that favour women are continually ignored (El-Nahhas, 1999; Mooney, 1998). For example, female circumcision is a cultural practice that has no basis in religious texts, yet the practice has been erroneously given a religious formulation (Alghamdi, 2002; Mooney, 1998). Unfortunately, these traditional views of women's roles and status have prevailed and are thoroughly embedded through different means, and Islam is persistently used to justify these views.

According to El-Nahhas (1999), the traditional and the progressive interpretations have remained two opposing paradigms since the early days of Islam. Each paradigm conceptualizes women's rights and public and private roles differently. One attempts to modernize women's status, rights, and roles based on the perceived inclusive, egalitarian nature of the foundation of Islamic society (El-Nahhas, 1999; Mooney, 1998; Stowasser, 1993). The other paradigm attempts to maintain the patriarchal nature of Arab society that existed before the advent of Islam, and was reasserted centuries earlier by a number of cultural practices (El-Nahhas, 1999). Supporters of this paradigm root their argument in a traditional interpretation of the Holy *Quran*, while the reformists root their argument in progressive interpretations. The problem lies in how the holy texts—the *Quran* and the *Hadith* that inform the *Sharia*—are interpreted. In many Muslim women's views, including the participants in this book, gender equality does exist in the Holy *Quran* and *Sunna*; as these women see it, however, the problem lies in the malpractice, or misunderstanding, of these sacred texts. Like Ali (2000), I argue that "many rights of Muslim women have become subsumed in the gendered institutions of society, including its legal institutions and the need to unravel these rights by interpreting the basic texts of Islam from a women's perspective" (p. 5) is crucial.

MARRIAGE IN ISLAM

Another crucial area of focus is women's rights in marriage—the *Quranic* perception of marriage—is worth mentioning in this context. The *Quran* exhorts all single people to marry if possible, and the purpose of marriage, as stated in the *Quran*, is, first and foremost, to bring life and mercy, which is interpreted as passion, friendship, companionship, understanding, tolerance, and forgiveness to the married couple (Dahl, 1997, p. 49). Islam views marriage as an institution in which human beings find tranquility and affection with each other. The *Quran* says:

> And among His signs is that He created for you mates from among your-selves, that you may dwell in tranquillity with them, and He has put love and mercy between your hearts. Undoubtedly in these are signs for those who reflect. (*Quran*, 30:21)

The Muslim wife is meant to be a companion to her husband, not a maid. However, many Muslims, both male and female, are unaware that the *Quran* stresses the importance of the human side of the marital relation-ship. Rather, they believe that the major purpose of marriage is to benefit the family and not the individual couple (Dahl, 1997, p. 103; Schvaneveldt, Kerpelman & Schvaneveldt, 2005):

> In many traditional families, girls are pulled from school before they reach puberty, are secluded, then married off. Young women are expected to suc-cumb to the traditional pattern of subordination to her husband and have limits placed on their outside activities. In many cases her parents make the final decisions, and she simply obliges—although Islam requires a woman to have her consent in marriage. (Dangor, 2001, p. 115)

In Islam, a woman must not be forced into marriage—her consent is always necessary.[13] For instance, "if a minor has been married without her consent, she can ask for her marriage to be annulled on reaching the age of majority" (Omran, 1992, p. 15). Nevertheless, "many Muslim marriages have been contracted in contravention of these injunctions as women are frequently married off against their will" (Harris, 2004, p. 32).

Through the institution of marriage, women's basic rights—such as the right to education, financial independence, and freedom of self-fulfillment—have been denied. A fulfilled woman was, in fact, viewed as one who married, served her husband well, and bore him children. This view is still common today, though it contradicts the Islamic view of women and marriage (Al-Hibri, 2000).

Extremist, misogynistic Muslim scholars view women's activities as be-ing confined to the home on the basis of their interpretation of the *Hadith*: "The woman is a guardian of her husband's home and she is accountable for

19

it." From this *Hadith*, traditionalists argue that women should be veiled and should leave the home only for urgent purposes (i.e., to visit the hospital) (Dangor, 2001, p. 121). This narrow interpretation suggests that the Holy *Quran* also implies that women are allowed to leave the home strictly for essential needs, yet many Muslim male and female scholars oppose this limited view of marital life:

> There is nothing in the scripture that women should limit themselves to the roles of wives and mothers. Indeed there is a great deal to suggest that women, as well as men, should be educated and women have the right to work even if men hold the primary responsibility for the family economic support. (Harris, 2004, p. 33)

Today, "Muslim women become aware of the influence of cultural, traditional, and patriarchal values on their status" (Dangor, 2001, p. 127). My research reflects a shifting attitude toward women's role with regard to public life and family responsibilities from Arab Muslim Canadian women's perspectives, yet for some participants in this book, "the preservation of their traditional Arab Muslim identity constitutes an essential element in their quest for a more meaningful existence" (Dangor, 2001, p. 127). These variations of Arab Muslim women's views could be based on "differences in age, educational background, economic position [class], and employment" (Dangor, 2001, p. 127).

EDUCATION

Prophet Mohammed's (PBUH) views on women's education are evident in statements such as: "The search of knowledge is a duty for every Muslim male and female," and "Seek knowledge from the cradle to the grave."[14] These statements serve as a platform to oppose the claim that seems to be dominant in the work of many traditional Muslim scholars—that, according to Islam, a woman's place is in the home. Education is a religious obligation for every Muslim, male and female, young and old. However, a clear understanding of what Islam teaches us should include explorations of how Islam views women's education, the limitations (if any) placed by Islam on women's education and access to knowledge, and whether the acquisition of knowledge is considered less essential for women than for men. Thus, to what degree does Islam affect women's educational pursuits?

Education, historically and currently, prioritizes males. Subjects have been categorized as male or female in nature.[15] In some Arab Muslim nations, girls and women are either excluded due to "customary practices that exclude girls from education" (Ali, 2000, p. 5), or they are confined to certain fields of knowledge. A common stereotypical notion is women's social inferiority in Islam, which is the justification used for providing differing opportunities within both education and employment between females and males. However, as a great deal of literature has proven, women's education in Islam has never been considered unnecessary or undervalued. In fact, the education of women has been highly valued and encouraged (Alghamdi, 2002). The problem—the devaluation of women's education based on misinterpretations of the Islamic texts—exists as a result of a single, restrictive interpretation by a certain group of male Muslims (Al-Manea, 1984; Alghamdi, 2002).

Other educators and scholars argue that the reason for this duality in gender roles and the prevalent assumptions with regard to women's education is based on a single and narrow interpretation of Islamic texts, leaving women no options but to stay in the home.

Mensch et al. (2000) rightly concluded that "education does not always challenge the expression of traditional attitudes for either sex or necessarily encourage wider horizons of girls" (p. 30). Furthermore, I argue that schools, whether sex-segregated or coeducational, are sites for producing gender biases through different channels (covertly within the curriculum). There is evidence to support this in Mensch et al.'s (2000) study in Egypt, where high school girls and boys believed "that a wife needs her husband's permission for everything" (p. 29).

Today, many Muslim women realize the need to be involved in the process of re-evaluating and understanding the Holy *Quran* and *Sunna* (Fernea, 1998). This has been argued recently by prominent Muslim scholars such as Wadud, Barlas, Barazangi, and many others. I stress that,

> Currently, many Muslim women raise questions about male domination, polygyny, and unequal norms and laws governing divorce and child custody. These women who have come to challenge their subordinate status within the family and within society, partly by engaging in a woman-centred re-reading of the *Quran* and of early Islamic history, have come to be known as Islamic feminists. (Moghadam, 2004, p. 155)

My research lays the groundwork for stressing progressive interpretations of the *Quran* and of Islamic teachings to women in general and may also act as a model for young Arab Muslim women. I argue that "Islam's universal message of equality and egalitarianism was delivered fifteen centuries ago, but countless generations of Muslim women have yet to see the final and necessary culmination of that aspect of Islamic project" (Noor, 2003, p. 330). This work highlights the emergence of both Arab Muslim and Muslim feminists, who are grounding their work in light of the Holy *Quran* and *Sunna*. Fernea (1993) indicates that,

> A growing group of highly educated, religious women see themselves as engaged in a new effort to use their education to, as they say, look deep into the spirit of the Koran and find there the gender justice they believe was the original intent of the Prophet Mohammed. Thus women have become today not only the subjects of intense religious debate, but also participants in that discourse. In the past, men interpreted the *Quranic* verses and the *Hadith* that described women's rights. Women themselves are now arguing for new evaluations of those older interpretations—and supporting their arguments with evidence from the sacred texts. (para 5, 23)

Women in many Arab Muslim societies are not acting out roles prescribed to them by misogynistic Muslim scholars. In fact, many are now questioning their rights and status in society while demanding social, political, economic, and cultural changes (Badran, 2005). I add that Arab Muslim women in North America, as indicated in this research, are finding agency within their Islamic identities and creating new paths for their hopes and dreams.

ISLAMIC FEMINISM: BRIEF OVERVIEW

There are debates on whether the term "Islamic feminism" represents a new feminist paradigm or whether it is a rearticulation of the *Quranic* mandate of gender equality (Moghadam, 2003; Wadud, 1992). Others argue that Islamic feminism transcends the secular and non-secular spheres, as well as categories such as East and West, and modern and traditional (Badran & Cooke, 1990; Vidyasagar & Rea, 2004). Muslim feminism is not a recent development; however, Muslim feminists and Arab Muslim feminists have been "debating issues of gender equality" (Badran & Cooke, 1990, p. 10) and arguing for women's rights and gender equity in Muslim and Arab Muslim societies for over a century.

Today, many educated Arab Muslim women legitimize their arguments regarding Islamic teaching to women by situating them within the framework of Islam (Badran, 1994; Yamani, 1996). Laura Nader (1994) argues that "the central difference between Western feminist ideals and Islamic feminism is that the first is based on equality between the sexes while the latter is based on complementarity between the sexes" (p. 90).

Many feminist Muslim scholars argue that the restoration of Muslim women's status, especially within the public sphere, would entail the need to refer to women's rights and responsibilities in the early Islamic era. Among Muslim feminists, "Haleh Afshar claims that the 'Islamist' women's return to the 'source' is the desire to return to the golden age of Islam" (Afshar & Maynard, 2000; Hendessi & Shafi, 2004, para. 24). Educated Arab Muslim women are able to negotiate existing inequalities and gender hierarchies within their cultural milieu (Ali, 2000; Baden, 1992). More progressive Muslim scholars, both women and men, are addressing the need to rein-stitute the Islamic laws and practices set in the discourses of early Islam (Afshari, 1994) and are attempting to encourage feminism within Islam as they examine scriptural sources and religious history to produce an Islamic theory of women's liberation (Ghadbian, 1997).

Shaheen Ali (2000) argues that Muslim women can and are pursu-ing feminist goals by challenging and redefining their cultural heritage; however, this does not mean setting aside all cultural norms. I contend that Muslim women need to redefine gender discourses, not by abandoning all aspects of their native culture, but by scrutinizing and critiquing aspects of cultural traditions that have no certain basis, that contradict the sacred texts, and are patriarchal in nature. Through her book, Ali (2000) provides an exceptional illustration, by a woman for women, of reviving Islamic law of women's rights. Her work, and the work of other Muslim women, is a significant contribution in ensuring that Islam is presented other than as a restrictive and retrogressive tradition (Ali, 2000).

SECULAR ARAB FEMINISTS' PERSPECTIVE ON GENDER: BRIEF OVERVIEW

It should be noted that the word "Arab" is frequently used synonymously with the word "Muslim." According to Abu-Laban (1980), "These errone-ous conceptions require examination and clarification" (p. 7; see note, Chapter 1). There is a wealth of gender analysis in Islam. There are analyses by scholars from many Islamic perspectives both Arab and non-Arab (i.e., Pakistan and Indonesia) and by Arab Muslim scholars.

A number of Arab feminists claim that they take a secular view of gender issues and women's issues. Nawal El Saadawi (1980, 1997, 1999, 2002), an Egyptian Muslim pioneer feminist, constantly re-evaluates her position on Islam and women's issues. Although she claims her secularity, she argues that,

> Islam has a progressive potential for women, and objects to conservative interpretations, which cast women only in subordinated roles. She also argues that the problems facing Arab Muslim women are compounded by the encroachments of Western cultural and economic imperialism. Women are therefore caught in repressive social controls of their own society, while they are also prey to some of the worst aspects of Western "commoditization" of women. [El Saadawi] also points to the impact of poverty and social inequality in determining women's status and opportunities, and contends that the overall lack of democratic rights has limited women's ability to organize. (Graham-Brown, 2001, p. 31)

Moroccan sociologist feminist Fatima Mernissi (1987; 1991) has been critical of Islam as a religion of sexual double standards in creating or legitimizing patriarchal power. She argues that Islam refers to women's sexuality as potent and dangerous and therefore capable of disturbing the social order and male morality. She claims that "Arab identity regards change as threatening to the moral order and thus impedes the development of democracy and Arab women's emancipation" (as cited in Graham-Brown, 2001, p. 31).

This brief overview of Arab feminist thought regarding gender discourse in Arab Muslim societies has been limited to El Saadawi and Mernissi, though there are many emerging Arab women feminists who are claiming a secular point of view.

WHERE ARE WE NOW?

According to Muslim women scholars in many fields (e.g., anthropology, religion, history, and literature), such as Omaima Abou-Bakr (2001), Sherifa Zuhur, (1992) Mai Yamani (1996), Ahmed (1992), Wadud (1999), Barazangi (2000), and many others, Muslim women are discussing and analyzing discourses and methodologies from within the authentic Islamic foundation, the Holy *Quran* and *Hadith*. Many Muslim women are returning to a more direct examination of the *Quranic* text and message while analyzing exaggerated gender distinctions. Many progressive

Muslims agree that the superiority of men over women attributed to a few *Quranic* verses should be superseded by the *Quranic* egalitarian world view and its repeated emphasis on ethical/moral religious equality (i.e., regarding distinctions that are strictly legal and functional and not inherent) (Abou-Bakr, 2001). Thus, Arab Muslim women's gender perceptions are not a result of individual, conscious choices, but are socially and culturally constructed. Cultural and patriarchal practices play a large role in many aspects in Muslim women's lives. I add that only when "women had the position of knowledge did they start to claim their rights and contest patriarchal interpretations of the *Quran*" (Hashim, 1999, p. 12) and imposed imperialist domination. I argue that this book would be a stepping stone for stressing the view of Arab Muslim women who are supportive of more progressive interpretations in understanding Islam and gender as well as the role of women.

25

NOTES

1.   Like Eileen Green (1998), my use of the term "discourse" in this context is based upon Foucault (1991): Discourses are structured ways of knowing that are produced within a culture, and that also help shape culture. They are always laden with power and institutionalized as practices, which help shape individuals as subjects (p. 183).

2.   "'Arab' in this study refers to individuals who trace their ancestry to the Arabic speaking countries of the Arabian Peninsula, the Eastern Mediterranean, and North Africa. The idea of an 'Arab nation' and the 'Arab world,' however, is problematic. The development of 'Arab civilization' is usually understood in the context of the medieval Arab-Muslim Empire, but the concept of an 'Arab nation' did not gain currency until the nationalist movements of the late 19th and 20th centuries (Antonius 1965 [1938]; Hourani 1991). Despite the wide appeal of Arab nationalism, it has rarely served as a truly unifying force, politically or socially. Moreover, the boundaries of the 'Arab world' are heatedly contested (e.g., between Northern and Southern Sudan), as is the position of minorities within these boundaries (e.g., in the case of Kurds, Christians, Copts, and Berbers).... Those considered 'Arabs' have different ideas about what constitutes Arabness and who may be considered Arab. So, while I define Arabs as my study population, I do not assume that an essential or uniform Arab ethnicity exists" (as cited in Nagel, 2002, p. 271).

3.   Any perusal of Islamic history indicates that women have played a prominent role in government, education, and politics. After reviewing progressive

Muslim views of gender issues regarding women's roles, one can conclude that Islam is an exceptionally dynamic, progressive, and egalitarian religion.

4. Many authentic historical resources documented that Khadija was at least 15 years older than the Prophet (PBUH) and had been married twice before.

5. To clarify my perception of progressive Muslim thinkers, I concur with Mooney's (1998) and Kandiyoti's (1996) definition of a progressive Muslim. Kandiyoti (1996) defines progressive Muslims as "women and men, who are challenging and undermining from within the framework of Islam the patriarchal notions that have influenced society [Arab and/or Muslim societies] for centuries" (p. 110). Also, Baksh (2005) defines progressive Muslims as "those who aim to revive the 'plural' Islam which has been buried under the debris of literal and dogmatic approaches to the faith" (p. 30). I add that progressive Muslims are those who argue for women's rights and gender equity within the framework of Islam. I argue, as do many progressive Muslims, that the *Quran* is specific about many issues related to women, including their status vis-à-vis men; however, Islam is frequently interpreted by men to the detriment of women (El-Nahhas, 1999).

6. Although Muslims accept the *Quran* as the primary and authoritative textual source containing the word of God, and *Hadith* as an inspired secondary source that can shed light on the interpretation of the verses of the *Quran*, when it comes to deriving laws from these sources, serious differences of opinion between the various schools of juristic thought arise (Ali, 2000, p. 80).

7. *Quranic* verses are often quoted repeatedly by extremist and misogynistic religious scholars to justify the idea that men are in control of women, and that they even have the right to physically chastise women if they are disobedient. These ideas have been reinterpreted by Muslim feminist scholars and progressive Muslim males. Gwendolyn Simmons (2003), in *Are We up to the Challenge? The Need for a Radical Re-ordering of the Islamic Discourse on Women*, references Amina Wadud's interpretation of the well-known *"Quwama* verse." Simmons (2003) notes that contemporary Muslim feminists have a different interpretation of the *Quran* than does the orthodox view. The explanation of this verse is found in the innovative work of Amina Wadud's *Quran and Women: Re-reading the Sacred Text from a Woman's Perspective* (1999).

8. On March 18, 2005, and most recently on October 17, 2008, Amina Wadud became the first Muslim woman to lead a Muslim Friday prayer in the United States. This was a controversial action and one that has since been an ongoing subject of discussion in the media. Wadud is an internationally known scholar on the subject of women in Islam. She is professor of Islamic studies at Virginia Commonwealth University; Dr. Wadud is also an expert on influences of Islam in America (*Frontline*, 2005).

9. The *Quwama* verse is most controversial; many Muslim religious leaders suggest that it is God's command for men to take control over women. Many progressive male and female Muslim scholars support Wadud's interpretation of the *Quwama* verse while many traditional scholars furiously oppose it. It is worth mentioning that Wadud's rereading of the gender discourse in the *Quran* is based on the Hermeneutical Model. Through that model, Wadud (1999) is

> Concerned with three aspects of the text in order to support its conclusions: 1. The context in which the text is written (in the case of the *Quran*, in which it was revealed); 2. The grammatical composition of the text (how it says what it says); and 3. The whole text, its worldview. (p. 3)

10. In Egypt, Algeria, Tunisia, Syria, and other Arab Muslim countries; yet for some gulf nations such as Saudi Arabia, there is no official, written so-called "family law."

11. This is long after the Prophet's (PBUH) time.

12. I contend the necessity to differentiate between fundamentalism and extremism in Islam. While the latter refers to narrow and extreme views with regard to diverse issues, fundamentalism refers to the foundations of Islam. These foundations are the Holy *Quran* and authentic *Hadith* and *Sunna*. Accordingly, Muslim extremists, and not Muslim fundamentalists, are those who support extreme views of the Islamic stance—for instance, women's status in society (Alghamdi, 2002).

13. In practice, in many cases, a father, brother, or male guardian would be proxy for the woman in signing the contract.

14. These phrases are attributed to the Prophet Mohammed (PBUH), who is presented as a messenger who delivered God's message and as someone who is followed by all Muslims.

15. In Saudi Arabia, for instance, women are not permitted to study engineering, law, physical education, piloting, geology, media and journalism, and political science.

27

Chapter Three

THE BEGINNINGS: ARAB MUSLIM WOMEN'S STORIES

THE WOMEN

In order to choose my participants for this book—Arab Muslim women who had been educated in Arab Muslim nations and who had then moved to Canada to continue their post-secondary education—I contacted various councils and associations, including the Society of Graduate Students' Council, the Arab Students' Association, and the Muslim Students' Association, all of which are affiliated with universities in southwestern Ontario, as well as with the Arab Muslim local community.

It soon became apparent that many of the young Arab Muslim women I knew did not match my research criteria. They had not studied in Arab Muslim countries because they had immigrated to Canada with their families at a young age. Almost all of their acquaintances and friends were first-, second-, or third-generation Canadians. One young Arab Muslim Canadian solicited participants for my research after *Jomaa* (Friday's) prayer.[1] Soaad,[2] who helped me select almost all the participants, became a valuable source in my research and showed me another aspect of community cohesiveness and communication.

The nine women[3] in this book range in age from 19–55. They are all Arab Muslim immigrants living in Canada. As Bateson (1990) argues, "Many women who are raised in male-dominated cultures have to struggle against the impulse to maintain complementarity without dependency" (p. 240). In other words, these women must project the idea that both sexes are capable of the same things, that one sex is not characterized by all that the other is lacking. This statement is reflective of the challenges facing my participants; however, the majority of the Arab Muslim women interviewed represent a certain form of rebellion against cultural norms. Fadwa's decision to stay in Canada and pursue her education while her parents are in the Middle East is an outstanding example. This woman with village roots constructed her life around her professional achievement and has attained her goals, undeterred by the negative gossip she faced.

Some of the women I interviewed were proud, while others were embittered and frustrated. Their composite lives and experiences, past and present, foster a better understanding of how Arab Muslim women make sense of interruptions and discontinuities in their lives. Moving from one place to another is one explicit aspect of discontinuity, but there are also implicit discontinuities, such as shifting dreams; for instance, in Ruba's and Fadwa's case, their dreams shifted from pursuing medical school to different paths. In each of these women's lives, there are discontinuities and interruptions within their thoughts, dreams, homes, and careers.

NARRATIVES WOVEN

One way for knowledge to accumulate—for the world to understand the hidden experiences particular to women—is through writing (Long, 1989). In the following chapters, I share and explore the narratives of nine women, weaving these autobiographies into a colourful textual quilt. These women's experiences in their native lands do not represent all women in Arab Muslim societies, nor do they represent the lives of all Arab Muslim women in Canada. They do not constitute a statistical sample.

The idea of having Arab Muslim women speak of their experiences was triggered by a number of factors. As a woman, I am interested in knowing how other women construct their life experiences. As an Arab Muslim woman, I am curious to hear the stories of other Muslim women, particularly the stories of their lives and dreams within a new social context. Bateson (1990) explains this affinity: "Women today read and write biographies[4] to gain perspective on their own lives" (p. 5). This experience was also challenging because

> ... narratives are potent ways of understanding relationships in motion and relationships from the past as they appear in the present; that narratives can help their tellers to feel happy and healthy or sad and sick.... Doing narrative research entails accepting that the subject matter of the field is a temporally and spatially sensitive cultural creation, produced in the liminal space between the teller and the told. As such, a narrative comes into existence as a facet of relationship. Not as a product of an individual. (Gergen, 2004, p. 274)

Narrative inquiry is not only a matter of interviewing and listening to someone's stories, taking notes, and remaining detached throughout it, but it also requires my personal involvement. There were times when I "interjected and clarified [their stories]. The spontaneous discourse and narrative accounts so co-produced reveal daily negotiations in Canada: theirs and to some extent mine as well" (Khan, 2002, p. 26). I was touched by all of the stories the women shared. While some stories disturbed me, others made me chuckle. These emotions lingered, especially as I played and replayed the interview tapes and read and reread the narratives.

The narratives offer provocative insights into the complex meanings of life and dreams for these women and their families; they show how the women view themselves as marked by a cultural perception of their role; they reveal their experiences, not only in Arab Muslim societies, but also as immigrants in Canada; and they reveal the ways in which the women dealt with the constraints they faced at various times.

The Arab Muslim women's self-narratives explicate certain aspects of their lives in their countries of origin and in Canada. There is no attempt here to explain or discuss their lives, but rather to explore specific aspects of their experiences that are related to their lives and dreams.

WHY THIS BOOK?

> Middle Eastern women have turned to writing as a way to participate in society when attempts have been made to mute their voices. Literary scholars have translated and studied some of these writings and made them available to Western audiences. (Gocek & Balaghi, 1994, p. 11)

This passage illustrates how I feel about my own story as well as those of the Arab Muslim women interviewed in this book. The stories are a potent means of self-expression from ordinary women—women who choose to express their hopes and dreams and the strength and sense of identity they derive from their Islamic faith. Just as Fatma Gocek and Shira Balaghi (1994) suggest in the above passage, I am trying to make both my own and these women's narratives available to the world.

In what follows, I include the demographics of the nine[5] women whose narratives are shared in this book. I have included their age,[6] parental background, schooling (sex-segregated or coeducational) in urban or rural areas, marital status, whether they have children or not, and their educational background.

TABLE 1: THE DEMOGRAPHICS OF THE NINE WOMEN INTERVIEWED

Name	Date of Birth	Profession	Marital Status	Year of Arrival in Canada	Number of Children (if any)	Location of School	Description of School before Arrival in Canada	Level of Education
Yasmine	1961	Family physician	Married	1984	7	Urban	Coeducational and all-girls	MD
Nora	1968	Exercise psychology	Married	1999	2	Urban	Coeducational and all-girls	MSc
Morooj	1956	Photographer (social worker)	Married	1999	5	Urban	Coeducational and all-girls	BA
Sahra	1973	Computer-analysis engineer	Married	1999	2	Urban	Coeducational and all-girls	MSc
Ruba	*	Computer-analysis engineer	Single	1994	None	Urban	Coeducational and all-girls	MSc
Fadwa	1979	Teacher	Single	1995	None	Rural and urban	Coeducational and all-girls	MA
Eman	1971	Teacher	Married	1996	3	Urban	Coeducational and all-girls	BA
Wafaa	*	Teacher	Single	1998	None	Rural and Urban	Coeducational and all-girls	BA
Nahlaa	1985	Engineer	Single	2003	None	Urban	Coeducational and all-girls	BSc

* Ruba and Wafaa did not want to reveal their ages.

Note: More will be shared about the participants as the book unfolds. I have provided this information in a table to make it easier for the reader to follow.

ARAB MUSLIM WOMEN

Morooj has an enthusiastic and vigorous approach to her life and her future as an artist. She plans to be a photographer and is taking college courses in portrait and landscape photography, an endeavour she finds inspiring: "I will be honest with you.... I never heard of a Libyan woman in her fifties who is interested in photography and studying it."

I asked her, "How do people react to this? Do you hear any negative comments?" Morooj roared with laughter and replied, "Yes, the negative comments, and the people I care less for." "You do not get hurt or bothered?" I asked. Morooj replied, "Not at all. I am convinced. I love what I am doing, so I do not care."

As a social worker in Libya, her country of origin, Morooj also loved what she was doing there, but in a different way. Now she is in her fifties with five adult children: three daughters and two sons. Her husband is in Libya; the sons live with her, and the daughters are pursuing their own paths. Her eldest daughter is in the United States working on a doctorate in immunology and pathology, while the other two are working in Libya. Morooj's new life in Canada focuses on art and photography because her social work expertise did not qualify her to work or study in that field here. She did not waste time on regret. She showed me some of her photographs—pictures of Tripoli, Libya's capital, taken from the window of a two-seaer plane, capturing the Mediterranean beach that runs through the centre of downtown and the ancient stone buildings in the city's outskirts. On that plane, while taking these captivating photographs, Morooj's dreams were flourishing and becoming a reality. Canada's natural beauty enthralls her and she recently joined a hiking group to give her more opportunities to take photographs of nature. She enthused, "Because the more you engage in the outside world, the more it opens new spheres for you, even in your connection and relationship with God, and that changed in me." Morooj seemed confident about her goals and herself.

Nora, a kinesiologist[7] and gymnastics teacher, is also passionate about her work and career. Nora was my first contact when I began my search for participants. During our first phone conversation, she told me about herself and her studies. Her strong voice and friendly Egyptian accent were inviting. She proved to be an eloquent and generous informant regarding herself and her cultural background. In her kinesiology lab at Alexandria University in Egypt, she found a correlation between low-intensity physical activity, diabetes, and high blood pressure. She was thrilled to discover the connection when she was least expecting it. Nora mused, "What if I knew the medical background of these women [the cases she was studying] and the scientific background of this idea?" Now in the final stages of a PhD in kinesiology,[8] Nora is a mother of a 13-year-old daughter and a six-year-old son. Her keen interest in people and in the Muslim community extends to a book she is writing, which features mainly Muslim women. She meets them in the lab, takes their medical history, starts a file for each one, and then she enrols them in low-intensity aerobic classes. Her studies are not her only ambition. She noted passionately, "I started classes in the Islamic school's gym with three women and now I have 50 women enrolled and 40 women on the waiting list. I also received letters of gratitude from Canadian physicians and Muslim physicians. I was asked to open up a class for Canadian women and also for women in the Jewish community."

Nora's story and her hopes extend beyond the parameters of the gym where she devotes her time to the women she is training. Nora's eyes sparkled when she showed me her photo from a recent interview with *The Londoner*, a weekly newspaper in London, Ontario. Suddenly, her narrative's subject shifted from ambition to anxiesty as she explained:

> I spent the first two years with no problems; it went like a nice dream. Then I began to be controlled. I was unable to go to the lab or do anything else, and was asked to wait. I remembered that my professor had asked me about my future plans, once I was finished my degree, and I was honest. I said that I was going back to my country. I was interested in continuing and doing the comprehensive exam (oral and written component), but I was unable to. I was told that the comps are the next hoop and if I passed them, I would have to write the dissertation and graduate. I did not think that my supervisor's questions about my future plans had been formed with bad intentions. When I sat with the committee, I found that my main supervisor was the one who was not willing to make things move along, while the two other members were encouraging. He asked me to do two more courses, although I had passed the courses stage.

Nora paused and tried to collect her thoughts. She resumed:

> I sat with Dr. X and she suggested that I change supervisors. The point of tension between me and the previous supervisor escalated because I started to be involved in the community outside of the university and I started helping people, … organizing free classes and handouts and arranging nutrition and physical health sessions. Everything I learn in the field, I offered to people in the community and he did not see the point and the benefit of doing that.

Nora also shared how having a supportive spouse made it possible for her to survive this exceptionally difficult time in her studies. In addition, women in the local Muslim community comforted her and bolstered her flagging confidence.

Sahra, sitting in her quiet, light, pink-painted laboratory, is a computer scientist who is finalizing her Master's thesis and is to begin a PhD a few months following this interview. She has a four-year-old daughter and is expecting a son. Sahra's work involves DNA computing. When asked to elaborate, she replied, "It is the pursuit of strategies to use DNA [deoxyribonucleic acid] for performing general-purpose computations, such as performing logical and mathematical operations and storing data." With a bachelor's degree in civil engineering, she worked in Egypt for three years before immigrating to Canada as a young bride with her husband, who is also an engineer. With two parents working in computer science, Sahra was encouraged to pursue the same field of study. She asserted, "I want to be an engineer, I want to be an engineer. I don't know why [laughs].... This is why I was motivated to get higher grades."

Ruba is another motivated woman. Her experience in designing and analyzing programs qualified her to work at the Canadian Ministry of Defence. Although her heart was set on medical school, after graduating from high school she was forced to reconsider her dreams. "This was not easy," Ruba said. In her temporary home, a Middle Eastern country where she lived with her parents, there were no medical schools, so she had to travel abroad to pursue her dreams. She explained:

> I was doing very well in school.... My grades were good enough to open the options for any kind of degree that I wanted to have, and my family was absolutely open to whatever I wanted, and there was no debate about what I could do.... I was 17 at the time.... I could go to medical school, which was something that I wanted to do.... I applied to many different countries, Arab countries as well, like Jordan and Egypt, but still the choices are very limited for Palestinians, especially Palestinians with no national passport....

Ruba had tackled a complicated dilemma that she and other Palestinians still face to this day. The displacement of Palestinians from their homeland and the resulting struggle for students to find a place to live and study is a common story: "Being Palestinian means, to me, being intimately connected to intense personal and emotional upheavals regarding place, location, identity, and desire" (Shalhoub-Kevorkian, 2002, p. 176). Ruba's struggle to fulfill a long-held dream is part of the dislocation narrative shared by many Palestinians. She shared the following:

> At the time, the opportunities for a foreigner to be accepted into a university were very limited, and we were foreigners in Abu-Dhabi.[9] I went to Madrid.... The only obstacle was the language; I had to learn Spanish before I could get into university. It was very difficult to communicate at the time, but my father spoke very good French ... he could communicate with them.... We did all the arrangements so I could get the language skills that I needed to apply to a medical school, ... but I was not very

comfortable in Madrid ... because I am conservative by nature and then there's my religion, which I have a fascination with.... I'm not going to tell you that I was a practising—a good practising Muslim—but I was very fascinated by my faith, so when we went to Madrid, the environment for me was shocking, especially the relationship between men and women; it was that the physical expression of those relationships was very public, and that, for me, was not something I was comfortable with, so I was concerned.... Then we went to Jordan to see what kind of choices I had.... I got accepted into science.... I had an aunt who lived there, though we're not close to her. When it was time for me to make the decision, I decided not to go to Spain, even though I know medical school was something I really wanted to do, ... there was no way I could get into medical school in Jordan.

36   Ruba struggled to explain the painful decision she had to make between living in Jordan and living in Spain. Being a science student put her in a position where she had to choose between teaching and her dream, medicine.

This illustrates that for some Arab Muslim women, life is often at odds with their dreams, yet we compose new dreams and live with what we are given.

Fadwa, too, had to readjust her dreams to suit her reality, although in a different way. In her native village, Fadwa was known as "Dr. Fadwa" among her relatives. Of the women I interviewed, Fadwa was the most articulate, and also one of the youngest. She is pursuing a Master of Arts degree. As far as becoming a physician, she explicated:

I grew up [and] their thoughts influenced me—my uncles, my aunts, and my relatives. I grew up being called "Dr. Fadwa" for as long as I remember. I still have uncles who call me "Dr. Fadwa," and I grew up being told that I'm smart enough to be able to become a doctor.... I pursued the sciences, and in the summer of Grade 11 in Canada, I went to a summer mentorship program for Black students at the University of Toronto, where I followed doctors and professionals. Basically, the concept of the program was to introduce Black students to the health sciences and let them know that, yes, you can be a health practitioner, whether it is a doctor, dentist, etc.... I did very well in that program. The year after that, they invited me to come back and work at a physiology lab. I hated it, absolutely hated it! Did not see the reason behind it, ... but I was there. I did my job because I wanted to represent the program well. It just didn't interest me looking at cells or doing the procedures.... I was very excited to go into science, and I didn't like biology, so I thought, okay, I'll do a physiology and psychology program, and I did that for a second and third year.... We were back into the labs, and we kept doing these labs and again. I hated the labs, so I found out that it's not in me to be a doctor.... I told my mom sometime in third year that I was interested in becoming a teacher, and my mother panicked....

As Fadwa and I sat in a quiet cafeteria, our talk was shaped by the fact that we are both teachers who share an interest and involvement in Arab Muslim women's issues. In addition, I come from Saudi Arabia—Madinah, specifically—where many Muslim families, locals of Fadwa's village, settle after their pilgrimage to Mecca and visitation of Madinah.

Wafaa is another village girl. An English literature graduate, she is the youngest of four sisters and a brother. She was raised in a Lebanese village before moving to Canada with her family. While almost all of the women I interviewed seemed excited about their current employment or the work they hoped to have one day, Wafaa is at a different point in her thinking. She said:

> You are not being educated for a career, but to be a good mother and a good housewife to raise healthy children ... [so working mothers] when they feel that they're slacking off on their families, they have to pay attention to their homes....

For Wafaa, a woman is educated in order to fulfill her primary duty as a mother and a wife. She felt that if work outside the home caused a disruption to a woman's family life, she should give it up.

Nahlaa, another engineering student, was the youngest participant. Both of her parents were engineers. Her move from the Gaza Strip in Palestine to Canada was a transformation for her. The noise of tanks and shells, and walking to school fearful of bullets, had been a part of Nahlaa's reality. Having lived in peaceful Saudi Arabia, I could only begin to imagine what it would be like to live in a war zone. During the second Gulf War in 1990, after Iraq invaded Kuwait, school in Saudi Arabia was cancelled for six weeks. Although the city where I lived was hundreds of kilometres away from the Saudi–Kuwaiti border, people in my city panicked and started storing cans of food and blankets for fear of war, yet Nahlaa, the confident young woman with broad shoulders and a sharp look who sat across the table from me, seemed calm and untroubled as she described soldiers checking her every 5 metres for her identification card in the Gaza Strip.

Yasmine, a family physician and a mother of seven, is no stranger to large families; she is one of nine children. Her soft voice and quiet demeanour first give the impression of shyness. Soon, though, it becomes evident that she is a self-confident woman with the ability to handle multiple tasks. I raise my eyebrows at her incredible capabilities. She said, "It is hard. If anyone tells you otherwise, they are trying to trick you. It is really hard to be a mother, wife, and a physician."

During our three-hour conversation, Yasmine often referred to verses in the Holy *Quran* and the *Hadith* to support an argument or elaborate a thought. As she spoke of her children, she mentioned how much each one of them knew of the Holy *Quran* and the *Hadith*. She proudly informed me about the awards they were receiving in school.

Yasmine's quick sense of humour was obvious during both of our phone conversations and in our face-to-face interview. A hard-working, devoted Muslim woman, she is also a poet and a writer of fiction, short stories, and plays in Arabic. A few days after the interview, she called me to suggest a few potential participants for my book, and then recited a poem about Muslim women. Her recitation brought tears to my eyes and was reinvigorating.

Diversity is a major theme in her life. She moved from the United Arab Emirates (UAE), first to Syria, then to Iraq and Yemen, before settling in Canada. After hearing about her adventurous life in Syria, where she was born, in UAE where she was raised, in Iraq where she went to medical school, and finally in Canada where she is a full-time practitioner, a wife, and a mother to seven children, I was amazed. I was reminded of Fenton's description of the relocation of people through immigration—people who neatly pack their roots and "transplant" them later in an orderly manner within a new society (1988).

Eman, a young mother of three, is an only child. Because of her highly educated father, she grew up travelling from one country to another, making many friends, gaining experience and diverse perspectives. When she was 16, she and her parents returned to their country of origin, where she attended university to study English literature. She came to Canada with her husband as a young married woman. Her eldest child has special needs, which adds an interesting twist to her life. Eman said, "He keeps us busy and thinking because, as a family, we want to be together, and at the same time find what's best for him as well because education is important and he's doing well at his school."

These are brief introductions to each of my participants. I try to make sense of their lives as women who "straddle two or more worlds and must negotiate various systems of beliefs that may not complement one another"

(Sarroub, 2005, p. 3). The way they presented themselves gave me insights into who they are and what is most valuable to them. Disentangling threads one after the other in my quilted narratives "enables one to see more clearly the nuances, details, and complexities of the women's lives, and the dynamic ways in which they manoeuvred traditional family contexts and their aspirations for self-empowerment and professional development" (Hertz-Lazarowitz & Shapira, 2005, p. 178).

SUMMARY

The sense of confidence and self-assertion in Morooj's tone is inspiring. Whatever questions were asked of her, Morooj answered eloquently, revealing an inner peace and personal strength. While others struggled with doubts, which were reflected in their responses, Morooj reflected what she believes it means to be a Muslim woman. Her assured self-representation was manifested in her answers, poise, and appearance.

Nora's narrative inspires me with the notion that nothing is an obstacle to a very determined woman. Attending national exams and purposefully skipping questions so that she could fulfill her dream of becoming a gymnastic teacher and health science book writer reveals how capable and confident Nora is.

Fadwa, inspired by early Muslim women, is able to challenge patriarchal aspects of social and cultural gender construction in Arab Muslim societies and in Canadian society. This was possible by the process of education in Canada, which encourages questioning and reasoning as opposed to mere memorization, as well as by having a network of confident, tough, and outspoken Arab Muslim women.

Their stories offered me personal growth. More importantly, all these narratives make sense of the formula "Education as a necessary liberalizing force" (Afshar, 1989, p. 269).

While reading, rereading, writing, and editing the narratives, I revisited my book's question numerous times. Morooj and Fadwa clearly indicated that their education in Canada had greatly influenced their outspoken, unique personalities. Nora, Eman, and I are extremely fascinated by the abundance of information that is available to students in Canada. The unique perspective of gender discourses the women presented is influenced by various factors. The main factor is their commitment to their faith. Other factors include their abilities to negotiate traditional boundaries that dictate specific gender norms; the freedom of speech and choice that is uniquely enjoyed in the Canadian context; their education in Canada; and, most importantly, their personal motivations and self-realizations. I highlight their knowledge of their faith and their education as playing a significant part in their self-realization, yet as a result of these various factors, the women became independent and influential, whether choosing to stay at home or to be part of the public domain. These women are becoming catalysts of progress in their families, communities, and societies. These women may also become catalysts of feminist and liberal movements in their native societies by supporting existing activists and taking part in development processes. Fadwa and Wafaa acknowledge the prospect of moving back permanently, or even temporarily, to their native societies and thus they may take part in advancing women's issues. Indeed, Fadwa explicitly indicated that her plan is to return and become fully engaged in social activism, which is long-standing and flourishing in Arab Muslim societies.

NOTES

1. A prayer held every Friday afternoon.
2. This is a pseudonym.
3. All the women who participated in the study were Sunni Muslims. Sunni and Shii are two major branches of Islam. The majority of Muslims practise Sunni Islam (Esposito, 1988).
4. I consider these women's narratives as mini-biographies.
5. I interviewed 10 women; the 10th participant's views have been omitted as she demonstrated views remarkably identical to that of another participant, whose views are, in this sense, now representative of both women.
6. Ruba and Wafaa wished to keep their ages confidential as a condition of participation.
7. Kinesiology is the study of human movement, and its goal is to discover strategies for enhancing human health and performance. The work of kinesiologists benefits all those who move, including high-performance athletes, people suffering from chronic injury or disease, and those wanting to improve their overall physical health (*Oxford Canadian Dictionary*, 2004, p. 579). See also the Wikipedia entry at http://en.wikipedia.org/wiki/Kinesiology.
8. Nora's scholarship was given by the Egyptian government to allow her to be in the United States, but she had it transferred to Canada.
9. Abu-Dhabi is a city in the United Arab Emirates.

Chapter Four

BORN FEMALE—ADVANTAGES OR LIMITATIONS?

IS IT A BOY?

Having a boy as the first offspring is, for Arab Muslims, the best gift a woman can give, not only to her family, but also to society. Everyone celebrates if a woman delivers a boy, for it is considered a blessing for the family to have more boys than girls. It was no different for me in Saudi society. Many families consider it noble to have a son and a disgrace to have a daughter. Yasmine, a participant, observed,

> Back home, or even here, an Arab is an Arab. I am having a hard time with Arab women here because every time I have a pregnant patient, she wants a boy, and I tell her, "Do not think or stress yourself about the baby's sex." Even when they go for an ultrasound, I tell them, "Do not overreact because the nurse will not be able to tell," and I have many cases where the paper will come back and the sex [of the baby] is not documented.

When asked how this bias affected her personally, Yasmine said,

> It did not matter; as a mother, it did not matter for the first or second. In fact, in *Hadith*, the Prophet [PBUH] says, "Those who start their offspring with a girl, they are blessed," so for me, it did not matter as long as it is a healthy baby.... My first newborn was a girl and when I had my first son, everyone was extra happy.... My husband got me a present every time I had a girl, but never did when I had a boy. I asked him, and he said, "Your prize is the boy, but whenever you have a girl, then I have to bring you something to make you happy."

When asked if she perceived this to be the case across Arab nationalities, Yasmine asserted, "All Arabs are the same, believe me, with regard to the gender of the baby. Some odd times it is the opposite," meaning that in unusual circumstances the woman would want a girl. In the Arab culture, a boy is not only capable of earning a livelihood, he is also a help to his father, the protector of his family, the bearer of his family's values, heritage, and name, and the one who will carry and continue the existence of Arab Muslim society. A daughter is an element within the family. The common concept is that after she marries, her personality is subsumed by her husband and his family. She cannot carry and retain her family name, even if she has many sons, because they carry her husband's name (Siddiqi, 1998). Morooj concurred:

> Preference to have boys is embedded in the culture. Some people like to have both.... We cannot interfere in that, but now scientists are trying to interfere in the matter.... In our Arab Muslim society, I hear that sometimes a couple divorces because of having girls and not having boys. When a woman has five or seven girls and no boy, she is abandoned by her spouse and family.... I had three daughters before my two sons, and I cannot explain to you how excited I was whenever I had a healthy baby....

She added:

> Having a boy to carry the family name is a necessity so that's why my parents, husband, and in-laws were happier when I had a boy.... It originated in the traditions because boys help their father in the farms or in businesses and it is not the same case for the girls. They are always home and in their families' minds.... Girls are always at home and are raised to be this way. When they are older, they marry and they also stay home and are therefore useless.... It is also in the tradition that the girl has to be always protected from a slip-up [doing something wrong]. Girls' misbehaviour brings disgrace and shame, while the boy's misbehaviour has a different consequence; the family will not be concerned.

When asked if she agreed with this perspective, Morooj retorted:

> Absolutely not. I do not agree with that.... Wrong is wrong, and I raised boys and girls. As much as I care for boys' behaviour, I care for girls' behaviour. Sometimes I am more protective of my sons than my daughters. The girls come and tell me things all the time. I know their friends and who they get together with. If they face a problem, they come to me and talk about it, but with my sons, I do not know all of their friends. They do

not like to talk about their lives. Religiously and socially, boys and girls should be looked at the same way. As a mother, I am always concerned about who they get together with and who their friends are. As a mother, I see them all the same and I protect them as much as I can, and this does not change as they get older. It stays the same.

Morooj's enthusiasm and support of her oldest daughter's educational pursuit for a PhD in New York reflects how she transcends gender boundaries and treats her daughters and sons equally.

Being an insider in the Arab Muslim culture, I know that attempts to break down some of the barriers within societal norms are challenging. The preference for boys as offspring in Arab Muslim societies is documented in literature:

> Islamic societies tend to be very patriarchal in nature (Walther, 1993). In most cases, the birth of a girl causes less joy than that of a boy. When a midwife or relative assisted with the birth, the mother knew immediately if the baby was a boy or girl. If it was a girl, the midwife said nothing. If it was a boy, the midwife would say, "Praise Allah."[1] The preference for boys is explained in that a boy would contribute to the family maintenance and protection. When a girl married, she left her family of origin to live with her husband's family and added to the strength of that family as she bore children. (Schvaneveldt et al., 2005, p. 81)

43

Shami (1988) adds that, culturally, a girl is a continuous source of worry, even after she marries, whereas a son is not a burden at all (p. 132). Thus, as an Arab Muslim woman, I do not have enough evidence to deny the fact that in Arab Muslim culture, boys are preferred over girls as offspring. It is my observation that many educated families in urban—as well as rural—Arab Muslim societies prefer to have boys.

Nora, too, suffered from this bias. She said:

> Once my mother had me in the hospital, they told my father that he had a girl.... He left without seeing me.... He was unhappy that he got a girl. He did not come and see my mother or congratulate her.... His reaction was really strange ... he really wanted a boy. Still today, my father is apologizing to my mother about it. My mother had a very difficult labour and I came [out] blue.[2] ... Forty days passed; it affected my mother psychologically; my father was really not accepting me ... not carrying me.... Soon after that, the picture turned ... and my father started to feel that he could

not be away from me.... Then the feeling of the first few days, the apologetic attitude toward me ... then love toward me. Now I remind him, "Do
you remember the first days?" and he always says that he is compensating
for that until today.

In my own large family of seven sisters and one brother, I recall how
neighbours, family, and friends gave condolences to my mother whenever
she had a girl. I do not remember my father complaining about this, perhaps
because he does not show his emotions, but I remember that my mother was
tired of trying to have another boy. I told Yasmine that in Canada, I have
noticed that some families favour boys as well. She replied that "Canadians
hope to have one of each, but there, in Arab Muslim societies, the more boys
you have, the better." Fadwa and I talked about this before my interview with
her. She mentioned visiting a friend who had a boy after having three girls,
and joked about the comments she heard from people about that friend's
"latest accomplishment." She heard comments such as, "Oh, finally" and
"Oh, that poor mother made it." Like Fadwa, I interpret these as expressions
of pity instead of congratulations. Sahra, who is expecting a boy,[3] looked
relaxed, and I wondered if knowing that she is having a boy contributed to
her peace of mind.

Even if one escapes this bias as a child, she or he will confront it as an
adult. For instance, traditionally a Palestinian[4] woman's status in society
comes from her relationship with her male relatives and *hamoula* (clan)
(McTaggart, n.d.). When a woman marries, she is effectively deprived
of status until she has her first son. At his birth, she becomes "mother of
[*Umm*][5] + [son's name]." The woman's civic identity in Arab Muslim culture
is therefore determined upon the birth of a son.

Thus, gender identity of a Muslim woman is constructed through cultural traditions, and not simply through religious teachings. A meaningful
understanding of the ways gender is constructed in Arab Muslim societies
cannot be investigated fully without examining dominant cultural traditions and themes, and the value systems that influence and shape the role of
women in these societies. An exploration of the ways these women perceive
the intersection of their faith and cultural traditions, as well as societal
norms, is necessary. This exploration involves asking questions such as the
following: Were girls treated differently than boys in the family? How is a
girl's achievement in school valued in the family in comparison to that of a
boy's? Where do religious teachings to women, cultural traditions, values,
and/or societal norms intersect, if they do?

44

LIVING ALONE

The concept of living alone is a useful category in understanding the way gender is constructed in Arab Muslim society. It is expected that a woman will live with her parents until she is married. In the case of divorced parents, a girl will live with her father. Even a divorced or widowed woman is expected to move back to the family house. There are a few exceptions based on the woman's age and class. Thus, a woman living on her own is rare, especially if she is unmarried. The honour and reputation of the girl and her family are at stake.

The Arab Muslim women I interviewed explained how they perceive their gendered construction. Yasmine observed, "For a single woman to live abroad without a support ... is extremely hard and difficult. I think the woman is the weaker sex and she needs the support of a man, in Canada or anywhere else."

Nora, who did not live alone, narrated her experience of travelling alone to a conference in Dallas. While on the plane, she was approached by two Muslim men:

> I asked them about something, and they said, "How come your husband left you to travel alone?" They told me that what I was doing—that travelling alone without my husband or a male guardian—is a sin. From that moment, I felt uncomfortable with what I was doing. I started questioning myself. "Can this be true? Is what I am doing wrong?" I spent 15 days in the hotel room without socializing, but thinking of what they told me. Other than attending the conference meetings in the same hotel, I went out once to buy gifts for my children and husband.

I wondered why Nora was shocked and felt less confident when two strange men told her that she was violating her faith. Why would comments from strange men cause Nora such profound concern? Could it be because women in Arab Muslim societies are brought up to give in to men's authority? Nora continued:

> When I went back to Egypt, I asked a few religious imams and they told me that I travelled for a good cause, especially since I was wearing modest clothes and wearing my *hijab*.... I believe that a woman travelling overseas by herself is fine, and the first thing we, in our culture, would care about is what others will say about us instead of thinking if it is a sin or not.

Sahra contrasted Yasmine's and Nora's views. She is confident that a woman living alone would not be an issue, aside from the feeling of loneliness. She said that any Arab Muslim person living on her or his own in Canada would feel overwhelmingly lonely, especially since we are from societies that are collectively oriented. Eman and Nahlaa agreed with Sahra's perception. I, too, agree with Sahra. People from Middle Eastern backgrounds can, at first, find it overwhelming to live in Canada. This may be because Canadian culture is individually oriented, while Arab Muslim Middle Eastern societies are collectively oriented. People in Canada seem to be content to live on their own. This is contrary to individuals in Arab Muslim societies who tend to be together more. I concur with Sahra that for a male or female Arab Muslim, it is hard to cope with loneliness.

However, Morooj, whose daughter is at a New York university to pursue a graduate degree in immunology, acknowledges that while it is difficult for someone to live alone, it may be beneficial as well. With regard to her daughter, Morooj noted, "It was a dream for her and if she wants to fulfill it, then she has to tolerate the loneliness." Morooj herself wanted to study to become a pilot before she got married, and wanted to travel abroad alone to pursue her education, but she was unable to: "At that time it was not something people would accept, but now some people are accepting it.... I knew of a few unmarried single Libyan women who are supported by government scholarships, ... travelling abroad to pursue their education, ... some in pharmacy, medicine, and in veterinary medicine...."

Morooj is delighted that now her daughter is fulfilling her dreams and continuing her studies abroad. Even Fadwa, who is living in Canada on her own, acknowledges it would be impossible to live by herself in the city where her parents live: "The cultural context of [the country where her father works] is not one that would permit a woman to live on her own without being intimidated, questioned, or threatened by people."

Interestingly, Ruba, who lived alone in Jordan and then in the United States while pursuing her master's degree in engineering, raised a noteworthy point about a woman living and travelling alone:

> Physically, I'm not as strong as a guy, so that's why I think sometimes the families could be reluctant to send their daughters on their own just for safety reasons and sometimes for cultural reasons because they think it's not proper for a girl to be by herself because they don't trust others, ... not because they don't trust their daughter, or because people talk ... or if she is single and living by [herself] ... that people will look at her as somebody that people could take advantage of.... When you are a girl by

yourself, there are more people who are looking at you. They can break in, ... they can attack.... When you have a guy in the house, it's not the same ... like if you're walking across the street, you by yourself, and there are people who intend to do you harm, there's more of a chance that you will be attacked than if you are walking with a man.... I would be driving from [city in the United States] to [city in Canada] and if I entered the wrong exit and if I am in the wrong neighbourhood, then that is it for a woman.

Like Yasmine, the woman's physical ability appears to be a key point in Ruba's perception. She overemphasized: "Women being a weaker sex ... she is in a form and a shape biologically that is different than men, so that's why it is not recommended that she travels or lives alone.... This is what I believe in...." Then she rationalized her comments by taking the conversation in another direction:

... what I'm talking about is not just the man as a financial provider, but being a man, it is his responsibility to take care of the household, the security of that household [and] the safety of people. And for me, the Quwama,[6] at the end of the day, is that the man's to be questioned ... for that safety, welfare, and well-being of the family.... Like in any kind of an institution or an organization, there has to be people who share the burden of responsibility. There are people who we question at the end of the day. When we have that structure in an organization, we do not question it. We do not question why we have a supervisor.... Somebody who ... all of the blame goes on to him ... I think the Quwama comes from him [the man] having more responsibility.

Ruba's analyses led her from discussing her perception of a woman living alone to the implications of male/female biological distinctions, to Quwama, and then to a man's superiority. Ruba drew a convincing analogy between the man as the head of the household and the supervisor of a company. The way she stated this implies an unwillingness to question these affirmed perceptions. The biological difference between the sexes seems to be an easier justification of women's inferiority. Woman as the "weaker sex" is an ideology rooted culturally and historically in people's minds. Without an in-depth investigation into the meaning of the word, and how it is mentioned in the Quranic verse, Quwama seems to be the religious licence that is used arbitrarily by any person to dictate and legitimize men's superiority. It was mentioned also in Yasmine's narratives; she said, "In the Quran, which I strongly believe in, the Quwama means equality [between the spouses], but it also looks at the husband as the protector. The husband is like the tent for his family and his wife...."

Unlike Yasmine, who analyzed the situation of a woman living alone from a religious perspective, Fadwa looks at the issue from a social angle. She is a living example of the "living alone" theme. Fadwa draws attention to class code, which plays a role in how people perceive a woman living on her own:

> It depends on what social class she belongs to.... There are social classes
> that are more liberal ... an upper class that is liberal that is known to
> be less religious ... and thus it is excusable or ... it is okay for a girl to
> leave and study abroad because ... they are not Islamically oriented, ...
> [although] this is the cultural norm.

However, being from a middle-class background, she recalls,

> The first time I went home to my country, ... I had been living on my own
> for just two months or so. Everyone in my extended family was in com-
> plete shock.... I got long lectures from mothers, fathers, and siblings,
> [all] telling me I should come back and get an education [there].... People
> took an offence to it.... They took it personally as if I was insulting the
> education system back home....

I asked Fadwa if her extended family's objections to her decision were based on religious reasons or gender discourse and she replied:

> Depends on who you talk to. My cousin ... made the implication that
> women should not be travelling alone ... because it is not Islamically ac-
> ceptable, yet she and her sister ... have lived in residence in their country
> of origin for years.... She saw her family very, very little. ... but it was okay
> for her to live alone because she was in ... a Muslim environment, but a
> non-Muslim environment away from my parents was not okay.

All the Arab Muslim women's perceptions of a woman living alone high-light aspects of contradictions and an overemphasis on biological difference as the reasons behind this patriarchy. Their perceptions also underscore the interlocking ways in which Arab Muslim women's gender discourses, roles, and perceptions are constructed in their native societies or abroad, and whether they live alone or with their families.

NOTES

1. "Allah" is God's name in Arabic.

2. "Blue baby" is a known case in pediatric medicine and described as a blue complexion and severe weakness that comes from a congenital, sometimes fatal, heart malformation. In blue babies, there is an insufficient amount of blood travelling to the lungs (Knobeloch, Salna, Hogan, Postle & Anderson, 2000).

3. Sahra told me during the interview that she was going to have a boy.

4. This also applies to women in different parts of Arab Muslim societies.

5. *Umm* is an Arabic word for mother. If a mother has three daughters and one boy (hypothetically named Ahmed), she would be referred to by family members, neighbours, and friends by her son's name (i.e., *Umm* Ahmed).

6. A controversial concept mentioned in the Holy *Quran*. Some conservative Muslim scholars interpret it as legitimizing man's power over woman. See also Chapter 2.

Chapter Five

RELIGION, CULTURAL TRADITIONS, AND SOCIETAL NORMS: THE PARADOX

Many aspects of gender discourses are based on societal cultural traditions and violate the teachings of the *Quran* and *Sunna* (*Hadith* and *Seera*). The following excerpts demonstrate how the Arab Muslim women interviewed differentiate between religious and cultural traditions. Understanding how Islam views girls and boys and the ways in which societal and cultural norms and practices construct and reproduce gender discourses provides an informative and essential framework for the discussion in this book.

Yasmine, who compared the application of cultural traditions with that of Islamic teachings, stated, "My father was religious and not traditional." She made a distinction between cultural traditions and the holy essence of Islam:

> I sense the difference between the two. When I talk about religion, I remember the Mothers of the Believers, and the Prophet's [PBUH] wives, but when talking about traditions, I only remember my grandmother and the ways she differentiated between me and my brothers. One exemplifies Islam and Islamic teaching to women, and the other exemplifies traditional ways of viewing women and girls.

Yasmine's paternal grandmother, who memorizes the Holy *Quran*, is a well-educated, well-known teacher of women in her community. According to Yasmine, her grandmother still has "traditional" ideas about women's education. Traditional ideas of women's education vary across Arab Muslim societies' subcultures. Some still prevail: For instance, a woman's education is a requirement until she is able to read the Holy *Quran*; higher education is considered a luxury for women or could spoil women; certain fields of knowledge are not compatible with women's nature; and women's education should be maintained in strict seclusion from men's.

Yasmine still remembers how her grandmother treated boys and girls differently:

> Some small incidents reflect how grandmother valued my brothers more than me and my sisters. For example, one day she asked us to mop the floor for her. While we were doing that, my brothers walked in from outside with muddy shoes.... We [the girls] screamed and yelled at them and it was such a big deal for her! I remember she said to us, "Don't ever scream in your brothers' faces! Let them do what they want to do. They have the right to do anything and all you have to do is clean again without screaming." For my sisters and me, it was a shocking moment hearing her saying this. My father used to treat us all, boys and girls, the same. He was strict with me, my sisters, and my brothers.

Yasmine also differentiated between religion and cultural tradition as a practitioner. She recalled an episode from her early years of practice: "The people in Yemen really were not practising Islam. They were practising sexist traditions. Very sad stories I encountered.... There were many dreadfully difficult moments in my life." I found it hard to imagine what kinds of difficulty Yasmine was referring to. The story she told me carries alarming significance, but it also describes the reality of some women's lives. She related the following:

> A 13-year-old girl came to my clinic with her uncle. The girl was having itchiness in her vaginal area. However, her uncle, who was her guardian since her father was working in Egypt at the time, was asking me to check the girl's virginity because he suspected that she was going out with someone [dating].... I remember that he was standing at the door waiting to hear from me; if she was not a virgin, then he was ready to kill her. Just imagine—a word from me would determine someone's life! The thing is, he is not her father; he is her uncle, so any male relative is a guardian of your life [and] will have the word if a woman deserves to be living or not. I said that she was virgin, and the uncle did not even believe me. He took her for an ultrasound.... A human being's fate depends on a word from, and a decision from, another human being [always male].

This story and many others supports my conviction that tradition, and not Islamic teachings, is the culprit behind this sort of patriarchal oppression, which prevails in many Arab Muslim women's lives. To value virginity to the point of threatening a life is certainly a violation of Islamic values and rights with regard to children. As Moghadam (2003) suggests, women's honour—and, by extension, family honour—depends primarily upon their virginity and "appropriate" conduct. In Yasmine's words, "These are not religious teachings. They are sexist traditions that benefit men only."

Nora's father did not follow the cultural norms in his treatment of her and her male siblings. She was given a position in the family and encouraged to think for herself and to assume responsibilities that were not shared with her male siblings. She successfully managed these responsibilities and appreciated her father's untraditional practices. During every summer vacation, Nora helped her father in his fabric factory, yet Nora admitted that living in a male-dominated society meant that her father's treatment opposed cultural traditions. She continued:

> His treatment created some jealousy between me and my younger brothers, who noticed that my way of behaving made me close to my father, so the family split into two camps: one is my father and me, and the other is my mother and my brother, who is a year younger than me. This created some balance.

While adolescents shape their gender identity through socialization, the way Nora was treated and socialized by her father gave her a sense of confidence and shaped her sense of gender, assuring her that she was no less valuable than her younger brothers.

Islamic teachings to women did not hinder Nora's involvement in her interests. Her interest in gymnastics did not contradict Islam. Up until high school, Nora had no issues with the *hijab* since she went to an all-girls' school.[1] However, at the university level, a few things changed. She recalled:

> College life was hard with the *hijab* because we have many university parties. I was the college's player in rhythmic gymnastics. The dean of our faculty challenged me because she wanted me to participate and told me, "Nora, you cannot participate with the *hijab*.[2] After consulting a few religious professors in my faculty, I designed an Islamic dress I could wear for the concert that would not hinder my movement on stage. Afterwards, all girls who wore the *hijab* had a similar dress. Indeed, the dean respected me for what I did.

Nahlaa knows that the way women's education is perceived is one aspect that distinguishes Islamic teaching from cultural traditions. She exclaimed, "Education is a must for Muslims ... males and females.... Culturally it's not. Usually men are the ones who are supposed to get higher education and women should stay at home...." Moreover, contrary to popular belief, Islam does not specify certain fields as suitable for women. Yet, culturally, some fields are considered predominately male just as they are in Western culture. For example, in Arab culture, engineering is considered a male enterprise. However, Nahlaa noted, "Although in the faculty here there are fewer women than men, there's a larger percent of women in engineering at the university in Palestine...."

Eman also noted that,

> Cultural traditions have nothing to do with Islam. I live Islam here in Canada. I lived Islam in the United States more than I lived it in Libya and Arab countries, and I don't want to generalize, but in Libya they live tradition, they live their customs. Their customs are like the social law—now this is what we do in weddings, this is what we do at funerals. It doesn't have anything to do with Islam.... The wedding is seven days. It's got to be seven days, overlooking the fact that it could be costly, it would be tiresome, but no, it's gotta be seven days.

Eman's frustration with many facets of cultural traditions revealed an important aspect of her narrative. She asserted, "Even though my father wasn't the man that followed the customs, he, at the same time, wanted to be somewhere in the middle: not the total radical over customs, but at the same time, in respect to our grandparents and our ancestors, he felt that we should follow some." Eman knew that educational achievement would contradict some cultural beliefs. She explained:

> To tell you the truth, cultural beliefs would have hindered my educational pursuits only because women can't be in certain professions.... For example, if you're a doctor, ... culture doesn't permit a woman to go out and sleep away from her home.... Culture doesn't permit a woman to travel on her own to continue her education. That's the cultural beliefs that were going on and are still going on regarding women. However, religious beliefs, as long as there is a sense of productivity toward society and towards your community, ... an intention is to progress and to develop, then there isn't a problem with that.

Eman's explanation makes a distinction between the Islamic construction of gender and culturally constructed gender discourse. Eman's view of Islam with regard to equality is an interesting one. She made the following distinction:

Equality is a relative concept, I have to say. How are women and men equal? Without thinking of law and regulation, and according to Islam, we are equal, in the way Allah sees us accountable for our actions and our responsibilities, we are equal in our emotions.... However, in our nature, we're not and a lot of people will probably disagree with me on this. Islam came to support the woman more than put her below the man. She's not below the man in any way, but in giving the man the responsibility of providing for the woman, that's in a way protecting her and treating her with respect because Islam acknowledges ... [for instance] Allah acknowledges the strain on her body after giving birth. Allah acknowledges the responsibility of taking care of a baby.... That's where I don't see that they're equal. A woman needs to stay at home ... to have her mind, her heart, her soul dedicated to the newborn.

With regard to cultural traditions, Eman acknowledges the instability of culture:

I really don't believe in culture.... Culture just varies from one year to another or from five years to another.... Sometimes society puts so many pressures on you, like you've got to finish building that house, ...you gotta work on that car, you can't be driving a car like that.... You've got to put your children in the best school, and, of course, the tuition can't wait for you ... to rest at home for 40 days.[3] Yes, lots of people are taking their infants to their mothers or their in-laws, so they continue ... providing responsibility ... to follow the culture's and society's law, what society wants from you, the image of society.... To fit is a cultural tradition in this century....

In this discussion, Eman pinned down an overwhelming reality. While Arab Muslim women are challenging patriarchal boundaries manifested in some families and in the workplaces, they are also confronting materialistic hierarchies that are imposing different sets of rules on women. The postmodern world is altering cultures and values and replacing them with values that are materialistic, where women's bodies are objectified and women's roles are recasting neo-patriarchy and gender hierarchy. "The mixture of traditions meshes" (Sahgal, 1992, p. 180) with modern ways, which probably hinders women.

Morooj took a different stance in differentiating between religious practices and cultural traditions. She argues that the perception that women are naturally suited to certain tasks over others gives men more control.

55

She blamed "traditions and old beliefs that, unfortunately, push women in certain directions" and added that,

> Cultural traditions keep woman away from other roads so men take them. It is not about men's and women's abilities. I am a believer in women—that women can do and are capable of doing anything if they are given the opportunity. I personally wanted to be a pilot, but I was unable to.

I asked why, and Morooj explained:

> At that time, in the 1970s, this was not possible and I do not think anyone would have accepted it—neither the society nor the government. Even if my father supported me, how is it going to be possible for me? Anything that will require women to be abroad was not possible or even negotiable. Now ... everything is possible.

Morooj indicated that culturally, people question a woman's ability to perform a task just because it is normalized as a male task. Morooj does construction work in her home even if "people look at me and think 'Why is she doing this?' But I do not care because this is who I am and this is what I believe in." Morooj added, "I raised my daughters the same way—my sons also; I told them that women and men are as capable...."

Morooj expressed her frustration with the private sphere, which is culturally constructed to be a woman's realm, and the public sphere, which is relegated to man:

> Culturally, men should always take control of everything, and woman should not know anything, ... should not interfere. Some women buy into that; they do not know how much their husbands earn. He is responsible about everything ... finance in the family. He could control pretty much everything about the children's upbringing and interfere in that.... Sometimes the mother has no role or say in her children's upbringing; only cooking, vacuuming, and cleaning and that's it....

I was raised in a patriarchal extended family in which the man looked after every detail and did not allow the wife to speak or voice an opinion, so I was surprised to hear Morooj talking about the issue. I asked, "Did you experience this?" She answered quickly, "No, I did not experience this, but I am aware because of my experience as a social worker. This is what I hear and see." I added, "Others had this life," and she replied, "Oh yes, a lot of people. The mother has no role, or very minimal." Then I asked, "Does a woman have a role in being treated in such a way?" Morooj answered:

> Yes, for sure a woman has a role in being treated in such a way, and education is important. This is the heart of the matter. Mostly uneducated women have this life.... A woman has a role in being silenced and ignored because she needs to know her rights and responsibilities, ... but sometimes this happens when a highly educated woman marries a very controlling husband. Then she will have no word in anything even if she tries.... Then problems start if she wants to have an opinion.... This problem prevails in Arab Muslim families.

I agree with Morooj that "education opens up opportunities for women," but I would also add that economic independence grants women freedoms that threaten this form of patriarchy.

"Religion and cultural traditions are influencing boys and girls.... I can speak for that." This is how Fadwa started this discussion. She spoke from her personal experience of the difference between Islamic tenets and cultural traditions: "... that's where both boys and girls are supposed to go through circumcision.... I grew up in a society where circumcision is a must and is believed to be something that the Prophet [PBUH] recommended that all Muslims have to do to their daughters and sons."

I listened intently to Fadwa, not expecting what was coming next. As she spoke, I was horrified[4] as I tried to picture what it would be like to be circumcised at seven years old. She explained:

> There are different levels of circumcision for women. There's Pheronic and *Sunna* and there is Sudanese.... There are ranges between those two, Pheronic being the complete closure of the woman's vagina, and *Sunna* being just taking a little bit out of her private parts.... My mother was unable to speak out ... and she convinced herself that it was the right thing to do. The thing here is, my father is absolutely against it, and he basically instructed my mom not to let me go through this, but he had gone away for the summer and we were in [home], and my [paternal] grandmother ... said that Fadwa must be circumcised because it is a religious practice, so my grandmother came all the way from the village to the city, ... and that's a three-hour drive, to ensure that I went through this process, and my mom was part of it. But what really hit me is that my mother refused to go and attend the procedure with me.... Looking back at it ... makes me believe that maybe she couldn't stomach it because she knew something wrong was

57

going on. I remember that they called her [the woman who performed the circumcision] a nurse. [laughs] My mother tried to justify that we had a nurse; it was someone that was qualified to do this [laughs].... And it was apparently a woman with a very good reputation. I remember my grand-mother holding me down and I remember just panicking and the fact that I was not anaesthetized—that was huge—and I remember thinking to God, as a seven-year-old, ... why are you letting this happen to me? And what I couldn't reconcile afterwards, right afterwards, is that everybody was so happy, and people were celebrating.... People came just to visit me and to tell me how wonderful it was, and I didn't feel that, ... so that was an interesting experience. And another interesting thing about that whole circumcision thing is that my mother made sure that she told me specifi-cally that I should never, ever, ever speak to this, speak to anyone about this. This is not something I'm supposed to discuss with anybody. Many, many, many years later, I found out that my mom actually did me a favour, which is to make sure that I got the *Sunna*[5] circumcision because her own circumcision was Pheronic....

As I listened to Fadwa, I wondered how many young girls must suffer this experience. This tradition is persistent in many villages in Sudan, Egypt, Somalia, and Yemen (IRIN, 2005; Althaus, 1997). Female circumcision is also referred to as female genital mutilation. El Saadawi (1980), as a femin-ist, psychiatrist, and physician who endured circumcision, differentiates between the Egyptian circumcision and the Sudanese. She explains that the Egyptian circumcision is a complete removal of the clitoris, or part of it, while the Sudanese circumcision is a complete "removal of all parts of the external genital organs. They cut off the clitoris, the two major outer lips (*labia majora*) and the two minor inner lips (*labia minora*)" (p. 9). Sally Baden's (1992) report on development and gender (1992), *Position of Women in Islamic Countries: Possibilities, Constraints, and Strategies for Change*, indicates that,

Female genital mutilation[6] is prasticed in 20 countries in Africa (in-cluding Egypt, Mali and Sudan) as well as in (south) Yemen and a num-ber of other countries and Muslim communities outside Africa. Within countries, some ethnic groups practise female genital mutilation while others do not, or practise different forms. There are various forms of female genital mutilation. The milder form of circumcision (known as *Sunna*, or tradition, by Muslims) involves removing the hood of the clitoris. Excision involves removal of the clitoris and all or part of the *labia minora*. Infibulations, the most severe form, which can induce many severe health complications, involves the cutting of the clitoris and most or all of the *labia majora*. The two sides of the vulva are then pinned together. There are also various intermediate forms of female genital mutilation. Female genital mutilation is traditionally performed by older women of the village, by traditional birth attendants (called *daya* in Egypt and Sudan), or by village barbers. (pp. 17–18)

Statistically, Sudan and Somalia are where the majority of girls are circumcised, and many reports indicate that 90 percent of girls are infibulated (Althaus, 1997). Fadwa, with all her sadness, was still thankful to her mother for refusing to have her daughter endure the same torture as she herself did. Fadwa explained:

> I'm happy that she [my mother] ... the best she could do is for me to go through a *Sunna* circumcision as opposed to the Sudanese, an entire closing of my vagina, because every time my mom gave birth, she was in pain. Every time she had her period, she was in pain. For her, the first few years afterwards of just urinating were painful.... My mom was very susceptible to infections.... My mom does not enjoy intercourse. These are all things that are very powerful that have been taken away from women for generations....

Arab Muslim boys are circumcised too, but when they are a month or a few days old. Through literature, including El Saadawi's autobiography (1999), I know that girls are usually circumcised between seven and nine years of age. I asked Fadwa if she knew why her family had to wait until she was seven, a question she could not answer. Some literature indicates that the reason is to make sure the girl remembers the pain. These girls' experiences of being circumcised affect the way their gender is constructed and the way in which their self-perception is formed. Fadwa related:

> My only relative on this continent is my first cousin.... I was curious to see what circumcision meant to her, and whether or not—she has a daughter—she would put her daughter through this. My cousin has the most interesting theory. My cousin, I think, also got a *Sunna* circumcision. But as far as her daughter's concerned, if she were to go back [move back permanently] to her home country ... with her daughter as an adolescent, she won't put her daughter through circumcision, but if they're gonna live here [North America] for a long time and her daughter's gonna grow up

here, [then] she will make sure her daughter is circumcised. The reason behind that is that, according to my cousin, circumcision is something that helps suppress women's desire—better than going wild. She's afraid [that] her daughter's gonna be bombarded by all these emotions, and the only way to make sure that her daughter monitors herself is by giving her a physiological mechanism....

I wanted to know how Fadwa, a young, articulate, critical thinker, responded to her cousin's rationale, but before I was able to formulate my question, she said eagerly:

Listening to my cousin I don't know if I said much. I think I explained to her that I don't agree with it. From my understanding of the religion, this is not part of the faith. I am pretty sure that this has nothing to do with the faith, and this is something that was added to it, and if you look at the history behind it, this is something that was started up by the ancient Egyptians. But she seems not to care.... It's not a big deal to her, and I think to my other cousins back home, it is not a big deal. So what? We're circumcised.... It's a given, it's understood. Part of me wants to let them know and inform them and educate them, and the other part of me wants them to just live life as if they didn't know that something was wrong with them, or maybe at least after they get married.... What if I marry someone who has no idea what circumcision is?

There was silence, as I had no answer for Fadwa's question.

Fadwa endured a great deal of criticism from her grandmother and other members of her family, not for discussing her brutal circumcision, but because her father provided her with the best education he could find. This is the other aspect of Fadwa's life in which religion and cultural traditions are paradoxical. She explained:

Cultural traditions didn't hinder me, but some of these things leave a bad taste in your mouth.... My dad looked into the Sister School,[7] the Unity School,[8] or public school, and my father decided to put me in the Catholic school because it had the traditional aspect, but it also was known for having, for several decades, taught girls a very high-level education. I learned. Probably some of the best math education I got was in that school. We were doing logic and reasoning and proving, in Grade 7 and Grade 8, which is very fascinating now to look back on it. My grandmother resented that, even though she had more education than her peers.... The

60

fact that my father paid so much money for me to get a private education ... she was appalled....

What caused a more serious reaction from her grandmother, according to Fadwa, was her father's decision to come to Canada so she could have a good education, yet her decision to stay in Canada on her own to study was an act that outraged everyone in the village:

My father in 1994 made a decision.... We were gonna go to Canada, and the number one reason—he had a series of reasons, like a platform, almost ... political platform to explain to the [extended] family why he's going to Canada—was Fadwa's education. It's huge. My father said to me, "It's your education; it is one of the biggest reasons why we're coming to Canada," which is another reason why I'm doing my Master's.... So for my father, the special person to the extended family, to be going all the way to Canada, so far away from them with his young boys because of my education, a girl ... so my grandmother said, "You are the reason my son is going away from me to a different country and it is all your fault, and you're selfish." And she just gave me a long lecture of how it is all my fault that her son was ... leaving. I know that much. The thing that I'm not supposed to know about in terms of me and my education is how much trouble my father went through with family members who ... really criticized him as a father figure for letting his daughter go to Canada [and] live alone. I didn't get much of that. I got a little bit of that—all they said [was], "Fadwa, you should just get educated here." But my father got the brunt of the criticism, and he will just hint to [say] ... "People might think that they know how I should run my family. It is none of anyone's concern." So I'm glad that I have a father figure that will take that responsibility and not ... hold it back from me. He supported me financially, emotionally, everything. And my mom, in turn, she's very proud of me and I'm really glad that that's happening. So thankfully, I don't know if it [cultural traditions] hindered. It just gave a bad taste in my mouth.

Fadwa narrated these memories bitterly, yet she emphasized that her religious background and deep understanding of her faith helped her keep everything in perspective:

Religious beliefs .... [have] supported my educational pursuits. Looking at the amount of strength and courage it took for Aisha, the beloved wife of the Prophet [PBUH], to lead a battle, given that she was born in a

61

generation of women who were buried alive as one of the misogynistic things that happened to girls, that she had the kind of character that she had as a woman. The strength of that character that illuminates throughout the ages.... So yes, they have helped; they've [religious beliefs] totally supported my educational pursuits. Another aspect of that is that my religious beliefs, ... from a personal perspective, is having lived on my own for five-and-a-half years, if I did not have my religious beliefs to ground me, I would have easily ... delved into different lifestyles that are valid for other people, but might have distracted me from my educational pursuits, be it drinking alcohol or other aspects that are not considered Muslim....

I felt I would not have been able to survive in Fadwa's position. Living as a lonely stranger in a foreign land would not have been an adventure for me. But Fadwa—who lived nearly as a stranger in her native land, challenged by cultural traditions, particularly battered by the circumcision trauma in her childhood—was capable of surviving the loneliness in Canada.

Fadwa's experience wither her first marriage proposal is another interesting narrative to show the paradox between traditional practices and faith. Fadwa indicated that being self-sufficient, which was encouraged by her parents, was a central impetus behind her pursuit of higher education. Fadwa's father, who has a PhD from a British university, is emotionally and financially supportive of her decision to live in Canada on her own and obtain her Master's degree. I understood from Fadwa's narratives that there is some pressure from her parents, especially her mother, to consider marriage.

Although raised by her parents to be independent, Fadwa remains burdened by social expectations of Arab Muslim women. This is also evident in her account of her first marriage proposal, when she noted that her aunt "ordered" her to be obedient and submissive when she met the prospective spouse. The meeting traditionally takes place in the presence of parents and relatives. When she met with the prospective spouse, Fadwa asked him some questions about himself, his life, and his interests. Fadwa's aunt, in total shock, told her that she should have been silent, that he is the one who was supposed to talk and ask questions. Fadwa related that,

My aunt told me that I am not supposed to say [to] him a single word and he is the one who is supposed to ask all the questions while I answer. I said, "What if he does not say anything?" My aunt said, "You sit and stay quiet for the whole time." I said, "But I need to find out." ... "Well, Islamically you are not even supposed to speak back to him or ask him a question," my aunt said. I replied, "No, Aunty. Islamically, I am supposed to, otherwise how I am gonna find out whether this is someone I can marry or not ... just by him asking me questions?" ... and [it] really took her aback that I actually had the nerve to question her, but she knew I was confident enough and I was old enough not to be intimidated.

The fact that Fadwa was expected to be silent contradicts her outspoken and curious personality.

After Fadwa recounted her first marriage proposal, I asked, "So what is your plan after going through that experience? Are you going to marry a Muslim who is from a different nationality, or one who is not from the village? How would your parents react to that?" She replied, "People who have not been exposed to different, multiple models of reality will have difficulty understanding my position ... and I've seen that even within our family...." Fadwa sighed and related this story about a friend of hers:

63

> The most academic girl I've ever met got some of the highest marks in engineering.... Halfway through her medical school application, ... she had gotten a proposal from a gentleman and her father said, "What do you think of this man?" She's like, "He's okay, I'll think about it." Before she knew it, her contract was ready and she was married to this guy. The point of the story is that she's been married to him for four years now and it's not the marriage she would have chosen for herself. This brought me to a point of understanding that women, depending on their context, they have very little room for negotiation.... It doesn't really depend on how educated we are, it depends on whether or not we're going to be given the freedom by our parents, our family, our culture to make that choice. Our education can only take us so far, but because we live in a collective society, ... maybe not Muslim—I don't know if it's just Muslim women, it's probably Middle Eastern Arabic women's—our choices are limited....

By sharing her friend's experience, Fadwa highlights the silencing of women's—even educated women's—voices, as well as the restrictions that determine many important life decisions such as marriage. Women are forced to abide by cultural traditions, many of which oppress them and their personal objectives. Even those women who have obtained an impressive education often fall prey to self-doubt. Fadwa confirmed this in her statement that "Our education can only take us so far.... We have very little room for negotiation." Is Fadwa's viewpoint realistic, or is she merely being pessimistic? Does her opinion reflect gender discourses that persistently reinforce patriarchy within various contexts (i.e., culturally and socially)? Many women are subjected to these gender discourses in a variety of ways and in a variety of contexts, sometimes even indirectly.

When it comes to compatibility of the level of education the married couple has and what that might imply within the marriage, Fadwa said:

> If a woman is very intellectual or articulate and she's chosen a companion that is not very compatible with her, ... it will be a problem. Some [men] are very educated men who went abroad, ... studied, ... got the highest degrees, and they're well-off, but their concept of what a woman's role is ... that a woman cooks, cleans.... I want someone I can actually sit and chat with and talk to and make decisions and articulate what life means.

In this example given by Fadwa, men are still viewed as the ones who decide how a woman's intellect is valued in the marriage. It is not about how assertive the woman is. Clearly, Fadwa—and many other interviewees—believe that compatibility in the level of education between couples would not guarantee a stable marriage, yet Morooj's daughter's former fiancé and Fadwa's cousin's marriage illustrated that the spouse's education does not guarantee that he will be understanding and supportive. Thus, I argue that the spouse's level of education is not a major factor in providing a stable marriage; how the couple views marriage within the "traditional box" or outside it and how a woman's role is defined within a marriage is what creates stability.

I was not surprised to learn that Morooj's daughter's former fiancé, who was educated in the West, still holds this patriarchal perspective about woman's education. Male chauvinism is embedded, although covertly, in the West as well. Further, Morooj added:

> I think it goes back to his upbringing, ... his family, and what kind of beliefs he was brought up with.... If he was brought up believing that a woman should be at a lower level than her husband and he fears [a] motivated women, then he would not accept that his wife is at his level of education.... Some men cannot and don't like to have women around them that are at the same level, whether it be at work or at home.... A motivated woman will always look at the better and best. I told my daughter, "This is your chance to do your PhD in New York," and she felt that he would not stand beside her. She left him....

So it is better for a woman to be educated. This will enable her to make the right decision for herself. I told my daughters, "Education first." ... Encouraging my daughters to obtain education is important because it is going to make me feel that my daughter is secure. I told my other daughter's husband [newly married] I do not want gold or money.[9] The only thing I want is that my daughter is able to have a job, if she chooses to. I made this request official when we wrote the marriage contract.

I also asked Fadwa about the value of education for men and women. Where does the importance of education lie? Was it economic security or prestige? Fadwa explained:

But when it comes to for whom education is more important—a man or a woman—I think two generations ago when education was scarce and men only had access and men were the only providers in the time, when men could provide and what they provided was sufficient to support a family and women were not allowed to provide, then I would have said perhaps it would just have been easier for men to get the education and maybe women, because they did not have as many opportunities ... at that time, just reading and writing might have been important, ... but now, economically, it is not very feasible to have men as the sole providers in the family.... Back in the day when women kept dowries ... gold as their insurance in case something happened, ... now we are in a different time.... I cannot expect my husband to give me a gold dowry and expect that to sustain me.

Today women's education, according to Fadwa, is an economic necessity. I add that women's education and economic stability would lead to women's independence, which would also result in their ability to control and maintain power. I then asked Fadwa to clarify whether she saw the purpose of a woman obtaining an education only as economic sustainability: "That's what culture teaches us.... My father needed to know what my profession was and he was very uncomfortable with me doing a double major.... He wanted me to be able to [have] a specialized trade...."

Both Fadwa and her parents expected that she would pursue an education to secure her life financially. Another reason for her to obtain a Master's degree was for self-actualization.

Although Ruba did not have as many struggles as Fadwa, she drew the line between religion and cultural traditions:

65

That Islam ... hinders women or holds them back is absolutely weird because to me, it's the absolute opposite. To me, it's the key to my freedom. I think if you're a Muslim woman, you're a free woman. That's my perception. You're free intellectually.... Even, like, our dress code is liberating because I'm presenting to you a person who you're actually gonna interact with on a level of equivalence.... You're not looking at me as an object. It eliminated a question; it eliminated a barrier that people sometimes find very hard to cross. When you're sitting across from a woman ... because of her physical appearance, ... somehow it's distracting.... That's the nature of human beings. We could deny it or we could just accept it and move on, so to me the covering is freeing, it's not restrictive at all. In terms of my ability to reach goals—educational, and even intellectual and spiritual— I've always found that religion opens the door for me without any limits.... When I grew up and we read the Holy *Quran*, some of the verses encouraged continuous thinking, so when you have a religion that tells you that you are encouraged to think and you are not limited, just look around you, think about it, and make the decision for yourself. So that, for me, is liberating, so it never hindered me at any time or by any means....

Ruba underscored that "my faith is liberating and culture is not affecting me very much because we did not live by culture."

When some of the interviewees reflected the idea that society is a masculine enterprise, dominated by "masculine ethics of rationality" (Chodorow, 1978), it clearly showed how cultural traditions are influential. On several occasions, the women argued that men dominate the "public"—the world of rationality, competitiveness, positivism, and linear thinking, while women occupied the "private"—the world of mothering, emotion, expressiveness, and imagination (Chodorow, 1978). Nahlaa, for instance, insisted that women are created to function in the private sphere. This is congruent with the predominantly historical trend.

This mindset is reflected also in Arabic literature[10] and in Arabic idiomatic expressions. For instance, the Arabic saying, "A shadow of a man is better than a shadow of a wall," emphasizes that a woman's life is worthless unless she devotes it to a man. Another perception that still dominates and was mentioned in Yasmine's interviews is that a "real" man is not expected to do any household chores. Society insists that a "real" man should not involve himself in the domestic realm as it is a woman's realm.

This is in contrast with Yasmine's and Nora's families' gender power arrangements. Yasmine and her spouse are sharing what is culturally known to be a masculine enterprise (i.e., providing for the family). Nora's family is scheduling household responsibilities. However, Yasmine, Nora, and other participants acknowledged that some traditional Arab Muslim families, "as a basic structure of society is among those culturally and legally shaped institutions that most pervasively curtail women's capacity for flourishing" (Hill, 2003, p. 5).

Many times during the interviews, Eman, Nahlaa, Fadwa, and Wafaa overemphasized that we are biological beings and therefore women, by their biological construct, are the weaker sex and should have a less public role. I am not denying that we are "biological beings." However, like Nancy Chodorow (1978), I agree that "women's physiological experiences—pregnancy, menstruation, parturition, menopause, and lactation—are certainly powerful ... in our society and in many others, and they are also given strong meaning socially and psychologically" (p. 16). Clearly, the women interviewed and others who attribute child nurturing to women reflect that they do not "separate child care from child bearing, nurturing as an activity from pregnancy and parturition" (p. 16). Many of them believe that "it is a woman's biological destiny to bear and deliver, to nurse and to rear children" (Jacobson, as cited in Chodorow, 1978, p. 11).

Fadwa clearly showed a degree of rebellion against some of the perceptions that subordinate a woman to a man. She acknowledged that her family's disapproval is related to the familial and social patriarchy and hierarchy, which are based solely on gender roles and expectations. She questioned that mentality, emphasizing that,

> The interesting, *interesting* [original emphasis] part is that my father, several of his brothers, [and] several of my cousins—all men—I can count about 12 people who left the country to study. No one said a single word, not a single person questioned their decision or even presumed that it would be an insult to the education system [back home]. Only when it was me—then it was something that insulted our fine educational system, but that was not my intent. I had just been [oversees studying] for so long, ... so culturally, I guess it is not ... acceptable.

Ironically, Fadwa's cousin, who was the most critical of Fadwa's decision, lives alone in a residence away from her immediate and extended family.[11]

From Fadwa's story and other narratives, I contend that women in Arab Muslim societies are expected to be obedient and silent—traits that are considered feminine. Conforming to gender norms, properly conducting oneself as a female, and submitting to the feminine traits is highly regarded in our native society—'*bent al-nas*'[12] is an Arabic term meaning "respectful woman

67

of a good family." In other words, living up to the traditional expectations of a woman in sitting, walking, and talking is all subsumed under gender discourses. I tried to conform, consciously or unconsciously, to these standards when I lived in Saudi Arabia and also during my short visits home over the past ten years, yet "we know that feminine girls sometimes grow up to be unfeminine women; we know that identity is not constant over time" (as cited in McQuillan & Pfeiffer, 2001, p. 18). This applies to Fadwa's experience.

Another interesting trend that I have noted in the narratives is that elderly women seemed to be perpetuating the suppression. Personally, I was subjected to these social norms. I remembered that when I introduced my spouse to my grandmother, after he left the room, she whispered that she needed to talk to me. She admonished me for "crossing lines" and she pointed out that a woman who is brought up in a "good house" should not talk loudly in her spouse's presence and should not call her spouse by his first name. Although I have not followed these rules, I note that elderly women in the culture feel it is their duty to perpetuate (with good intentions) the cultural traditions of gender discourses.

Sorya Altorki, a Saudi anthropologist, was also subject to the patriarchy supported by elderly women. Her anthropological research, entitled "At Home in the Field," involves various discussions with elderly women. In her research, Altorki was constantly reminded by elderly women that "education is good, but women are weak. No matter how much money they have, no matter their education, they cannot manage without men. May Allah save your father and your brother. But you have to start your own family" (Altorki, 1988, p. 53). When I read the above quote, it resonated with me and I was reminded that the foremost expectation for a woman in Saudi society is to be a mother and a wife. While attending university, I, along with my sisters and other female relatives, were relentlessly reminded of our role by elederly women. According to them, the only way a woman can contribute to society is through marriage and children, and a woman's life is meaningless unless she is devoted to a man.

Personally, I have wrestled with how to interpret and construct my environment at different points in my life, particularly in times of transition or change (i.e., moving to Canada). I draw from my personal experiences as a Muslim Saudi woman who grew up and completed undergraduate studies in a conservative, patriarchal society. My gender has been constructed by my Islamic faith and the Arab culture of Saudi Arabia. I read and memorized the Holy *Quran* from a very young age. The *Quranic* text does not contradict scientific discourse, which I found fascinating; indeed, the *Quran*'s teachings to women contradict some cultural traditions, practices, and patriarchal societal norms I have experienced and observed. For instance, while I found the *Quran* supports women's leadership, powerful male elites in most Arab Muslim societies prevent women from practising that right. In addition, while female genital mutilation is a cultural practice that has no basis in the *Quran* or in the Prophet's teaching (PBUH), it is perpetuated by cultural traditions in the name of Islamic teachings to women. (Fortunately, female genital mutilation is not practised in Saudi Arabia.)

In Saudi Arabia, I questioned the contradictions I perceived between the *Quran* and the patriarchal cultural traditions and societal norms I experienced. These cultural traditions and practices were imposed, justified, and carried on in Saudi society and still prevail today due to the hegemony of male power. Some cultural traditions and practices have prevailed by keeping women illiterate.[13] Morooj alleged that women might tend to be passive if they do not know their rights and responsibilities in light of Islamic teachings. "If Islam gives rights to women, it remains that they [women] need to know these rights in order to defend them" (Ramadan, 2001, p. 55). This puts a great emphasis on education and the ability to think critically.

Morooj, Eman, Yasmine, Nora, and some other women interviewed for this research were aware of the differences between the actual Islamic teachings to women and cultural traditions and values. All of my interviewees are Canadian immigrants, born and raised in Arab Muslim societies. I noted that all of them stressed Islam as reconciliation. In looking at Arab Muslim women's perceptions of their gender roles, one should bear in mind that "beyond all social norms stands Islam, the tenets of which are ultimately the arbiter of all community standards" (Harris, 2004, p. 24). Islam, in their view, gave them power and authority to bring equitable social order within their communities as well as in Canadian society, where they can discuss issues of all inequality, including racial biases.

Interestingly, these women presented Islam as a counterperspective to the prevalent gender discourses and practices in Arab culture. They also offered alternative perspectives to many dominant Western notions of Muslim women. The women are constantly negotiating gender discourses and gender social relations, as well as re-evaluating gender ideologies perpetuated in the name of Islam to pursue their own interests, which is to reinitiate the status granted to women in Islamic texts. They are exerting and creating new social and cultural ideas for inclusion "as participants and as producers of new cultural ideologies rather than passive recipients" (Limon, 1989, p. 476) who merely reflect and transmit cultural norms of gender.

Although the women interviewed made a clear distinction between patriarchal traditional and cultural values, and Islamic teachings to women, some seemed to be caught up in, or highly influenced by, certain aspects of these patriarchal societal norms. For instance, Wafaa, who lives with her parents, stated that she needed to ask her fiancé, who lives abroad, for permission if she wanted to go for errands. Wafaa mentioned that her older sister does not agree with this practice. Wafaa told me that her sister doesn't agree that she needs her fiancé's or spouse's permission for anything. Wafaa's married sister informed her that a woman is wise, mature, and knows what she's doing and therefore should be able to move freely. I asked Wafaa if she agreed with what her sister said. Wafaa responded:

> No, no, because Islam tells us we have to ask the permission of our husbands. Let's say I wanna go to Windsor with my friend. I don't just go. I call him, although he's far away.... I'm responsible, I call him. "Can I go to Windsor? Yes? I go. No? I don't."

In the same breath, Wafaa stated that a good wife in Islam is not the obedient wife portrayed by the culture. I asked her how she differentiates between what is Islamic and what is cultural tradition. Wafaa said, "In culture, the good wife is just committed to obey, but that is not right.... A good wife can be good by being a good mother to her children; she can be good by having a welcoming home, by being good to her husband." Wafaa's contradictory points of view indicate that she is caught between two conflicting ideas, yet she does not seem to realize that some of her views are echoing cultural values that were inculcated as we grew up at home and at school.

Also, while all the participants saw themselves as intellectually capable as men, some of them stressed that there are differences between males and females when it came to performing certain skills. They attributed those differences to biological distinctions. Most of the participants conveyed a belief in the separateness of men and women, particularly in terms of employment. In contrast, to support their views of men's and women's equality, they all cited *Quranic* verses that a woman and a man are equal and created from the same soul (i.e., the *Quran* presents God as saying, "Your Lord who created you from one soul"). However, the women did not cite any religious texts when referring to the distinction between men's and women's spheres. This, according to Nahlaa, was a matter of personal observation.

Fadwa described the struggles she endured while living alone in Canada so that she could obtain a better education. She resisted the rigid oppression and harsh discipline of the patriarchal system that attempts to dictate her life, a system that treats her differently based on her sex. Fadwa's decision to remain in Canada to study, and her confidence in challenging this patriarchal system, demonstrate her determination to live by the principles of her faith, not by patriarchal criteria. In her view, however, biological differences still render a woman more nurturing and caring than a man. Along the same vein, some participants also emphasized that women embody nurturing characteristics while men embody logic and rationale. Further, they argued that women are not objective enough to hold political positions, and women are too "emotional."

The issue of women holding leadership positions is another example of how Islamic teaching contradicts the prevailing patriarchal cultural traditions and societal norms in most Arab Muslim societies. In the history of Islam, there are many examples of strong female political leaders, yet that is not the case in most modern Arab Muslim societies. This is giving the public the impression that it is neither expected nor desired for women to occupy leadership roles. These contradictions between religious and some cultural values greatly influenced the participants' perceptions. Some double standards the women held became evident in attitudes toward the value of education for sons and daughters, as mentioned earlier. For instance, Nahlaa asserted that a man's education is of more value than a woman's. She was strongly influenced by tradition. It is troubling to watch "women … internalize these negative beliefs leading them to lack confidence in their ability to perform challenging tasks. Research suggests that women may lack confidence in their ability to successfully complete nontraditional tasks" (Betz & Hackett, 1981, as cited in Dickerson & Taylor, 2000, p. 192).

Although some of the interviewed women expressed the extent to which the culture affected their choices, they did not passively agree with some traditions, especially the ones that contradict Islamic tenets (i.e., Fadwa regarding female circumcision). The women interviewed are aware of the conflicts among some aspects of cultural traditions and societal norms, some of which are patriarchal, on the one hand, and some of which are Islamic teachings to women, on the other. Yet they have a sense of comfort and confidence by being religious, reading the texts constantly, and staying close to the *Quran* and the authentic Islamic texts. Yasmine emphasized, "Only religion makes someone good or bad, no matter what the religion be [*sic*]."

As much as some of the women interviewed are influenced by their traditions, they are also working to contest and resist the negative and patriarchal aspects of them. In this I concur with Buitelaar, Ketner, and Bosma (2004): "The [women] are not only influenced by their tradition and religion; they have an influence on these ideologies as well" (p. 166). Thus, I argue that the women interviewed in this research are creating new traditions that are Islamically authentic.

It is significant to appreciate how cultural traditions and religious practices are intertwined yet contradictory in these Arab Muslim women's narratives. Morooj, Fadwa, Ruba, and the other women believe that in all life matters, Islam is pro-woman. They all acknowledge that there are many aspects of cultural traditions that differentiate between a woman's and a man's role. In Islamic essence there are no prescribed roles for men and women. In each of these narratives, the women have distinguished between traditional practices and religious teaching, noting how both construct their gendered self.

Through their education, Fadwa and the other women in this research managed to move beyond the goal ascribed to Arab Muslim women by cultural traditions, which is to be mothers and wives. Although there is a tone of self-limitation echoed in Fadwa's examples, the way she dealt with her marriage proposal suggests sophistication in renouncing and disavowing the traditional role of woman—of submissiveness and silence. These Arab Muslim women made a great effort to separate Islamic teachings from cultural traditions and values. They highlighted the tension and the contradictions between the two, especially with respect to gender discourses. The women distinguished between Islamic teachings and cultural practices. Indeed, some of the women referred to some traditional and cultural practices as merely "sexist traditions."[4] Also, the women developed cognitive strategies to deal with contradictory cultural norms and Islamic values to avoid and/or reconcile contradictions. Moreover, they rejected certain elements of traditions, especially with regard to gender, and used their knowledge of Islam to denounce unfavourable traditions. The gap between the Islamic construction of gender and a cultural construction of gender discourses runs like a thread through the texture of the participants' narratives.

NOTES

1. Muslim women are required to wear the scarf only in the presence of male non-relatives.

2. This happened in an Islamic country. In some colonised Arab Muslim nations, such as Egypt, Tunisia, and Algeria, the *hijab* was not encouraged when the colonisers were in power. However, at "a turning point in the 1980s, it became a form of protest against Western intrusion and religious reconversion" (Fernea, 1998, p. 234).

3. Forty days is the cultural maternity leave for new mothers from all social and religious obligations.

4. Although I read and researched female genital mutilation, this is my first encounter with a woman narrating her personal circumcision experience.

5. Although *Sunna* refers to the actions and sayings of the Prophet (PBUH), female circumcision is not documented in the Prophet's (PBUH) traditional practices. However, it is mentioned once in a saying that not many scholars authenticate.

6. "Female genital mutilation" is preferred to the misleading term "female circumcision" because the latter practice refers to the mildest form of operation, which affects only a small percentage of the millions of women operated on. Most of this section is based on the Minority Rights Group (1992), "Female Genital Mutilation: Proposals for Change" (as cited in Baden, 1992, p. 17).

7. Sisters' School is a Catholic all-girls school, which used to be run by nuns (sisters) from Italy.

8. Unity School is an American secular international school.

9. It is in religion that a man gives a dowry to his prospective wife. A dowry is a obligatory in Islam and is like a gift. It is a cultural tradition that a man also has to give gold, but this depends on the social class of the families.

10. For more on Arabic literature on the silencing of Arab Muslim women, see Ahmad Jamal (1980), *Qadaya Moasera. Current Issues*. Damascus: *Dar Majlaat Althagafea*. It is important to mention that that book was part of my curricula in Grade 8.

11. Fadwa's cousin's parents lived in a Gulf country.

12. For more details, refer to Yamani (2004).

13. Official schooling for women in Saudi Arabia was initiated 40 years after men's education (Al-Manea, 1984; Al-Mohsen, 2000).

14. These are Yasmine's exact words.

73

Chapter Six

TALKING EQUALITY: CREATION FROM ONE SOUL

"The *Quran* clearly indicates and asserts that human creation comes from, or is made of a *single* [italics in original] soul and grants human trusteeship for all" (Barazangi, 2000, p. 24). If the Holy *Quran* states that a woman and a man are created from the same soul, where has the second-class status that women hold in most Arab Muslim societies originated from? Barlas (2002) states that the *Quran* does not say that males embody divine attributes and that women are, by nature, weak. Canadian Muslim scholar Jamal Badawi (1995) argues that nowhere in the *Quran* does it state that one gender is superior to the other. Why, then, is there an oversight of Muslim women's potential? Why do some Muslim families choose to finance their sons' educations at the expense of their daughters? Why do some women, when discussing the subject, implicitly support the notion of male superiority? I argue that misogynistic interpretations of the texts that prevail in most Arab Muslim societies are deeply entrenched in the minds of many women and men across the generations.

In Islam, there are defined roles for men and women. There is no sense of competition between the sexes; instead, they are complementary to one another. They excel in different areas and they are able to perform different functions. Women and men only complement each other in the biological reproductions, not in other functions (religious, moral, social, etc.) (see Barazangi, 2004). Men and women are different but equal, as Ruba has stated. Wafaa also perceives the need to treat boys and girls equally, stating that this is an Islamic tenet. Sahra added that from an Islamic point of view, women and men are equal: "They're not the same. There are still some differences—biological differences and psychological differences—but still they are equal. They should have equal access to education and jobs...."

Yasmine suggested, "I believe in equality between sexes—both sexes have rights and responsibilities. They are equal in the eyes of God, not equal in their abilities. There are certain jobs men can do, but a woman cannot do...." Yasmine was unable to determine what her perception is, nor was she able to firmly decide on equality between the sexes. I argue that the contradictory tone in her discussion of equality exemplifies the tension between cultural traditions and religious points of view.

Fadwa observed that although many Arab Muslim parents may claim that they view the two sexes equally, they continue to differentiate in how their children are socialized at a young age. Fadwa narrated a story:

> My father always *always* [with emphasis] said there is no difference be-
> tween a boy and a girl. Sometimes girls can be better than boys, and he
> humbles me by using me as an example, saying to me that the fact that
> I've been here [in Canada] and I've maintained my faith and at the same
> time done a good job with my education is something he takes pride in
> and something that confirms belief that women and men are essentially,
> or inherently, equal or capable of the same things. My mom, on the other
> hand, even though she didn't grow up in the village like my dad did, is
> more aware of that cultural socialization, differentiation for genders in
> the local sense of it....
>
> Socialization is another thing. My mother made sure I knew how to
> do my own laundry, how to cook, how to clean, and it was all about me
> knowing how to do girls' things by a certain age. And when I went to the
> village, my aunts, whether it be my father or mother's side, a lot of the
> time gave me the lecture: "You should be able to cook such and such, or
> clean such and such. You're eight and nine, and girls who are five- and
> six-year-olds in the village can do this already." ...

Certainly, there is no doubt that the way individuals are brought up in their native society influences their thoughts and actions later in life.

Eman confirmed that even though there are many slogans about equality, the slogans vanish in practice: "... in most societies I have lived in, from the outside you can see that they're equal, but when you really look into certain issues, ... a woman is not considered equal."

When speaking of equality between the sexes in terms of gender roles, Ruba asserted, "To start with, women and men are different: I don't think we're physically compatible.... Men are physically different.... Emotionally we are different.... Men can do things better than women and women can do other things better than men." However, she emphasized, through her personal experiences, that her interactions with intelligent men in the family and in the workplace were unlike her encounters with women who, according to Ruba, tend to be emotional and manipulative. She also concluded that "Men have proven to be wiser because they tend to be calm and less emotional when they are trying to reason with things."

Fadwa continued to talk about the differences between women's and men's abilities and cultural perceptions regarding the gendering of their roles:

> From a physiological and psychological perspective, the differences between men and women would logically make sense ... because women are the ones that get pregnant for nine months.... [They have] that relationship with the baby that a man never, never will have, and they're [women] physiologically prepared to be the nurturers. Part of me would want to say, like, I don't see women as lumberjacks. They wouldn't be as good lumberjacks as men are at cutting wood, for instance, but one of my earliest memories is of my grandmother when I was six years old. I would wake up to this drumming sound and it was my grandmother cutting wood.... There was no electricity in the village, so my grandmother needed the wood to [start] a fire to make breakfast.... So, I guess it might not make sense that women would be better than men at other things.... It's just a sociological construct.... I seem to be a little ambivalent and I acknowledge that because part of me wants to say, "Yes, we are different." The other part is the equality between men and women.... If men can do it, we can do it too, so ... I'm a little in-between.... They were created from the same (soul) or the same spirit, so their origin is the same. Men wouldn't be men and women wouldn't be women if they weren't different. Then we would be all the same.... I think our biological differences might result in our societal differences, but intellectually I ... think the only reason that we are different intellectually, or believed to be different, is because society makes it out to be so. I think intellectually, we're not different at all, maybe emotionally, emotionally of course.... Again, biological differences might result in emotional differences. We have our monthly visitors [menstrual cycle].... But they [men] don't have estrogen; they have testosterone and these hormones do relate to some physical aspects and perhaps emotional aspects. From a religious perspective, according to Islam, we're going to be judged equally based on our individual actions.... Our actions are based on our reasoning and our thought processes and our logic.

77

I did not interrupt Fadwa during this part of the interview, nor did I divide her narrative, so that it would truly reflect her self-analyses and perceptions. It is amazing how she was thinking out loud—she was trying to analyze her thoughts, which point out contradictions between her reasoning and her emotions. Fadwa wants to think that women and men are equal—a thought that was supported by her grandmother's woodcutting and by referencing the *Quran*'s teaching—yet she kept convincing herself that women and men are different. Her statements reproduce an acceptance of the inevitability of women's inferiority. In admitting women's weaknesses, biologically and physically, she appears unable to contradict the cultural norm. The main reason for the difference between the sexes is the biological structure. She knows that her position is ambivalent, but she is unable to alter it since society is widening the gap and reinforcing it:

> Society-wise, though, men can get away with way more than women can. Men can do things that would be deemed inappropriate for women, like me living here on my own without my family.... My extended family has known me since I was a young child.... But if [it was] in a different context, with a different family within the same culture, ... a female living alone would be considered immorally [and] ethically impaired as opposed to a male who's pursuing what's best for him so he can provide for his family.... A girl, what is a girl doing alone in North America? So, you see where the culture comes into play. Yes, mentally we might be equal [and] actions might be the same, but the way society evaluates us is not the same ... as the way God evaluates us, and that's what we have to deal with.... If someone lives in a context where her reputation and her honour are very important, she might have to adhere to society's norms just to make sure that society doesn't outcast or ostracize her.

This part of Fadwa's narrative is extremely powerful. Not only is she illustrating the double standards with which boys and girls are treated, but she is also pinpointing the reason for that mentality—female "honour." Fadwa's comments here best demonstrate the social construction of gender in Arab Muslim societies. The gap between what a woman can do and what a man can do is profound. In Arab culture, if a man decides to live on his own, there would be no concern about his desire to be independent. A woman, on the other hand, cannot leave her parents' home unless she is married, and if she divorces, she will have to return to her parents' home. Thus, it is deeply embedded in the minds of Arab Muslim people that a woman cannot live alone, perhaps because she is thought to be less capable, less competent, and less moral, and therefore cannot conduct herself appropriately. I acknowledge that this argument might be similar, to a certain extent, to that found in certain parts of the world, but it prevails strongly today in Arab Muslim Middle Eastern societies. These kinds of restrictions on women can be detrimental to women's education, as Fadwa noted:

My understanding is through both my parents, through the way they've promoted my education by telling me since I was very, very, very young that I need to be independent. Even living here on my own is just a part of their experiment for "Fadwa to learn independence." ... It shows that, in theory, my parents want me to [be independent]. My parents believe that men and women are intellectually equal. In practice, however, things might be a little different. Maybe part of it is because of the higher rank that is given to men culturally, ... so that if a man's idea comes through and a woman's idea is a little different, ... [the] man's idea will be the one to win.

I wholeheartedly support Fadwa's conclusions—they reflect the way in which we are socialized in school and in society at large.

When referring to equality within education, all the participants agreed that education is important for men and women alike. However, some emphasized that education is still more important for males. Through the following discussion, I explore how strongly these women feel about the importance of women's education, whether or not they feel that males' education is prioritized within the school system, and to what extent they have asserted their perceptions.

When I asked Ruba about equality, she laughingly recounted her memories of an engineering professor:

He made a comment in class while he was talking about his education in England at Oxford University. He proudly said, "Back in the good old days before females were allowed in engineering." And I thought that remark was kind of weird.... We were only two girls, me and another one. He said it in a very subtle way.... I was so surprised that he made that kind of remark or comment.... This is a professor who is White, middle class, with jeans and long hair, ... so he's supposed to be the hip and cool guy, but still, his mentality was a little bit different.... Another incident was in the engineering lab while I was assisting a male instructor.... He was uncomfortable answering my [casual] question.... I realized that he was avoiding eye-to-eye contact.... Later he told me that he thinks that women hinder the progress of things.... He thinks they're a distraction.... These two incidents did not bother me. It surprised me, and actually I expected it.... There are a lot of free sentiments about equality out there, but I don't think a lot of people believe [in] it.... But there was always a push to get more females into engineering, ... which I found very strange....

During the conversation, I was interested to know why Ruba stated that encouraging women to enter engineering is "strange." At the time, she was one among very few females in the faculty of engineering. Two or three girls, at most, were enrolled in the faculty of engineering at the Canadian university she attended in the late 1980s. Ruba compares this with the faculty of engineering in Jordan, where she was previously enrolled. She affirmed, "In Canada, the majority of the class is made up of men, unlike in Jordan, … [where] you could actually see that the class was split between girls and boys in engineering school." She recounted:

> It was an event at [my home university in Canada] at the engineering school, an all-day professional day for girls, where girls visit from high school and inquire about engineering and women's positions in engineering.… I remember that I participated and, just to be honest and truthful, not for the cause of women because I'm not like that. I'm not trying to raise awareness of women's issues or anything like that. I'm absolutely actually not interested in that, but to me it was an extracurricular and I needed it as a credit.

Ruba also expressed that "It's very sad when we get into this competition of trying to actually do everything because men do it.… If you want to explore something, try it, but don't do it just for the sake that men are doing it." As much as I admire Ruba for her honesty, I argue that this is a risky attitude for her to have. I examine why Ruba and many other women, Eastern and Western, do not perceive that there are women's issues, and why they overlook the need to support women's causes. Is Ruba denying something about her life? Is she overlooking her femaleness? Or is she discounting the fact that she is an engineer now as a consequence of other women's struggles, mostly women who created the early feminist movement in the West? Another possibility is that Ruba and other women who disclaim the existence of women's issues are relieving themselves of their responsibility toward other women. I contend that by taking this approach, Ruba and other women who oppose women's issues are limiting their options and narrowing their world view.

Unlike Ruba's experience in the faculty of engineering in Jordan, Sahra remembers that in her engineering faculty, the proportion of women was lower than that of men, both in Egypt and in Canada. When she made the decision to become an engineer, many of Sahra's friends told her that engineering is a male enterprise and that being inquisitive in math and geometry is one thing, while pursuing engineering is another. Also, "some traditional faculty members in Cairo treated me according to the assumed inferiority of women in engineering.... I avoided taking their courses [laughs] and that's it." I asked Sahra if she personally ever felt that engineering is a man's field. She replied adamantly:

> No, no, absolutely not. I worked in civil engineering for three or four years in Egypt, and one year I was my husband's supervisor [laughs] kind of, or at least my job was to make sure that he's doing his job correctly.... In the same year I graduated, it was a female who achieved the top highest mark.... Eventually, she got the department's support and was hired as a part-time faculty member....

Sahra told me that the number of women in engineering differs according to the branch of engineering: in the "electric engineering department, you find the ratio of male/female is 50/50 and you find lots of female professors. In architectural and in mechanical there were no females at all at the faculty or student level, ... " yet, according to Sahra, in computer science, in which she was doing her graduate work, the ratio is equal between males and females. Sahra contrasted Ruba's perception: She asserted that women are needed in engineering and need the encouragement to pursue their studies.

In terms of the male-to-female ratio within the arts and sciences, Eman did not think that there was an issue. When she studied English literature in Libya, the male/female ratio in her faculty was evenly distributed, yet for Fadwa, who had been to both science and arts faculties, "Ratio-wise, there are way more males to females in science.... I had four professors who were women, of all the years I was in science." An interesting aspect of Fadwa's observation is the stereotypical images of female arts and sciences students. Not only did the participants discuss differences, but they also inadvertently supported stereotypes within the conversation. Yasmine stereotypically asserted that there are differences between boys' and girls' abilities in school:

> Boys are generally good in sciences and math; girls are good in art and languages.... I think that there is some scientific evidence behind that. Girls do better at university than in high school, and boys do better in high school than they do in university because of hormonal changes.... Scientifically, we believe that men and women have menopausal lows, ups, and downs. Girls have their period and they have lots on their plates. I believe that girls are not the smartest in all subjects, and the same with boys. They don't master all subjects.

In the next breath, Yasmine added:

> Boys are not smarter in all fields, but they are smarter in some areas like
> business, for example.... My cultural beliefs and religious beliefs tell me
> that boys and girls should be treated the same and both be educated....
> However, we cannot generalize their abilities according to gender.... In-
> dividual abilities come into play.... There is an exception to everything.

As an educator, I revisit Yasmine's statement that "boys are good in sciences and math; girls are good in art and languages," and I argue that there
is no definitive evidence for the claim of innate gender differences affecting
the educational achievements of boys and girls. I question whether or not this
perception translates to the reality of boys' and girls' schooling. Many scholars argue that the differences between boys and girls achievements,[1] when
noted, is insignificant. I contend that the differences between boys' and girls'
performance in school, when noted, are related to socialization rather than to
genetics. Also, Fadwa, along the same lines, highlighted the following:

> Well, science girls aren't as pretty as social science girls because science
> girls are the nerds.... They're the articulate ones, so articulate, smart
> girls aren't usually as pretty. The girls that aren't so smart are the pretty
> ones, which are the girls in social sciences.

I argue that these kinds of stereotypes have a lot to do with the way we are
socialized and cultured. I perceive these stereotypes as a platform to discourage girls from pursuing science. These stereotypes create "invisible
barriers raised by socialization of boys and girls and old norms against
women's pursuit of wholeness, of autonomy, and of authority ..." (Aisenberg
& Harrington, 1988, p. 142).

For Nora, although elementary school was her only coeducational experience, this perception was a reality. She remembers a few incidents where
boys and girls were not treated equally:

> My girlfriend in elementary school was getting the highest marks, yet
> some of the teachers used to give another boy in our class slightly high-
> er marks than her so he would end up before her on the honour list, but
> my girlfriend used to argue that a lot with the teachers. She used to go to
> teachers and ask them, "Why did you give me a lower mark?" In Grade 6
> she was at the top of the list in the class and in the school list—far from
> the boy....

Hearing these aspects of the narratives, part of me is thankful that my schooling in Saudi Arabia was segregated by sex—not that I consider myself incapable of competing with males, but I suspect that the situation would be worse as Saudi society is male-dominated and males always receive more attention.

When asked the question "If you could not financially afford to support both your sons' and your daughters' education, which would you support?" all respondents agreed that their sons would be the ones they would foremost support, justifying that, according to the culture, the man is the one who must work and provide for his family. They were then asked, "What if your sons were not doing well in school? Would you still support them financially?" Here, they felt the parents' financial support should go to whoever was doing the best.

Yasmine, for instance, felt that university education is valuable and necessary to both men and women, but if faced with limited resources and she had to choose, she would support her sons, unless they were not succeeding. She spoke to me earlier about her eldest daughter, who is exceptionally intelligent and has won many awards; however, she did not mention her son's educational achievements.[2] She added, "I even told my sons and my daughters that whoever is not doing well in school is not going to get my financial support."[3] From these responses, I infer that girls' education is considered as secondary in importance to that of boys by most of the women in this study.

Morooj, a mother of four, perceived no difference in the importance of higher education for men and women. "What if you have limited resources? What would you do?" I asked. She replied:

> My sons need to be educated as much as the girls. This is a difficult question. It did not occur to me before, ... but I don't like to give that a thought.... I'd like to think that I am capable of sending them all to school. Culturally, the boys have to be the ones because they will start a family, but in case they are not doing well in school, then my daughter, who is doing well, deserves it.

I asked, "So you will decide according to their level of success and how well they are doing in school?" Morooj nodded.

In a closing statement that provides a sort of justice within such a topic as equality in education, Nora stated: "In my family ... my father wished that he had three girls after me instead of three sons because he is not satisfied with their educational achievements." Nora's father, in stating this, gives weight to the argument for equality within the educational system for both sexes—that both boys and girls have equal likelihoods of academic success, provided they are given the opportunity and necessary support to achieve it.

FAMILY HONOUR AND FEMALE VIRGINITY

In many regions of the Arab Muslim world, the notion of family honour facilitates patriarchal power by circumscribing women's sexuality and movement in social arenas and, to some degree, within economic opportunities. Women are not only socialized to feel inferior, they are also brought up with the fear of dishonouring their families if they fail to follow restrictions. This enhances the power of fathers, grandfathers, uncles, brothers, and male cousins over women (Josef & Slyomovics, 2001, p. 199).

Arab Muslim parents worry that a daughter may conduct herself inappropriately; for instance, a daughter may risk interacting in a flirtatious manner with a male. This may lead her to lose her virginity and disgrace her family. In contrast, a boy's virginity is not an issue, since when he marries, no one will know whether or not he has had sexual intercourse previously. Clearly, this is a double standard in the way boys and girls are treated:

> Women are expected to behave in ways that would not bring shame on themselves, and destroy the honour of their community ... the underlying issue in the definition of shame was the sexual control of women. If a woman refused an arranged marriage, for example, had an affair outside marriage, flirted with men, or dressed in a provocative manner, then she caused shame. This does not merely reflect badly on her, but also on the people who were supposed to be controlling her. (Tett, 1994, p. 137)

Although this statement is about women in Muslim societies, it can be applied to Arabic culture as a whole.

In terms of physical proof of female chastity,

> The hymen myth involves the notion that patriarchal honour is dependent upon female virginity, thereby putting the sexual aspect of women's roles at the forefront, ... and marrying so as to prevent dishonourable engagement in premarital sex. (Schvaneveldt, Kerpelman & Schvaneveldt, 2005, p. 81)

An intact hymen is a proof of a woman's virginity, which is vitally related to men's honour and self-image in Muslim culture (Hassan, 1999; Mernissi,

1982). Blood loss has been required to prove that the woman is a virgin at marriage. In some Arab Muslim cultures, a bloodstained cloth would be given to the groom's family on the wedding night to verify the bride's purity. If a woman did not bleed, the repercussions could be severe, so it became vitally important that the hymen remain intact as a sign of virginity because the family's honour was at stake (Ali, 2006).

With the importance placed on an intact hymen, it is clear that much emphasis is consistently placed on the control of female sexuality. Thus, both men and women are taught to diligently guard their families' honour—the women by abstaining from sexual activity and any form of contact with male strangers; the men by controlling the women's actions and, in a sense, their bodies.

Unfortunately, if a female grows up in Arab Muslim societies, she will most likely be warned of the importance of keeping away from the opposite sex and will receive constant warnings about any activities (i.e., bicycle riding, horseback riding, gymnastics) that may jeopardize the condition of her hymen.

Marrying girls off at a young age is thought to ensure their virginal status, yet early marriage is a hindrance in women's "intellectual maturity, educational pursuits, and other areas of growth and educational development" (Mernissi, 1996 as cited in Schvaneveldt, Kerpelman & Schvaneveldt, 2005, p. 81). In other words, having women married off at a young age, circumcised, living with the family, or prevented from pursuing an education are all intended to protect them from losing their virginity, and thus destroying their family's name and reputation.

Mernissi (1987) and Moghadam (2004) agree that "the whole concept of patriarchal honor is built around the idea of virginity, which reduces a woman's role to its sexual dimension" (Moghadam, 2004, p. 153). Historically, the honour of an Arab family "has been tied to the purity of its women ... even today it is important that women maintain their virginity until marriage ... [thus], segregation [between the sexes] is perceived as a means of controlling female sexuality" (Strickland, 1994, p. 68). Additionally, Buitelaar, Ketner, and Bosma (2004) explain that,

> Girls are supposed to show chaste behaviour and to not bring shame on the family. A girl would bring disgrace to the family if she does not behave herself. Not only would she make herself and her family a topic for gossip, but her behaviour would also indicate that her *father and her brother* [emphasis added] do not keep her in control. Traditionally, a girl should obey her father. In short, the family's reputation is at stake. (p. 152)

Although the above statement was drawn from a study by Buitelaar, Ketner, and Bosma about adolescent girls of Moroccan descent in the Netherlands (2004), it mirrors, unambiguously, the struggle within Arab Muslim societies, as in Yasmine's experience in Yemen, and in immigrant communities in the West. Yasmine narrated her experience practising as a doctor in Yemen. An uncle brought in his niece to have her virginity inspected. The uncle, according to Yasmine, was ready to kill his niece if the doctor denied the girl's virginity. This incident indicates the prevailing obsession with female virginity in many parts of the Arab Muslim world. One of many indicators of masculinity in Arab Muslim societies is having a strong "clean" reputation with regard to the females in the family. If a woman interacts with men in school or in the workplace, she risks becoming the subject of gossip, which in turn shames and disgraces the family. In many cases gossip justifies parents' restriction on their daughters' freedom.

This explains why many Arab Muslims are opposed to a woman living or travelling on her own (as indicated earlier in Nora's and Fadwa's experiences). If she does, she may risk her virginity and thus her family's reputation. To prevent neighbours or friends from gossiping about her, an Arab Muslim woman must always travel in the company of a man, preferably a husband, a father, or a brother. For example, Arab Muslim men told Nora, who was travelling on her own to the United States, that she was not a good Muslim woman since she was travelling without male companionship and protection.

Thus, virginity is a central value in Arabic culture and is the primary reason for restricting women's behaviour. The fact remains, however, that,

> There is nothing particularly Islamic about the weight placed upon pre-marital virginity and marital fidelity. We are dealing here with an aspect of a social system in which family alliance played and still plays a major role in political, economic and social life.... (Khalidi & Tucker, 1996, pp. 12–13)

In addition to virginity and a family's honour, in Arabic tradition, it is a widely held belief that women's sexual purity is the basis and sustainer of the family honour. Some double standards remain because it is more acceptable for a man to initiate dating than for a woman to do so (McMurtire, 2001). Also, a man would not be socially prosecuted if it was known that he had premarital relationships. Patricia Kelly (1999), in her research, concluded that,

> People are much more afraid for their daughters than for their sons. If a boy goes out and does whatever he wants, that's much less serious than

if a girl goes out and does the same thing. Another told me about a Tunisian proverb that acknowledges this double standard, "Put a boy in water and he comes out clean, put a girl in water and she comes out dirty." This shows, she explained, that whatever a boy does will be forgiven, but whatever a girl does "sticks to her" and will be not forgotten. (p. 210)

Accordingly, for some parents, the danger of moral and sexual "corruption" has, primarily, implications for girls only. Indeed, in many families, teenage boys are free to have sexual relations (Moghissi, 1999, p. 213).

Yasmine, for one, did not treat her children with double standards, especially with regard to dating. She critiqued some Muslim Canadian families who are raising their children—boys and girls— using different measures. She metaphorically explained that,

> Even here, some Arab Muslim families, unfortunately, allow boys to get away with things they don't allow girls to. They say that boys are softer sticks; you move them and bend them. But girls are like hard sticks—if you bend them, you will break them. This is why in many instances, girls are not allowed to date while families allow their sons to date.[4] I believe this is wrong. Boys and girls should be treated the same. Wrong is wrong, whether it is a boy or a girl. With my children, I put one rule for all. For my daughters, no male should be phoning at home, and no dating for both my sons and my daughters.

While growing up in Saudi Arabia, where the segregation of men and women prevailed, my favourite childhood playmates and elder role models were males. My pre-teen association with boys caused me some trouble with family members. I realized by the age of 15 that I was not supposed to talk, play, or associate with males, including relatives. As an adult, and before moving to Canada, I did not have the opportunity to interact with males because of Saudi's social law.[5]

I asked the interviewees about the ways in which they interacted with males outside the family. Most interviewees responded that if a Muslim woman must associate with men in school or in the workplace, she has to be respectable and limit interaction to work-related issues when dealing with male colleagues. Unfortunately, the women interviewed did not elaborate on or recount any stories with respect to their interactions with male colleagues. Nora described the agony she felt in choosing between professions that her parents, especially her father, wanted her to pursue and her own motivation to become a nutritionist and a gymnastics instructor, both of which involve interaction with men and working long hours. Only Fadwa mentioned that when she was a student in high school,[6] she usually walked home with a group of males and females, which troubled her mother greatly because she feared gossip, which may destroy a girl's reputation.

Thus, I argue that shame, honour, and virginity are tools to propagate patriarchal discourses. This statement goes a long way in explaining beliefs surrounding interaction between the sexes.

THE DANGERS OF FEMALE SEXUALITY

In Arab Muslim societies, there are strong implications between women and seductive sexuality, "which is at once dangerous and threatening; the antithesis is male spirituality and rationality" (Shaikh, 2004, p. 103). It is also believed that the mingling of males and females could lead to *fitna*,[7] which refers to moral and social misconduct, and the dangers inherent in female beauty and nature. For instance, the notion that a woman is a destructive sexual creature or that "A woman running for office may use her physical attributes of beauty and so forth to gain more votes ..." (Amawi, 1996, p. 153) is firmly set within many people's perceptions. Al-Tabarı, a well-known Muslim historian, voices his conviction that,

> Female sexual desire is a potential source of danger to men; it will cause them to sin, because it will come between them and God. It must, therefore, be punished. Only when satisfied within the bonds of marriage is female sexual desire redeemable, and, indeed, rewarded, bringing happiness and sons to man. What more could a good woman want? (as cited in Leo, 2005, p. 137)

The depiction of woman as temptress—and the conviction that she is indeed one—lends further power to oppressive patriarchal discourses that can severely, and sometimes permanently, distort women's overall perceptions of sexuality.

With such a view of female sexuality, the practice of female circumcision is perhaps not surprising. According to El Saadawi (1997),

> The patriarchal system is, of course, historically based on a double standard. Because the whole idea [of circumcision for girls] was, and still is, to diminish the sexuality of women [by] forcing monogamy upon them ... [make them] monogamous to attenuate the women's sexuality. (p. 65)

88

In cultures[8] in which female circumcision (also referred to as female genital mutilation) is performed, such a practice marks both female sexual purity and male control, both of which are closely associated with male honour (Baden, 1992, p. 18).

Female circumcision is usually performed between the ages of seven and nine,[9] as indicated in Fadwa's example, before puberty; male circumcision, in almost all cases, is performed at infancy. As indicated by El Saadawi (1980, 1999, 1997), girls are circumcised between ages seven and nine to make them remember the pain and to impress upon them the value of being chaste.

The underlying motive of female circumcision is to control female sexuality, which, in turn, is related to notions of honour and shame. Berkey (1996) connects that tradition to medieval and modern misogynist discourses, which present females as having an aggressive sexual appetite that must therefore be curbed by the removal of the clitoris. This practice was also believed to prevent adultery. Berkey notes that this kind of discourse is common to patriarchal societies in the Mediterranean and Near East (p. 23, as cited in Leo, 2005, p. 136).

Although shame of one's body or a negative self-image has no basis in Islam (Bouhdiba, 1998), the way in which some Muslim parents refuse to address sexuality sends a conflicting message. Some Muslim parents constantly emphasize that their children should not touch their own bodies and discourage them from exploring their sexuality. Societal norms in most Arab Muslim societies dictate that parents should discourage their children's sexuality by sending negative messages about sexuality, thinking that by doing so, they are protecting them from premarital sex. Children, especially females, may misunderstand their bodies and may experience a sense of shame, which may negatively affect their self-image.

These attitudes toward girls' sexuality may affect their self-image and self-worth. In Arab Muslim cultures, many women are unable to experience sexual fulfillment once married due to feelings of shame regarding sexuality (Muslim Women's League, 1995). Most girls learn that because they are born female, they will have such experiences: A girl cannot participate in activities enjoyed by boys, and she may, depending on the geographical location, have to endure female circumcision.[10]

Islamic teachings and values do not differentiate between men's and women's chastity. For instance, "Islamic perception confining sexuality to the conjugal relationship is not applied solely to female but also to male" (El Saadawi, as cited in Badran, 1994, p. 141). What Islamic teaching strongly discourages is premarital sexual behaviour for both men and women.

Shahid Athar (1996) argues that the concept of shame or disgust regarding one's body has no basis in Islam. Furthermore, Bouhdiba (1998) contends that "in Islam, sexuality enjoys a privileged status" (p. 88). Indeed, within Islam, one can identify elements of a very "sex-positive" religion, which affirms the spiritual value of sexuality (Shaikh, 2004, p. 102).

Fadwa, Eman, Ruba, and the other women's narratives join together to weave complex and contradictory meanings that demonstrate some aspects of girls' and women's socialization processes at home, at school, and within society.

NOTES

1. There are numerous articles and books about gender and education and girls' and boys' achievements in school. I recommend Arnot, M. (2002), *Reproducing gender: Selective critical essays on educational theory and feminist politics*, London: Routledge Falmer. Reay, D. (2001), "Spice girls," "nice girls," "girlies," and "tomboys": Gender discourses, girls' cultures, and femininities in the primary classroom. *Gender & Education, 13*(2), 153–166. And Blair, M., Holland, J. & Sheldon, S. (Eds.), (1995), *Identity and diversity: Gender and the experience of education: A reader*, Clevedon & Philadelphia: Multilingual Matters, in association with the Open University.

2. This supports my earlier arguments that women's achievement is a source of pride and a chance for respect in society.

3. In Arab Middle Eastern societies, it is expected that parents financially support their children's schooling.

4. This same mentality is prevalent in Middle Eastern Muslim societies (Baden, 1992; Mensch et al., 2000).

5. Saudi Arabian schools, universities, parks, and banks are all segregated by sex.

6. She was in Canada at that time.

7. *Fitna* has many meanings in the various texts, such as female desirability, female power, male weakness, social chaos, and social disorder. Its implications for women as a gender group are that they are quantifiably less intelligent than men, physically weaker, and prone to emotional instability. In the modern Islamic world, women's bodies and beauty are seen as great temptations to weak men, who cannot curb their desires. Women are temptresses who have more sexual power than men. Women are therefore burdened with the responsibility of controlling male desire, thereby saving their community from *fitna*.

8. Female circumcision commonly prevails as a practice in rural Yemen, Egypt, Somalia and Sudan.

9. In almost all Arab Muslim societies, male circumcision is a must and highly preferred for both religious and health reasons. However, it is performed a few days after birth.

10. I did not suggest parents' educational backgrounds because Fadwa's example negates that parents' backgrounds—both of her parents are highly educated— have an effect on whether or not a girl goes through circumcision.

Chapter Seven

EDUCATION AND SCHOOLING TALES: A TAPESTRY OF SHARED EXPERIENCES AND ASPIRATIONS

A few centuries ago, and in the name of religion, women in some Muslim societies were deprived not only of societal participation but also of an education. Many women were and still are, though to a lesser extent, confined to their homes. Some Arab Muslim cultural traditions claim that women's participation in the larger society is a violation of the Islamic tenets, and that higher education corrupts the morality of women. However, the essence of Islamic teachings in the Holy *Quran* and *Sunna* suggests that women and men are commanded by God to achieve social responsibility, uphold morality, and combat vice as the following verse states: "Believers, men and women, are protectors, one of another: they enjoin what is just, and forbid what is evil."[1] The command here, and in many other verses, denotes that women should acquire the knowledge to be eligible for such active leadership. In the Prophet Mohammed's (PBUH) time, women were free to go to the mosques to pray, listen to the preaching, and hear lectures. These practices meant that women stayed connected to the sources of education because at that time, the mosques were functioning not only as places to worship but also as sites for education (Al-Manea, 1984). By seeking education and educating others, women contributed to their advancement in society.

Nonetheless, the discussion of women's education in Arab Muslim society is not a straightforward one. While Islamic texts such as the *Quran* and *Hadith* are supportive of education for both sexes, traditionally, men have been given the priority in education. In fact, some Arab Muslim countries explicitly restrict some faculties, such as engineering, law, and geology, to men. What women can and cannot pursue, in terms of their education, is implicitly controversial in Arab Muslim societies. Which subjects and fields are "women-friendly" and which are not?

When writing sections of my autobiography and thinking about my schooling experiences, I thought about the gender role ascribed to young girls in Saudi Arabia. My elementary school experiences were regimented; I had to conform to the teachers' authority. Elementary school days were full of fearful moments of being caught doing something inappropriate, which could be anything but schoolwork. I have strong memories of formidable teachers whom I had to obey without question. Teachers in Saudi Arabia's educational system are usually considered mere instruments to carry out the instructions received from the upper administrative level (Al-Manea, 1984). "There was little or no recognition of the diverse histories of each student, neither of the classrooms, nor of the many thoughts and ideas which infiltrated our minds" (DeLuca, 1996, p. 143). Thus, teachers were expected to act as they did. Their behaviour was neither accidental nor personal. The education system in Saudi Arabia,[2] for instance, fosters a power hierarchy in which males dominate women. Decision-making positions at the school board level are restricted to males, and all top positions are assigned to men. Male perspectives prevail in textbooks, especially religious ones. Although the school administration, which is female, may not seek to oppress women and girls, it makes no efforts to change the status quo. Gender ideologies that have long been perpetuated have convinced many Saudi women and men that a woman's nature is different from that of a man's. This has led women to believe that men have more value, therefore women must prescribe to the assigned gender roles. Also, many women accept that women's education should be limited to what is helpful in becoming good wives and mothers. Therefore, women in Saudi Arabia do not have access to the same job opportunities as do men. This explains why only certain jobs (i.e., teaching and nursing, as opposed to engineering) are open to women.

Living in Canada for the past 10 years, and being a student for eight of these, I also acknowledge that the education system in Canada does not seem to challenge socially constructed gender divisions. The education system seems to maintain the stereotype that women are most suitable for nursing and teaching careers, while men are most suitable for engineering. The Canadian educational system does this to a notably lesser extent than the Saudi Arabian educational system, however. Also, the Canadian educational system seems to de-emphasize the authoritarian role of the teacher,[3] while placing a greater emphasis on students' assertiveness, involvement, and interdependence, while promoting an informal social relationship between teacher and student (Pai, 1990).

The Saudi education system is, in my experience, authoritarian in contrast to the Canadian education system. Also, like that of other Arab countries, the Saudi education system is influenced by the Egyptian and the British education systems, which are authoritarian and emphasize the role of teacher as a "knowledge transmitter" and text as "the Knowledge." In such a system, the student is expected to be a passive recipient. On the other hand, some theorists such as Die (1996) and Zine (2001), for instance, argue that despite the multiethnic, multilingual, and multiracial demographics in Canada, public school education remains Eurocentric. The Canadian public school curriculum, as some Canadian scholars argue (i.e., Zine, Cummins, and Die), superficially embraces multiculturalism and overlooks the histories of minorities that comprise the majority of the student population in Canada.

I concur with Apple (1999), Whyte, Deem, Kant, Cruickshank (1985), and hooks (1994) that boys and girls develop firm ideas about their prospective lives and roles at an early age (hooks, 1994, p. 19). As a result, I contend that gender discourses and prevalent gender ideologies are manifested and maintained within the classroom. The progressive class-room is the core site for individuals to practise, experience, and acquire critical thinking and consciousness, and to take up a commitment to end domination and inequity in all its forms.

In some respects, there are similarities between the education system in the East and West. The education system in almost all Arab Muslim societies, as in Western societies, is merely "an instrument that is used to facilitate the integration of the younger generation into the logic of the present system and bring about conformity"[4] (Shaull, 2003, p. 34).

From my experience as a student and as a teacher in the Saudi education system, critical thinking was neither encouraged nor preferred. Teachers were expected to teach to the test, and students were expected to memorize course content and regurgitate it for exams. There is no critical thinking involved in the learning process. By critical thinking, I refer to two aspects: First is the deeper understanding of issues and problems; second is the ability to analyze, evaluate, and examine an argument from different points of view (McPeck, 1981).

My education in Saudi Arabia was a series of lectures given to girls who were expected to sit in silence with their hands folded. Indeed, silence was a trait for which we gained extra marks. As early as Grade 1, students sat in rows with the teacher standing at the front, lecturing and writing on the board. No one was allowed to leave or speak unless first given permission by the teacher. Physical education classes were not part of my experience, and even today are not part of the public school curriculum in girls' schools. Since segregation by sex is pervasive in Saudi society, all my schools were all-girls' schools. The differences between boys' and girls' curricula are many. While boys enjoy physical education classes, the home economics curriculum[5] is limited to girls. Until recently, males took more advanced math and computer classes than females. In fact, computer science was introduced in boys' schools many years earlier than in girls' schools. Subjects such as geology are still restricted to boys' schools. A lesser amount of the budget was allocated to girls' schools, universities, and colleges than all-male schools. Girls' schools were not only separated from boys' in terms of buildings and curriculum, but also in terms of management. Girls' schooling at all levels—elementary, secondary, high school, and post-secondary—was put under the control of the General Presidency for Girls' Education, while the education of boys was overseen by the more prestigious Ministry of Education. The GPGE was, and still is, led by conservative male scholars. This was to ensure that women's education did not deviate from the purpose of making them good wives and mothers, and to prepare them for "acceptable" jobs such as teaching and nursing—careers that men believe suit women's nature.

As a child and young adult, I fully engaged with my school courses. I obtained the highest marks in almost all subjects, arts and sciences alike. I was known as an excellent and highly motivated student. My favourite part of school was reading about various topics before the teacher told us to, or solving math problems before we discussed them in class. Perhaps I read ahead because the teacher was too slow for me, or maybe I had more time to study. Perhaps I needed the challenge to discover the course content by myself. For certain, I did not like to be silent. In the early years I was talkative, but as I grew older, I chose to be silent for fear of being punished and sent home with the red sheet that misbehaving students had to have their parents sign. A student who argues, analyzes, and discusses is considered a misbehaving one, and thus a problem that needs to be addressed with the parents.

In elementary school, we learned that the world is black/white, Muslim/non-Muslim, and good/evil. I was taught that there was only "one answer" in the book, which was known by the teacher. I was taught that there were no choices, no options—only "one way" of doing things. Everything else was deviant and wrong. I had to live these binaries for a very long time. The school system I experienced also reinforced the notion that any knowledge is given as fact, and "truth" is fixed; this knowledge, which is non-negotiable and sacred, is selected and chosen by powerful elites within religious realms. Additionally, religious texts (i.e., the *Quran* and the Prophet's [PBUH] narration) are taught with the same philosophy. A student is prohibited from asking questions related to religion or cultural traditions. Everything in that regard is taught as "the best and only." We were taught that the "true" version of Islam is the one practised in Saudi Arabia and that anything else is derivation and incorrect. Since school knowledge is dominated by men, it does not "challenge the gender division of labor or the social constructs of what is legitimate and proper for men and women" (Stromquist, 1989, p. 175). Therefore, I contend that the education system and teachers play a significant role in reinforcing rather than challenging prevalent gender ideologies.

In Grade 4, like any naive nine-year-old girl, I looked at my teacher with eyes full of hope. I had two long black braids, which my mother combed and twisted every morning. I sat in the front row of the classroom, sometimes by choice, other times because the teacher told me to.[6] I remember the day my teacher talked about divorce. She explained to us that if parents divorced, a daughter as young as nine years old would be taken to her father's house, while a son, at the age of 15, would be given a choice between his mother's custody or his father's. I was horrified when my teacher said that this is an Islamic rule. I insisted that she show me in the *Quran* where the rule is mentioned. My teacher took this as a challenge, which was an "unforgivable *sin*." "To pass opinion against the way of the elders, whether it be teacher or parent, according to the *school system* [italics in original], might fall into the category of *SIN*" (DeLuca, 1996, p. 144). It is not only in school that we are not to challenge a teacher or an elder, but we are not supposed to challenge any authority in society. My teacher furiously demanded, "Why are you disturbed by this decree? Are your parents divorced?" I said:

> No, but what if that happens to me? Do I have to be with my father even if I want to stay with my mother? What I cannot understand is why girls and boys are not treated the same. Why would a boy my age get to choose what he wants while I will be silenced? Why do I have to listen to something without question, even if it is nonsense?

The teacher's action in this instance and many others followed the "banking system of education" (Freire, 2003) in which "the educator's role is to regulate the way the world 'enters' into the students" (p. 57). The teacher taught with an assumption of control over class discussion. She or he also controlled the manner in which a student was expected to engage in class discussions (DeLuca, 1996). This is what I learned, not only "from my first educational encounter with silencing" (p. 143), but also in my first educational encounter with gender discourse in my society. For me, this incident was the beginning of my realization of a gender inequity that is manifested throughout education. My analysis of what I was taught in elementary school about child custody shows how schools transmit patriarchal ideologies. Teachers' practices and ideologies affect girls' views of themselves. Sexist stereotyping and restrictive gender ideologies limit and constrain girls. Thus, I argue that progressive education is the way to question gender ideologies and discourses in Arab Muslim societies that are perpetuated in the name of Islamic teaching..

I began noticing that school subjects like history and language rarely included female role models. This was ironic, considering the ample number of female Muslim role models in early Islamic history, yet history taught in higher grades focuses solely on men's triumphs and is reported from a male point of view. Hence, education tends to be traditional, with little or no room for innovation, especially with regard to women's status.

After Grade 10, all students could choose between two streams: social and natural science. I had to choose between the art stream and science stream. I chose science. I thought that my curiosity and questions in science classes (i.e., math, physics, chemistry, and biology) would seem "reasonable" and "non-controversial," and therefore acceptable to my science teachers—more so than my questions in arts and social science classes. My constant wonder about the things I was taught in social science classes seemed, at least in my teachers' eyes, horrendous. Ideally, in natural sciences there is always room for wonder and inquiry. Before long, I discovered that the same boundaries that existed in arts classes existed in science classrooms as well. I wondered how these boundaries were created, and by whom. At that time, it was a difficult question to answer. In the science stream, I chose to be creative, but I was disappointed by the limited and inferior scientific equipment, and inadequate access to proper laboratory facilities. Our lab periods were short; we received lectures and were not allowed to touch the equipment. The medium of inquiry was, again, lecturing, but instead of a classroom, there lectures were given in the lab where we sat, not in rows of seats, but on benches.

I agree that "The school community is a microcosm of the world and, as such, models the expectations that society wants students to have in order to participate as adults" (Farmer, 1996, p. 38). Now I understand that not being able to interact, ask, and analyze in the classroom as a student, whether it is in science or the arts, is a discipline and a cultural norm. This is the expectation of girls in wider society. Watson describes this kind of learning, which lacks self-reflection, as a "formula approach to people, objectifying, codifying, and reifying human experiences with 'official knowledge' that takes on a life of its own—a life that is separate, decontextualized, rather than connected" (as cited in DeLuca, 1996, p. 149).

After Grade 12, I finished my national exam for high school, and my high marks provided me entry to any field I wanted to pursue. As a teenager, I still was not completely aware of the massive social constraints I would face if I tried to fulfill my dreams beyond the norm. Indeed, my sensitivity to gender discourse was not yet fully developed. However, intuitively, I knew that as a young woman, my choices were restricted and limited. "The policies and ideologies that permit or disallow female education within any society also affect the entry of women into various professions" (Mohammed, 2003, pp. 106–107). The limitation of women's professions is pronounced in Saudi society and I had only two choices: education or medicine. With only these two options, I felt like I really had no choice at all. At that time, I had to think not of what I was capable of doing, but of what was socially and culturally available and acceptable. I ended up in teachers' college, which was not my first choice. The closest medical school was a five-hour drive from my city, and living in residence was not traditionally acceptable for a young woman in my family. Not being able to live in residence prevented many girls from pursuing their dreams. After a summer-long debate with my father, who insisted that a "good girl" does not live away from her father's house, I attended my first lecture at the teachers' college in tears.

On a different note, ever since my childhood, I have been attracted to literature. I have a profound interest in languages and literacy. In search of knowledge and literature other than that available in the schools, I went from one bookstore to another, hunting for books by famous Arab authors, but this search was in vain. I searched for literature in my leisure time during summer vacations. Because of the great emphasis on science and mathematics in the school environment and the fact that science and mathematics subjects are associated with higher intelligence, I seldom thought of literature in the school context: School was reserved for "serious" and "beneficial" knowledge. I would, as a result, read literature only during my free time.

My interest in topics such as politics, science, and history—topics that are considered by cultural norms to be associated with masculinity—was noticeable to my peers and family. I did not find my interests to be contradictory to my Islamic identity, yet by the age of 15, I had comparatively astute questions about a variety of subjects. I had plenty of questions that I was unable to find answers for in the books available to me. Also, I had been disinclined to express my views freely in the presence of my parents or my teachers.

I, like the Arab Muslim women I interviewed, was encouraged by my parents—especially (and ironically) by my father—to pursue education.

In my situation, I was encouraged to seek education that would not violate the norms, education that would not require me to mix with men, or travel and live alone. Unlike Fadwa, I was unable to cross or negotiate traditional boundaries and maintain my self-interests. Some of the participants in this book were compelled toward specific fields, as in Nora's case. Others were encouraged to choose their fields of study.

In the interviews for this book, I explored the educational experiences of these Arab Muslim women. I encouraged their narratives through probes such as how much their parents encouraged them, whether they were excused from household chores, and whether there were any differences in the ways parents valued their education compared to that of their male siblings. In response, Yasmine noted, "My parents supported me and my sibling's education and did not excuse us for house chores; my parents were very social. We would have 40 people over for dinner close to exam time, but I still had to help my parents. Boys and girls were both required to take part."

Nora did very well in all school subjects and was especially talented in math, science, and gym classes. Her parents were encouraging, but a conflict occurred as a result of her desire to pursue her interest. She explained:

> I always wanted to go to physical education and I always did gymnastics. Since I was a child, I was training, and I loved my trainers and my physical education teacher so much.... I wanted to be like my gymnastics teacher.... All my family was against my interest.... They did not value the field, they told me, So what (hip hop 1-2-3)?[7] Unfortunately, there is still no appreciation for these kinds of fields. They call it "games" and the faculty of physical education there does not have the same weight as it does here in Canada. I was positively inspired to know that the department of health sciences and kinesiology here is one of the best and most difficult faculties to get into.... Here students need high grades to go into these fields, ... whereas in Egypt, the lowest grade will go into the field of physical education....

Yet Nora was determined to pursue what motivated her most—physical education and health science research. Nora's father, mother, and brothers, and, in some ways, society all opposed her aspirations. Clearly, she did not want to fit into the moulded script, to match up with the ready-made category of a "typical woman." She told of going to the national exam and purposely skipping questions: "I used to go to the exam and skip questions. This way I wouldn't get high marks ... and I would be guaranteed that no one in my family would convince me or force me to go into science. This way I would be able to go to physical education."

A major reason why Nora's family wanted her to study science was that her father owned a textile factory. Thus, if Nora studied chemistry or accounting, she would be able to assist him in his work, especially since she worked as an accountant in her father's factory during summer vacations. She explained, "There was no other way for me to escape this plan.... Everyone in my family was opposing my goal, and they would not agree unless there was something big, and the big thing was the grades ... the percentage. This would determine the department that I could apply for."

In spite of the obstacles Nora faced in choosing a field that was neither respected in society nor desired by her family, she managed to be one of the top five students in her college. When her father saw that she did well in the first two years, he realized that she took her field seriously. He became more encouraging and was the most supportive, as Nora happily acknowledged: "He was finally enthused by my idea and my choice. All I used to ask for, he would do." Nora proceeded in physical education, winning many medals, awards, and a scholarship to the United States. Her interest in the human body's movements flourished in the physical education department:

> I used to look at my trainers while they were training me and I would ask myself why she or he is asking me to do this movement or why the trainer is switching now to stretching.... I was always interested in these kinds of questions. In fact, my trainers were the ones who encouraged me to pursue the physical education field.... My teachers and trainers instilled this in my mind.

Unlike Nora, Sahra's struggle was not so much with her parents urging her to follow the norm, but had more to do with transferring from the "banking system of education" to an education system that focuses on students' creativity and not memory:

> The difficulty I faced when I first started in Canada had to do with my way of acquiring knowledge. Education in Egypt highlights memorizing.... The ideal student is the student who memorizes lots of stuff.... It's different in Canada—here the ideal student is the student who can think.... Here, I face this problem; study is built on the way of thinking—how far you can imagine and how creative you are....

Morooj's perspective on acquiring knowledge and education is worth mentioning in this context. When she volunteered at her friend's private school, her approach to teaching was that,

> Education is not memorizing a book, but education should be obtained through experiences. I worked as a volunteer to teach Grades 5 and 6. I took my class to museums and I organized trips to the mail offices in the city to show them how the mail is being organized and distributed.... I took them to arts exhibitions. Also, I organized meetings with artists so students could meet them. Of course, we cannot do these things in a public school because of the regimen of the system and the number of students we have in each class. Unfortunately, children are not being taught from the "hands on" and "experience first" approach....

Nahlaa highlights a concern about parental pressure, especially regarding their child's abilities and interests. She says, "My parents, especially my Dad, were encouraging me to get the highest marks and he would get me awards or prizes if I got an A mark." Then she added, "I didn't like math or physics." I asked, "Why did you choose engineering if you did not like math and physics?" She replied, "I actually wasn't that interested in engineering, but my father is an engineer and he encouraged me. I would have preferred medicine more, but I thought it's much harder and engineering is good. I went to engineering."

This is common in Arab Muslim societies; parents impose certain subjects and professions on their children, regardless of their sex, overlooking how important it is for a son or a daughter to find his or her own motivation. Sahra, for instance, emphasized that her father was particularly excited that she was going to be an engineer: "... my father was not pushing me, but he was very, very excited. He wanted me to go [to engineering] and was very, very proud of me...."

The uniqueness of Wafaa's educational experience stems from her village roots in Lebanon. According to her, in every village there are stereotypes about the value of boys' education. Boys are the ones who should go to school, while girls should stay with their mothers to be socialized in a way that makes them ready for the nurturing role of a mother and a wife. This puts Wafaa's statements about classroom arrangement into perspective. Wafaa said:

> I went to an Islamic school. It was coeducational.... They put the boys in the front [rows] and the girls at the back because we were teenagers, so ...

the fact that hormones kicked in and stuff, ... it's good to keep the boys at the front and the girls at the back, which was very good to us girls.... We're just sitting, relaxing at the back, ... so that was the case from Grade 6 till Grade 9 in that school.

As a naive child, Wafaa felt that girls who stayed at home and did not have to go to school were fortunate. She observed:

Yes, I would be going to school and other girls would be staying home, so at first when I was young, I would say, "Oh, they're so lucky, they get to stay at home!" But then as I grew up, I realized that every girl should have the right to even just finish high school, but that changed with time. Now if you go to my village, almost 80 percent of the girls go to school and they are forced by their parents to finish high school, so culture changes. It doesn't stay the same.

Also, multiculturalism made Wafaa's schooling experience exceptional. Her primary memory of school in Lebanon is that it was multicultural and heterogeneous. It was her first experience mingling with students with diverse belief systems. For Wafaa, this made school more exciting. She said, "It was the first time I got to be with people from other religions: Christians and Druze.[8] I always looked forward to going to school every day. I never liked to miss [school], even when I was sick. I would just wanna go."

However, Wafaa shared her frustrations that "doing well on national exams was one major way to prove that one is doing well in school." Only the national exam percentage allows a student to study the subject that she or he feels passionate about. The work completed throughout one's school career does not count. At the end of Grade 12, in almost all Arab Muslim countries, all students write the national exam. The results of that exam determine what subject a student can study. Those who get 95–100 percent will be able to study whatever they want.[9] Those with lower percentages will be registered, arbitrarily, in different faculties, usually arts and languages. In my experience, choosing my field and my profession was determined by many factors, one of which was the percentage I earned at the end of the national exam. Wafaa elaborated:

High school is divided; you're either in the literary section or the scientific section. I took the literary because of my parents' financial situation; I had to find a field that would not cost me to move far away from the village.... Islam tells us to go to India or China[10] to study if we have to. It doesn't matter, but we should learn, and it doesn't matter if it's a girl or boy in question.

When Wafaa went to university in Lebanon, she faced many obstacles in the first year. She travelled an hour each way, every day, from the village to attend lectures, while her colleagues were unable to attend because they needed to work in order to make a living and to afford tuition. She mentioned another obstacle: "I was taught English, but in Arabic.... Everything was translated. Also, authoritarianism of the teacher was a problem.... If you asked a question and the teacher did not like it or if she or he felt that you are challenging her or him, then it could get pretty bad."

This resonates with my experience in elementary school. This authoritarianism, which persists at all school levels, reflects the hierarchies that prevail in Arab Muslim societies. Totalitarianism is the way to describe many aspects of schooling and education in our native societies.

While Nahlaa, Sahra, and Nora were encouraged to pursue the interests of one or both of their parents (e.g., engineering), Morooj's parents encouraged her to follow her own interests. Her parents' encouragement made Morooj's educational experience positive: "My parents were never imposing things on us. Whoever liked something, she or he studied it." After high school, Morooj worked in a bank at a time when women were strongly discouraged from holding a public position, yet she noted that her parents motivated her to do what she wanted. Morooj's inspiration to pursue more education is relentless: "I like education.... I go back to being a student whenever something new interests me." When she decided to pursue photography, she noted cautiously that "[Arab Muslim Libyan] society in general is not enthused about older women pursuing any kind of activities or education."

For Ruba, school was an exciting place to learn about the human body and the world around her. She excelled in school, especially in biology. Ruba remembers that her parents used to encourage her to take time off to play, but she was determined to get the highest grades: "It [school] was very competitive because your name is even announced on the radio with your grades sometimes.... It was more the girls than the boys.... I think the expectation of the boys is that the boys can handle themselves, but we want our girls to be better."

Ruba's comment highlights how girls' identities are constructed around schooling. Yet is Ruba implying that girls are more vulnerable and need to protect themselves with education? I wonder why girls are expected to perform better in school and how this affects boys' performance. Are girls expected to excel in school to overcompensate for not being born male? In Ruba's statement that "the boys can handle themselves," I sensed a gender-insensitive tone. This is one of many implicit cues prevalent in gender discourses in Arab Muslim societies. I hypothesize that because boys are given opportunities to lead outside the school setting, girls are more motivated to focus their attention on excelling in school. Girls' high educational achievement, which recently became the focal point of theorists' and educators' attention in Middle Eastern school boards," stems from the girls' sense that education is a way to attain status and respect in society. The higher proportion of women obtaining post-graduate degrees in Arab Muslim societies suggests that women are seeing education as a "springboard" (Hertz-Lazarowitz & Shapira, 2005) to status and leadership. Yet are their societies able to negotiate cultural traditions that exclusively assign males to leadership positions?

Eman, too, excelled in school, but experienced difficulty adjusting to new schools and making connections with totally new environments whenever her parents moved to a different city or country. At the beginning of her schooling in the United States, in Grade 4, the biggest hurdle was the language:

> When I was in Grade 4 in New York City, and everything around me was in English, it was a bit overwhelming, but I thank my father for standing beside me and helping me a lot with that. He had daily exercises, building my vocabulary, working on my grammar, and talking to me in English until little by little, it kind of changed the way that I perceived the language and how I acquired the language, and I think that was one of the most important turning points in my education because certainly I learned English.

I can relate to Eman's comments that her father's help improved her English. My father also assisted me with my Arabic writing homework. Although I enjoyed his help very much, it did not last long because of his work schedule. Also, in contrast to Eman's experience, my one year of school in the United States was one of the best I had as a child. In my school, I had music classes, free reading periods, and, best of all, gym classes.

Eman could not overemphasize her father's help. She grew up in a family where, in the 1960s, her aunts had attended university. "So I grew up with a father who encouraged education and who was a professor in the '60s and had women students," noted Eman. She elaborated, "My professors in the university, some of them were his [my father's] students, so it was an ongoing process of women learning and developing their education and going to other countries to learn, and then coming back to Libya and becoming professors in the university."

Another aspect of Eman's educational experience is the way in which she acquired the knowledge. She explicated:

> I remember that I knew English that year and then I was at high school and it was different because of the way of learning, the way of acquiring the knowledge. I very much enjoyed the independence that I found in high school, and how you would go out and you work out with the encyclopedias yourselves, and the dictionaries yourselves; you would pick your books and your own research and you would be responsible for that, and so, again, that taught me how to acquire knowledge.

Eman's parents encouraged her to explore the world and did not place boundaries or limits on what to do or where to go. She was excused from housework and her parents expressed pride in her accomplishments. Her parents had also always been highly interested in her schooling. Part of Eman's success, according to her, was the teacher-parent collaboration:

> There was always interaction between parents and teachers, from my parents asking the teacher, "How is she doing?" "Where does she need help?" "What can we do?" ... But for them to sit with me and do the homework with me, ... I don't remember that....

Eman's favourite school subjects were English, arts, humanities, and history. In these subjects she found no boundaries. "I mean, you can go anywhere, you can ponder with any thought and it's valid...." When asked why this was so, she answered quickly: "I think science puts a limit.... The answer has to be what it has to be." Further, she stated that,

> In English, you can just explore yourself ... and write what you feel as an individual. It's not something for everybody.... Certainly everybody can write, but you as an individual have your own style, like thumbprints, in whatever you write and that's what I enjoyed. [I liked] history because it just takes you places and you meet new people and learn what happened and how people lived. The consequence of people's actions and how they lived in the past, and it's interesting....

Another reason for Eman's interest in English literature is where her country was historically in 1984:

> English literature in a place [like] Libya ... it was a treat to find a litera-
> ture book. We always have libraries in Arabic and Arabic books. I was
> fascinated because English literature took me far away from the reality
> that we were living in Libya. Also for me, it [choosing to be a teacher] was
> interesting to see there were people coming in and wanting to learn
> English, whereas in the 1980s, they saw that as taboo in Libya.

Eman's early education was abroad, while her university education took
place in Libya. Her educational dreams grew as she did. Eman's career
choice is interesting. She cheerfully said,

> According to customs, everybody should be either a doctor or an engi-
> neer, or somewhere in between—a pharmacist, for example, a dentist,
> whatever.... Some family members wanted me to take that route, but I
> have to go back to my father, where he said, "You're the one who's gonna
> work and you're the one who's gonna deal with your life, so you choose
> because if you're not happy in your job, then you'll never be good at what
> you do," and I followed that advice and I'm very happy that I did because
> here I am, doing what I like the most—teaching.

Fadwa's educational support was inherited, in a way. Many years ago,
Fadwa's paternal grandfather raised the money to build the first women's
school in the village, something unheard of in that region. Thus, Fadwa's
family has a long history of supporting women's education. Fadwa, with a
sense of pride in her grandfather, observed:

> There were people who threatened him, basically cursed him, because
> according to those people, my grandfather was spoiling the women in the
> village. And I grew up hearing those stories about my grandfather, and
> realizing that my father took from my grandfather these qualities, and
> that's why my father, unlike a lot of other men in our family, appreciates
> me learning and studying, which is why I'm here in Canada on my own.

Fadwa's parents' did not differentiate between the importance of her
schooling and her brother's schooling, which encouraged her. Her parents—
her father has a PhD; her mother will soon obtain a college diploma—are
both supportive of her endeavours:

The extent to which my parents were interested in my schooling was that my father said that my education, my brother's education ... is the biggest investment to him, and my mom also really values my education, and they come from different angles. He has his doctorate in business management or accounting, and his education has helped him out.... My father's family had lived in poverty. My mom, at the opposite end, when she just graduated from high school, married my father by proxy—my dad was in England—and she was at home.... One of my mother's regrets, lifetime regrets, is that she was not able to pursue her education....

Recently, Fadwa's mother went back to school. This, in itself, delivered a positive message to Fadwa, who said, "She [mother] started five years ago a program and she will be finishing soon in Islamic education. When I was a child, she used to tell me, 'Fadwa, when you are in university, I hope I will be in university, too, so we can both be studying.'"

Fadwa's parents valued her schooling. "For them," said Fadwa, "school came before and above everything else.... I was not allowed to watch television until I finished my homework." The message reinforced that education was the way to please her parents. Her father, in particular, was helpful with schoolwork. She says:

This is where my brothers come in, and my parents are a little more lenient with my brothers—my brothers get to do their homework while they're watching TV, sometimes. My mom, for the first few years of school, she would sit down with me at the table and make sure I was doing my homework. And now I have that sense of discipline that I know this is my homework time or my assignment time. I'll sit at the table and do it on my own. My father was very helpful with math. Even though I loved math, word problems were a bit difficult for me, so we would sit and we'd discuss them and talk about them, and he made math very, very interesting. I really enjoyed school. I liked math and science and English and Arabic.... I loved religious studies. I hated gym! I hated physical education class! And I always found myself out of breath, and this goes back to the concept of a "good student." The gym teachers used to think I wasn't trying my best and that I was giving up, and I would tell them I couldn't.... I did have a lot of bronchitis attacks. It was only when I was 15 and came to Canada that I was diagnosed with asthma, and the doctor said, "You can't do this, you can't do that," and I look back and I think, maybe if those teachers were a little kinder, I might have liked gym.

The "cultural dichotomy" in Fadwa's elementary school in Kuwait is a dichotomy of us versus them, Arabic teachers versus English teachers. She explained:

> We would call our Arabic teachers who were, all of them, women ... by their first names, and all our English teachers, we'd call them by their last names, so even though we didn't articulate it, we were very aware that we talked to our Arabic teachers from our own culture in a different way than the way we spoke to our teachers who were from a Western culture. Then I went to school at home, and I spent two years there, and I was in a Catholic sisters' school, an all-girls' nun school, one of the most disciplined schools I have ever been in. The nuns were Italian, ... so there was also a cultural dichotomy at different levels. There was the Muslim—Christian dichotomy, where in religion class we were separated into Christians and Muslims and we studied our respective religions. There was an Arab/non-Arab dichotomy, mainly within the local community because it is a very multicultural country. I mean, there are those who claim to be Arabic and speak that language as their mother tongue. The girls from the south were mainly Christian, and we would find a dichotomy there between southern girls and Arabic girls. And then we found a few girls who were not Arabic, but Indian, and they would stick together, too. I was categorized as one of the girls who had lived in the Middle East all their lives; I acted in a manner that is very reminiscent of how someone would have acted 15, 16 years ago.

I, too, know about the importance of fitting into both Saudi society and Canadian society. As a teenager, I wanted to fit with the school norm and to belong. That same need arose when I moved to Canada. As a young woman, I wanted to fit in and took steps, such as working on my accent, to do so. I asked Fadwa how she fits into two such dichotomous cultures. She expanded on her experiences:

> I was in Qatar for three years. I was in an American International School for two years, and those two years were the years where I actually started thinking in English, and my accent—I used to have a stronger Arabic accent when I spoke English—my accent started changing at age 13.... There it was different from my native home school. At school in my home country, I was rewarded socially for being as authentic a local as I could be. In the American school in Qatar, I would have been rewarded for being as American as I could be. I really did not fit in with that concept of American. I was wearing

the *hijab* at that point, and there weren't many *hijabis*[12] around, and I had never been to North America.

Changing schools from year to year may have caused some adjustment issues, but this was not Fadwa's only struggle. The discontinuity of school culture and the absence of the Islamic component in the new school disturbed her the most:

> That really affected me deeply because I felt that there was no commitment to my faith, and I was upset by that, even though I understood that most of the students there, their families, even though they might be Muslim, their families were not committed to that faith and it hit me very hard that there were different ideals here. I grew up in an environment where the Ministry of Education wasn't just the Ministry of Education, it was the Ministry of *Tarbea*,[13] "Upbringing," and education and "Upbringing" was in the Islamic way ... and they lacked that. To sort of make up for the missing Arabic language, I actually took some Arabic classes on Saturdays ... but those were a joke ... and my religious education stopped right there, and I realized that if I were to learn more about my faith, I would have to go about it in a different way.

After Fadwa's second year of university, she told her mother that she was interested in becoming a teacher:

> My mother panicked. She said, "No, what kind of work is this, being a teacher? Teacher! What kind of a job are you gonna get? They're not very well respected! You're not gonna get enough money!" My father said, "Fadwa, years ago when I was a kid, teachers were the most important people in our community. They were well respected, they were revered, but these days, teachers apparently don't have the same level of respect." So I said to him, "Well, I could be a lawyer or someone in business, but I really, really want to be a teacher." He's like, "Well, I don't want to force you to be something that you're not, but maybe a teacher at a university level."

Many aspects of Fadwa's narrative underline how her father was encouraging her motivation. Indeed, there are many implicit messages in Fadwa's narratives; they are extricated through the themes in her discussions.

From these narratives, it is clear that parental involvement is a significant part of women's education, whether encouraging or discouraging. Almost all the women I interviewed were excused from household chores during exam times. Almost all the participants were encouraged to excel in school, and fathers played a major role in that support.

Many studies indicate that "Gendered practices are strongly influenced by school life, religion, ethnicity, and language" (Sarroub, 2005, p. 7). However, I strongly advocate that gendered practices are also influenced by parenting, as is evident in the narratives of the participants.

COEDUCATIONAL VERSUS ALL-GIRLS' SCHOOLING

Sex-segregated schooling is a controversial topic in both Eastern and Western education systems. Arabic literature on the topic does not exist, or may not be published, but there is a plethora of Western studies on the topic of sex-segregated or coeducational schooling:

> It is often assumed that there is no particular advantage to girls or boys in single-sex education, at least as far as achievement is concerned. It is probably true that many single-sex schools have a tendency to reinforce the traditional aspirations of boys and girls. However, there is also some evidence that single-sex schools may help boys and girls to separate subjects from gender and that girls in girls' schools are likely to have a more positive attitude to "male" subjects. (Ormerod, as cited in Whyte, Deem, Kant & Cruickshank, 1985, p. 18)

I argue that there are advantages and disadvantages with both coeducational and all-girls' schools. As a student in Saudi Arabia, I did not consider sciences like physics and math as male subjects. However, in Saudi Arabia women are not allowed to pursue engineering, law, and some other professions, not only because they are considered men's fields and do not suit a women's nature, according to the traditional view, but also because study in those fields most probably requires women and men to mix. Amalgamation of the two sexes in schools is a huge taboo in Saudi society, yet when I came to Canada, I noticed the scarcity of women in fields like physics and engineering. I wondered why this is so. While the gender discourse is overt in Saudi society and manifested through schooling and education, in Canadian society the discourse seems more covert.

Yasmine noted that her schooling experiences prior to university were segregated by sex. She then analyzed the advantages and disadvantages of each type of schooling through her perspective. I was interested in exploring the differences between boys' and girls' schools, though this was not one of the themes around which I organized my interview questions. Yasmine gave me feedback anyway, and many other Arab Muslim women diverged to talk about their perception of their experience in coeducational schooling. In regard to this, Yasmine observed that,

> All my schooling [was] sex-segregated, and now after I had experienced both, I can see the difference. Girls have their emotional time, their periods, so it is better for them to be separated from boys. They have their ups and downs and I think it is healthier to have them separated.... As a student back home, I used to be creative in sports and I was really comfortable not having to worry about the dress [the *hijab*]. And I used to be very active without having to worry about boys taking over. All my schooling I was like that—a funny, smart, active kid, but in university it changed because I was more conservative in a coeducational setting.... I have to be strict when I am in a mixed setting.

Yasmine continues:

> Here in Canada, I think my daughter is ripped off of awards because she is with boys in coeducational schools. My daughter is excellent in academic work. She is socially active, very polite, but she was not involved in sports and that's why boys won over her. She earned four or five academic awards at least, and I believe that if she was in a sex-segregated school, she would do even better. Her stories are published in books.... She was unable to participate in dancing class and in swimming classes because she wears the *hijab*. All extracurricular activities she was unable to do because the mixing contradicts with the *hijab*. Now, in university and because of the Muslim Students Association, she is able to do more. She organizes sports occasions and swimming for Muslim girls or all-girls' occasions.... I am pro-sex-segregated schooling....

Interestingly, studies show that in Muslim countries, the widespread practice of female seclusion encourages women to pursue non-traditional fields in a separate female sphere (Matsui, 1991, p. 37; Merriam, 1979; Youssef, 1977). In general, "Studies have documented higher academic outcomes among students in single-sex schools as compared to students in co-educational schools" (Proweller, 1998, p. 183). Such studies concur with what Yasmine noted about her daughter and the fact that her achievement seems to be overlooked in a coeducational environment in a Canadian school.

On the other hand, Nora, like me, stood in the middle of the road between the two kinds of schooling. Nora believed it was important for girls and boys to mix:

> My school experience was excellent and healthy.... It gave me confidence in myself.... I knew some women would be awfully intimidated to talk to or present an argument in men's presence, but that was not my case. I can say that the elementary school had a very good influence on me.... I continued with all-girls' schools in both junior high and high school, though I like the idea of having all-girls' high schools because girls can be apprehensive about their looks and it is good to be comfortable out of men's ways, yet I was always around boys in the neighbourhood and the family.... Then my university was sex-segregated. Because we were taught swimming and gymnastics, women need their own space, and also we want to be able to wear swimming suits and be comfortable. But there were always mixed parties—boys and girls—on the main campus, and I always participated.... Men and women always got together.

Nahlaa reminded me of myself when I first came to Canada because I had been in an all-girls' school up to my undergraduate years. Sex segregation is pervasive in Saudi society, so the transition to coeducational Canadian universities settings was not an easy one for me. In the college where I did my undergraduate studies, I was able take off my *hijab* and move freely; however, I was unable to do that in Canada. Like me, Nahlaa believed that "being in an all-girls' school gave me more freedom than being in a coeducational school." In contrast, Sahra never minded that she could not remove her *hijab* in a mixed setting:

> I knew for some girls, this was like a huge step because they weren't allowed to interact with men, and suddenly when they are teens and enter university....[14] I used to interact with men all the time, although I went to an all-girls' school, but the university was mixed.... I had a bachelor's degree in civil engineering. Probably that's a bit of a hard field for women to enter.

Eman had a different perspective of her all-girls' and coeducational schooling experiences. She made an interesting distinction between the different schools she experienced:

In Libya, there isn't really a gender segregation of any sort. With regard to my schooling, ... having boys around was just unconscious because our goal in school is just going to learn and getting the best grades you can.... I don't feel that the coeducational schooling had influenced me in any way, ... [yet] in all-girls' schools, the girls were demonstrating a lot of rebellion.... Discipline is a relative concept and it was different in every school setting. For instance, you had girls talking back to the teachers sometimes.... This was new to me.... This was 1984. There was a lot of rebellion going on and I was in the centre of that, but it was a good school, and some of the girls, yes, were wild, but certainly there were some who demonstrated the discipline that I was brought up with and the ethics, ... but it was definitely different from the school that I attended before ... maybe because some girls matured before others ... and they just wanted to test their limits....

Eman's example illustrates the cultural norms girls are taught to abide by. Although some girls, according to Eman, demonstrated resilience, she asserted that she maintained the cultural discipline. Discipline here is the cultural expectation of what it is to be a good girl. It is an aspect of Eman's schooling and the influence of different school ideologies she experienced.

Wafaa had an interesting point to contribute to the coeducational schooling discussion when she mentioned earlier that the classrooms in the village school were arranged so that the boys sat in front while the girls were sitting "relaxing" at the back. She did not question why boys were asked to sit in front; rather, she thought that it was better to have it that way. I perceive that this reflects how the education of girls and boys was valued. Boys sitting in the front of classrooms while girls were arranged to sit at the back denotes the importance given to boys' schooling over girls'. In no uncertain terms, I describe this as an implicit way to emphasize female inferiority and male superiority in a coeducational setting. This is why I remain ambivalent toward coeducational schooling. In coeducational schooling, there is a greater possibility that boys would be favoured or would be given more attention and therefore would achieve better results than girls.

Morooj was pro-coeducational and felt that boys and girls should grow side by side:

My social surrounding was free ... compared to the surroundings I saw in my extended family and relatives. For many people, going to university back in the '60s was forbidden and unthinkable because universities are coeducational.... Girls from conservative backgrounds would finish high school and then go to teachers' college.... [15]

While Morooj supported coeducational schooling, she analyzed the advantages and disadvantages in both situations:

> For girls from families that are highly conservative and that do not allow girls to mix with men—even within the relative circle, and even when they are young—they tell them not to play with boys. It is hard.... When the girl goes to university, she would face difficulties interacting with men, or would not know how to interact and deal with men and therefore problems would arise. Some families are not that strict so they encourage the girls to mix with the outside world, and they do not see problems in girls interacting with boys in relatives' and friends' gatherings and in the playground, so when the girl goes to a mixed university or setting, then the transition is easier, so they do not find as many problems in interactions as much as others with no experience do.[16] Mixing between the sexes may also have some disadvantages, especially with teenagers.... In junior high and high school, I, as a social worker, encountered some of these problems.

When Morooj volunteered at her friend's school, she noticed how some teachers exaggerated a few negative aspects of coeducational settings. She contended that some teachers were uncomfortable and tried to censor and control students. Morooj asserted that all-girls schooling contributed to the prevention of women from entering certain fields of knowledge. Further, she analyzed that the seclusion of women originated in the "Ottoman and Turks' ruling period over Muslim countries, when female slaves existed.... Ottomans and Turks were the ones who introduced seclusion and the *harems*, and that women have to cover and be locked up." However, Morooj argued,

> The positives of coeducation are that the girls know about the other sex—how they think, how to interact with men, their activities, their interests, and are enabled to compete with them.... This will advantage the girls in broadening their own perspectives, and then they have experience when a man is introduced to her or when she gets to that stage, she will be able to know for herself how to choose her future partner. Whereas the negative aspect is that ... girls might be more apprehensive about how they look, how they sound, and how they move, and so on.

Fadwa had a cogent reaction to all-girls' schooling. She promptly responded, "I hated being in an all-girls' school, absolutely hated it!" Fadwa continued:

It's a very strong feeling because I found that girls around guys are a little more cautious. They, even in Grade 1 or Grade 2, girls were more careful about how they behaved themselves around guys because they just didn't wanna show their evil sides, but when they were with each other, they could be so vicious! And I was bullied a lot in the all-girls' school, mainly because the girls, even though I had a very authentic self, the fact that I had lived in Kuwait, and the fact that my dad came and picked me up in a brand-new model car every day, ... and the fact that we lived in a really upscale place, and we had travelled all the way from another city to my city to study, and that teachers viewed me as a good student—these things put me in that category of spoiled nerd ... and the girls picked on me as a result. In [coeducational] schools, there were girls that have picked on me, but it was not as bad when guys were around because I always found that boys don't like that kind of—excuse my language—crap.... Boys defended me more than other girls did ... maybe also because I was a bit of a tomboy and I could actually, as a kid, play with boys in a more fun way than girls.... To look at me right now wearing very long *jelbab*[17] and my *hijab* probably wouldn't give that impression, but I was a tree-climber, so that was why I wasn't comfortable with the girls.

The differences in academic expectations between boys and girls are a concern for some theorists when talking about coeducational schools; this, however, was not an issue for Fadwa. She suggested that,

When I was in high school, I used to get some of the highest grades in my classes, and part of it was because we were in the diaspora and we didn't have a big social life, so I spent most of my time studying. So for me as a girl, getting very high marks and getting honour rolls and all these things, I didn't find a different expectation between me and the next boy because sometimes I excelled. I got higher marks than those boys, but having said that, I didn't find that all my other girlfriends had the same expectation of themselves. I don't know if that's because their families didn't see them as having the same degree of ability as the boys, or the teachers didn't encourage them as much, but generally, there were very, very excellent girls or excellent students, and there were excellent boys who were very good students, and then there were students who did well and possibly could've been "A" students, but just for one reason or another (i.e., personal circumstances), they weren't interested, just weren't at that level.

These narratives show how attending an all-girls' or coeducational school affected the way the women perceive themselves or the life routes they chose to take. Fadwa had a strong opposition to all-girls' schools. As these discussions show, the majority of the women in this study were not channelled, explicitly, into certain professions because they were female.

EDUCATIONAL EXPERIENCES IN CANADA

Fadwa, who is doing her graduate degree in Canada, where she also earned her Bachelor of Science degree and a teaching certificate, narrated her educational experiences in Canada. She was socialized by her father, not her mother or society, to believe that critical thinking is important, valid, and beneficial:

> Looking back at it as a teenager living in Canada, I realized that I was ... always reproached or scolded for being too philosophical, and too philosophical [there] meaning "questioning authority" ... meaning "Why do you need to ask that question? ... It's just something that you should obey." And that's why someone who does her Master's degree or a PhD degree, depending on where she does it or how she goes about it, might find difficulty in my native society....

Critical thinking and freedom of thought and speech are aspects of my educational experience in Canada, as well. However, in Saudi Arabia, I was not free to question school knowledge, social dictates, and cultural rules—all of which are considered sacred.

Yasmine spoke of the difficulties in being a student here. She noted that her educational experience, while training in a Canadian medical school, was hard because she was a woman and a Muslim. She explained what it was like getting ready to enter the operating room:

> I used to be very strict about scrubbing and rolling up my sleeves in front of everyone, so I would wait till everyone left the room and then I would do the scrubbing. At first they thought that I was nervous, but ... I explained to them. I asked a few Muslim (imams),[18] and they told me that it is my job and this is a good cause, so it should not be an issue. I actually thought of transferring to internal medicine because it does not involve OR and I will not have to do the scrubbing, but then I thought that I could modify. I remember that one day the chief nurse saw me in (the winter time) while getting

ready for OR.... I had worn a high neck and long sleeves and I did not take them off to wear the special OR dress. She screamed at me and said to me, "You are going to contaminate the room!" And it was a really hard time for me. I went to the residence room and I started to cry like a baby.

Yasmine remembers that it was also hard when she was in residence, training in Iraq:

> *Yasmine:* I have to be fair, though: I remember that it was hard also in Baghdad. I remember a professor in the final exam used to pick the women with the *hijab* to ask them to do a hernia checkup in front of 30 people. That was really mean of him.
>
> *Me:* You don't have to take it this way. Maybe that was an important part of your training as a doctor, which does not necessarily mean that he was a mean person.
>
> *Yasmine:* I agree with you, but if he is picking those with the scarf and asking them to do that specifically, then, yes, this is being mean. Thank God, my patient was an eight-year-old boy.... [laughter]

Yasmine noted that her family's support enabled her to overcome many barriers: "Thanks to my family's encouragement—my husband, my parents, and even my eldest daughter. I remember her saying to me once, 'Mama, it is time to go back to medicine.'" Another aspect of Yasmine's difficulties has to do with her conservative views of interacting with men, which is part of the educational experience in Canada. She was concerned about going to educational conferences because of handshaking. Yasmine and many other Muslim women are conservative about shaking hands with males who are not relatives. She explained:

> I am really uncomfortable with it. This is why I don't go to conferences and big gatherings, and I don't socialize with Canadians out[side] of my work, not because [of] hostility or anything, but it is just how conservative I am with handshaking and with silly jokes.... I do not have time to explain every time I am in these situations.... Males and females are still different and usually at conferences I have to find a female colleague to be my companion. I feel more comfortable and relaxed, and get more from what I am here for ... if I am in an all-women environment.

Wafaa also had an issue with handshaking. Nora's own challenges as a student in Canada differed:

I had some difficulties, partially for being a Muslim woman pursuing science. Although the first two years for me were smooth and productive, I started feeling an unexplainable discouragement from my supervisor (who is a male), but then I have some male colleagues and there is no preferential treatment…. In fact, I feel that a lot of people admire me for what I am doing. I am the first Muslim woman in the faculty…. One other female professor (one in particular) had helped and supported me…. She made me realize how the desk arrangement in the first lab I worked in (with the male supervisor) was hierarchical. For instance, the women's desks were left in a small space at the back end of the lab's corner…. Now all my committee members are women and my new supervisor, in fact, took me as a challenge to prove that women are capable and that women will support each other's causes.

Wafaa benefited academically from being part of the Canadian educational system. Actually, she did not only gain greatly in terms of academic knowledge, but a Canadian education also helped her to be more confident in herself and her abilities. "My education in Canada made me a different person…. When I came here, I knew very little…. I was confused with the 'add and drop' system and I did not know where I was going." For Wafaa, it was a difficult task to adjust to university here. The system and the language were all new to her. Everything was hard for her, including course registrations. A counsellor completed her application so she could obtain admission to school. Wafaa felt she benefited greatly from the education system and also from knowing other Arab Muslim women colleagues. She said:

I've always thought a Muslim girl is shy. This is what we were taught there…. I'm very shy and not good at public talking. I did my first presentation here. It was—oh God! I almost cried. I'm not used to that. They told me you have to give a speech about [a topic] and when I was speaking, I didn't look at anyone. I just put my head to the paper and I read it off. [I said] "Thank you!" I got a good mark on the information I provided, but I got 0 marks for eye contact! 0 marks for having a position up there. [laughter] And it helped me a lot knowing Arab Muslim women on campus and in the prayer room because after seeing what they can do, it kind of encouraged me to become like them. I will never reach their level of courage, but I was able to do a presentation by my second year and third year. And with that presentation, I had some eye contact and in my fourth year, I was outspoken. I would say anything…. I opposed if I didn't agree with something and I would argue, and I would participate in class without any fear.

Wafaa needed to see role models, outspoken Muslim women, which encouraged her to be herself. It was not enough for Wafaa to be inspired by Muslim women as role models in the early days of Islam. Her real motivation was a combination that stemmed from the education that encouraged her to speak up as well as meeting assertive Muslim women of the same generation.

Although Sahra struggled to transform her learning style, to use her imagination and think critically, to not depend solely on memorization, she still found many similarities between her university education here and her education in Cairo. She pronounced that the only difference she felt was that the emphasis in Canada's education system is on creativity whereas the education system in Cairo emphasizes memorization. This was her main struggle. With regard to other difficulties in her education in Canada, she observed that,

> Well, when I think of my experience here and there, it is almost the same.... If I talk about old-fashioned people [in terms of their views of women's roles] in Cairo, I ... find some old-fashioned people here.... People everywhere [meaning East and West] stereotype Muslim women.... They think: "What is she doing in a faculty of engineering?"... and I have to deal with it.... I have to prove myself....

So Sahra is resisting the stereotypical idea of Middle Eastern Muslim women by proving her capability as an engineer. She disavows the prescribed image in both worlds.

Morooj, like Sahra, admired the focus in Canadian education on creativity instead of memorization. Although she spoke little English, this did not hinder Morooj in studying or fully engaging in student life. What is special about Morooj's educational experience in Canada is that it offered her what was not feasible for someone her age in Libya:

> What I appreciated the most is the fact that there is no limit on the student's age. In Libya,[19] whenever you graduate from high school or university and work, ... it is extremely hard to go back to school.... However, in Canada, as long as you have the motivation to continue your education, then there is no limit and you can gain new experience in any field you want.... Although my English is very basic, I was welcomed, stood by, and encouraged.... My education here opened new possibilities for me. I entered a new world.... When I started photography as a hobby, I knew so little about pottery and photography.... I was encouraged when I enrolled in some clay classes, pottery, and sculpture.... What I admire the most

here is the politics of education, ... [the] methods of education. All this combined opens new choices and opportunities that were not available for me before; also the way a student is valued and assessed.... The education system here encourages creativity and critical thinking.

Uniquely, Eman felt that the differences between being a student here in Canada versus being a student in Libya are internal; that the differences are in her feelings and her expectations as a mature student: "What is new about my experiences here is me.... I'm 34 now, and my classmates are all in their 20s. Also it's more competitive here.... There are more and larger libraries here. We didn't have many [books and libraries] in Libya, unfortunately."

Also, Fadwa's educational experiences empowered her. She pointed out that being able to give back to the school and being an active member in the school culture built her confidence and gave her insight on what she wanted to do in the future:

> What I love about Canadian schools is the ability to be socially active. In high school, I learned about all the associations that I could participate in. I could stay after school [for extracurricular activities]. There was leadership ... a choir, I was a peer mediator, I was a teaching assistant.... It is giving back to the school. Also in Canada, volunteering is a big theme, and being able to participate at the organizational level—not only be at the receiving end, but actually produce as a student—was a very empowering feeling.

This freedom of choice can be difficult to handle sometimes, according to Fadwa. She remembers that there were issues that she faced as a student. What was most difficult for her was choosing what she wanted to specialize in, and choosing a profession: "choosing the final career was a little hard."

These were the Muslim women's experiences in Canada, including their perceived advantages and disadvantages of being part of the education system here. In my experience, I have had many educational advantages as a student in Canada. I have been introduced to a wealth of knowledge and endless resources of scholarly work. Like Eman, I am astonished by the size of the libraries here, the affiliations with universities and public libraries, and their accessibility. In Canada, I am, as a Muslim woman, contributing to the production of knowledge, going to conferences, and publishing my work. I aim to continue to produce knowledge that affirms my identity as a Muslim woman in the Canadian context.

IDEOLOGIES THAT CONSTRUCT GENDER THROUGH WOMEN'S EDUCATION

Some aspects of the women's narratives, like those from Wafaa's schooling, reflect the prioritization of male education. This is not surprising to me. I was astounded, however, to hear the women's comments about implicit gender patriarchal discourse. For instance, Wafaa's comments about how comfortable she was sitting at the back of the classroom revealed an implicit acceptance of male superiority. Furthermore, when I asked the participants if they considered education as a necessity for men and a luxury for women, Eman disagreed, explaining that—and justifying why—it is important for each to obtain an education. Nonetheless, she differentiated between the men's and women's realities:

122

> Well, education is a given right to every human being, and I believe that women have a more important role than men in building society, thereby building civilizations. Now, I mean if a woman was ignorant and she wasn't educated, then how is she going to penetrate [sic] any knowledge to her children or any education, or any discipline, or any ethics? Even the women before our time, when schools didn't exist, they were educated, and education was passed down by fathers, by brothers. It was passed down by anyone in the community who was willing to give an education. It doesn't have to be an institution of a school as we know it now, as long as knowledge ... is passed down to women or girls and boys the same way because they both have important roles.... The man is gonna go out there in the world and he's going to provide for his family.... He's going to basically be a productive entity in the community, and the woman is too. Whether she worked outside the home or worked inside the home, her role is very important in that she needs to educate her children. I mean, she's the one that they're created in her, they're born from her, and she nurses them, so it's just her nature to look after the children....

Eman stresses the idea of a woman as nurturer and a man as provider. She continues:

> Yes, a man can nurture them [the children] as well ... and some people can disagree with me and say, "Well, a man can do that," but it's mothering. I mean, even the verb says so. So education is important for a woman, just as it is important for a man. And for her to acquire knowledge, it can be anywhere, really. I mean, if it was in the institution of school as we

know it now, or in any way or form, but she has to be educated. She must be educated. She must be exposed to knowledge and it is a crime, really. I consider it as a crime if she is not educated, if she is not given that right to be educated because, in the long run, she will affect more individuals in society.

Morooj rightly argued that in Arab Muslim society, the man's education is still given more importance than the woman's, the main reason being,

... he will be responsible to feed a family, so the higher grades he gets, the better his future will be. Although my parents were happy and encouraging me, they would be more concerned if my brother fails a course. They were more concerned about his education than the rest of us [girls]. The consequences are different: If a girl fails, she will stay home and wait to get married.... If the girl repeats a year, also, it is not as a big deal as if the boy failed a year. At the end he will be responsible for feeding his family.

Morooj continued that this should not imply, in any way, women's inferiority and seclusion from obtaining education, or taking public roles:

Personally, I believe that when a man secludes a woman and locks her up, he is being selfish and because when a woman has education, it is not for the man's advantage ... because then she will start asking, arguing, and discussing. An educated woman will start talking with the man at his level, and the man has a desire to control and does not allow a woman to be better than him. This is, unfortunately, a complex problem in some Arab Muslim men's minds. Still, until now, Arab Muslim societies, even the advanced ones, are still suffering these kinds of problems. Most of the time this is the case, but sometimes men are respectful of women and they like to deal with educated women. For instance, when I got married, I was still in university and my husband encouraged me a lot to finish my education and his family helped me with the children. Thanks to Allah, I think this has to do with the level of education of even my husband's parents. Education always makes a difference....

I asked Morooj, "Where do you think the double standards about men's and women's education exist?" She asserted:

Islam, I do not think that it values men's education more than women's because the more you are educated as a woman in all fields, religious knowledge or science, the more you are protecting yourself from abuse and strengthening your background. Does the religion differentiate between women's education and men's education? Absolutely not. Education is for both boys and girls and there are no limits, but both sexes have to be aware of morals and manners. I would think that in some fields, women have to be cautious in entering because they would be more vulnerable, and so she could try to avoid these things or situations. As long as you are strong and have morals, I believe that no one or nothing is going to stop you from what you want to achieve. The reason is, sometimes, women are not as strong.

When asked to give an example, Morooj said:

For instance, in space, in being a plane pilot, or in a war, or in the military, it may put a woman in a position that she is not ready or prepared for, although in early Islamic days, women did all that, but the difference, in my perspective, is that in the early Islamic era, Islam was still strong and fresh in Muslims' hearts, so the religion was alive in women's hearts, but now it is different and, for a believing woman, it will not be hard to pursue any field.

Ruba said, "I did not face the experiences that other women say that they faced in that they were treated differently than their brothers.... I would hear stories like the girl would have to do this and the boy would have to do this." Ruba's narratives noted that some families focus on girls' educational progress. I perceive this as a double standard toward boys' and girls' education. Ruba's statement that "the boys can handle themselves" emphasized such double standards, which may be transferred to other matters. She elaborated on girls' safety versus boys' safety:

There's restriction to your freedom where you could go.... It's a matter of being afraid for the safety of the girl and the perception of the community and the culture to her.... It's not perceived proper conduct or behaviour when a girl just goes out at night.

Ruba continued, "For me, the way we were raised is the same as everybody. Boys and girls are the same." Yet, equality between the sexes is another point of tension among Islamic teaching, patriarchal cultural traditions, and societal norms of Arab Muslim societies. Ruba made the distinction: "But I believe that Islam gives us the same rights and duties in general. I believe I'm equal to a man because this is what my faith tells me."

In the workplace, women are faced with this patriarchy and sexism. It is a stereotypical perception that a man is better at some jobs than a woman; that a woman is better than a man in domestic jobs, or that a man is more intelligent than a woman. However, Morooj disagreed with such views:

> These are all wrong beliefs. First, intelligence is partly inherited, but mostly gained, so if a woman had an opportunity to learn, whereas the man did not have the opportunity to learn, then the woman will be more intelligent than the man. The belief that women should be only educated to a certain age or degree is discriminatory for women. I believe that there are no limits for women's education in all fields and in any fields. If a woman could obtain all the education she wants, then why not? A woman is the principal and the basis for her family.... The more she is educated, the broader her perspective is and the more she will benefit her children. By raising a good generation of citizens, or participating in the workforce, or both, she is gratefully benefiting her society. The woman and the family is [sic] the focus, or need to be the focus, because that's how society progresses.

Nahlaa related all the dominant traditional perceptions of women's education to culture. This dichotomous thinking of man/woman, reason/emotion, and superior interlligence/inferior intelligence should not be applied in today's world. According to Nahlaa, "It's actually cultural thoughts. Women now should get educated so that they can help themselves in the future and get jobs ... for a better living.... I don't believe that boys are smarter or girls are smarter. It doesn't depend on being a female or male."

Ruba believes that men and women deserve to enjoy equality in pursuing education. Parental financial support should depend on merit regardless of gender:

> When it comes to mental and intellectual growth, unless the girl is not really into education or the guy is not really ... you see these situations in some families, then of course you put [support] the money toward the one who is interested.... Why should anybody be deprived of an education?

Fadwa did not perceive that higher education was a luxury for women:

> Higher education is very highly regarded. It's been told to us that girls or boys should go to university and get an education because you don't want to live life without an education. It's just not an option. We all knew we were going to go to university. The other thing is, my father

tended to make the comparison between educated people and influential people, so he would say to me as a kid—I would be seven or eight years old—and he'd say, "Margaret Thatcher, Fadwa? I want you to be like her. She is a powerful, strong woman." But at the same time, there are drawbacks to being very, very well educated as a woman because as much as they want you to be educated and have that status, when it comes to issues of getting married and playing a certain gender role, there were certain expectations....

I agree that Fadwa's explanation of the importance of education to both sexes depends on social class. Statistics on education and gender in Sudan[20] and Saudi Arabia show that there is some gender disparity. For example, the Gender Parity Index[21] in 1999/2000 was 0.09 in Sudan. In Saudi Arabia it was 1.47 in 2002/2003 (UNESCO Institute for Statistics, 2005). Gross enrollment ratio[22] of tertiary[23] education in Sudan in 1999–2000 was approximately 6 for males and 7 for females. In Saudi Arabia the gross enrollment ratio in 2001/2002 was 18 for males, 25 for females, and in 2002/2003, 21 males to 26 females (UNESCO, 2005). The UNESCO report (2005) indicates that "Saudi Arabia and Sudan are among the countries where the gender parity has been achieved in access to secondary education, but these countries will face a trend towards greater gender disparity" (UNESCO, 2005, p. 28). Therefore, I conclude that education still depends on social class. I agree that "class remains a relatively unspoken descriptor, commonly filtered through discourse of gender, race, and ethnicity" (Proweller, 1998, p. 69). Not only are class and social status factors in women's education, but the father's education is also a major factor in whether children are encouraged to pursue education.

I would like to revisit Fadwa's last statement: "There are drawbacks to being very, very well educated as a woman." I asked, "How can education be disadvantageous?" Fadwa replied, "Men tend to be threatened by it [woman's higher education]." She continued that some men favour less-educated women. A good wife, culturally, according to Fadwa, would be the one who "cooks, cleans, raises the kids, and leaves [her] husband to do his stuff. It's not about your effort, it's not about your thoughts or how you interact...." She asserted, "The drawbacks of having this education, for me, is if I were to go back home and marry someone who's living back home, then it is an issue." I contend that Fadwa's observation is true. Some married men feel threatened if they have professional wives or successful partners. This may disturb some men's pride and might destroy family harmony. This certainly pinpoints how patriarchal societal norms emphasize men's education and encourage men's success, while giving women the least possible level of education, yet none of the women interviewed are content with the least: They are looking for the best.

Through the next thread of the women's narratives, I investigate further what Fadwa has observed about women's higher education and family stability. I also explore how marriage contributes to women's gender construction.

NOTES

1. *Quran*, Sura IX, 71, p. 461, translated by Abdallah Yousef Ali.

2. The education of women in Saudi Arabia started 34 years after men's education and has been given secondary importance (Al-Manea, 1984).

3. Some Canadian students' experiences indicate that Canadian teachers tend to accept only those critiques that agree with their ideologies, and, thus, many are authoritarian—it is simply more covert.

4. An example of this is that education for women tends to emphasize that a woman's primary role is that of a good mother and a good wife.

5. From Grades 4–9, all girls are enrolled in home economics class. In Grades 10 and 11, girls have the option of specializing in one branch of home economics classes: cooking, sewing, or drawing.

6. Teachers always requested that short students sit in the front rows.

7. Implying that it is not serious.

8. The Druze faith is a branch of Muslim faith.

9. Many restrictions apply for girls.

10. It is documented that the Prophet (PBUH) says, "Seek knowledge even in China."

11. In Canada it has been discussed extensively.

12. *Hijabis* are girls and women wearing the *hijab*.

13. An Arabic word meaning "discipline."

14. Universities in almost all Arab Muslim countries are coeducational, except in Saudi Arabia, where they are exclusively sex-segregated.

15. Teachers' colleges are sex-segregated in Libya.

16. Universities are coeducational in Libya, while public schools are sex-segregated.

17. *Jelbab* is a long dress worn by some Muslim women.

18. A Muslim imam is a religious leader,

19. In Saudi Arabia, too, whenever a student graduates from high school or university and works for a while, it will be hard for him or her to be accepted into education programs as priority is given to new graduates.

20. Sudan is Fadwa's country of origin.

21. The ratio of female-to-male values of a given indicator.
22. The general level of participation at a given level of education.
23. Tertiary education refers to the third stage in education.

Chapter Eight

THE IDEAL WOMAN: ILLUSIONS OR REALITIES?

THE IDEAL WOMEN IN SOCIETY AND CULTURE, AND WOMEN'S OWN VIEWS

"All societies define sex roles according to their images of the ideal man or woman. It cannot be too radical to assert that no human being is unaffected by these definitions, or can escape being measured according to these cultural images" (Epstein, 1970, p. 20). This statement asserts that a society, whether Eastern or Western, measures a man's and a woman's performance according to its ideal roles. Although the characteristics of the ideal woman change over time and from culture to culture, the ideal woman in Arab Muslim culture is still an obedient and submissive woman, one who does not cause any trouble in her home through abiding by the cultural norms.

When defining an "ideal woman," almost all of the Arab Muslim women commented that Arab Muslim culture defines who an ideal woman is; they claimed that "it is the culture and not the religion that is our problem." Ironically, when I asked the Arab Muslim women about their views of an "ideal woman," almost all of them focused first on the cultural expectations. According to them, the cultural perception of an "ideal woman" is one who occupies the margins of society in relation to a man, both in and outside the home, but particularly in the public sphere.

Fadwa, by sharing the story of her aunt, explored the features of the "ideal woman":

An aunt of mine is educated and has a liberal mind, but she married a traditional village guy who, yes, is highly educated, but he's a traditional, traditional man [with emphasis], ... but she questions and she's an intellectual woman and because of that, they [people] thought that she was disturbing the waters and that really troubled them in their marriage a lot. They've had a lot of tumultuous times in their marriage because of that characteristic. She was seen as *lameeda*,[1] like one of those wives who talks back at her husband and questions his authority....

Fadwa's aunt did not meet the criteria of the "ideal woman," or even that of a "good wife" because she argued with and questioned her spouse. Aisenberg and Harrington (1988) argue that the institution of marriage is constructed to repress women. Similarly in Arab Muslim culture, the institution of marriage encourages men to repress women because of the idea that women's instincts must be controlled. The ideal result of this control, in Fadwa's example, is a silent and submissive wife. Culturally, these are the traits of a good and peaceful wife.

Fadwa philosophized about the "ideal woman" in marriage. She suggested an analogy between the "banking system of education" (Freire, 2003), marriage, and society's expectation of an ideal woman. This can also serve as an example of how Fadwa compared social expectations and individual desires when choosing a spouse. She spoke of the connection:

> That environment back home ... is an environment that does not promote critical thinking in the educational system.... The best answer is the answer from the textbook, and if you can provide the textbook's answer, you're an excellent student.... And that's, again, the relationship in a marriage. The best wife is the wife who does things by the textbook, meaning the social conventions: cooking, cleaning....

Fadwa also acknowledged that when it comes to an ideal wife, the village's definition is the most culturally prominent:

> Yeah, ... the village and the roots in the village is just what are going to be the ideals. A woman who can take care of her house and let the man know that she's in charge of the house is a good wife.... This is our cultural belief. For me, ... if I have my children, I wanna be at home ... if [it is] financially possible, ... and I think that is something that our culture overlooks—that being a mother is just being a mother. That's it.... No, I wanna be a good mother to my children because that is my religious duty, I believe.... Being a good mother is probably directly related to being a good wife ... in kindness and compassion ... and caring and consideration from both spouses.

When I asked Ruba about an ideal woman, she thought of a specific example of a woman whom she knew and idolized:

> What makes this local Arab Muslim woman ideal is ... what fascinates me the most about her is her strength and her sense of justice and fairness, ... the way she looks at things, and the fact that she is not a selfish human being. She always wants to do something for others, and that to me is fascinating because I think the key is actually being concerned about people around you.... It's amazing because she's religious ... and she was raised in a very religious family. She, for me, was the way a Muslim woman is supposed to be; an independent thinker, strong, powerful, and creative— because she's very creative—and instills her sense of confidence in her children ... she dresses properly when it comes to Islamic dress, she's knowledgeable in her faith, she's knowledgeable in the Holy *Quran*.... She lives by that.

131

Ruba later emphasized, "In Islam everything you do is considered some kind or form of worship ... your responsibility as a mother, God is gonna reward you for that." Thus, in Ruba's views, a woman approaching her life from that perspective is an ideal woman.

Eman referred to society's characteristics of an ideal woman. She immediately acknowledged that a woman in our Arab Muslim Middle Eastern society should be moulded in a certain way in order to be considered ideal:

> An ideal woman in society would be a woman ... that works outside [as a professional], and that has a spic-and-span clean house, well-mannered children who are always clean and never forget to say please and thank you, ... that lives in a three-storey house and drives a Mercedes or a BMW and her husband is well off and she's kind of strong-willed, so I think that's, yeah, in the Libyan society.... This is not the ideal for me.... Some people see a good wife as ironing shirts and cleaning the house and, but no, again ... [my husband] irons his own shirts and cooks lunch for us. So a good wife in my standards would be a person who stands by her husband in good or bad, just as he would be expected to do the same for me, ... [and] thereby be called a good husband. [laughs] A good mother is just a mother that sees to the needs of her children's needs.

Eman's view did not overlook the materialistic aspect of an ideal woman in the world we live in today, whether it is Eastern or Western. The traditional notion of an ideal woman who can clean and cook is substituted, certainly in middle-class families, with a woman who can provide for the family to keep up with luxurious matters. Eman is able to live outside the traditional and the new, materialistic framework of how to be an ideal woman for her own family.

Wafaa, who at the time of the interviews, was engaged and would marry in a few months, differentiated between the Islamic and the cultural perception of a good woman. She offered, "Culturally, being the obeying wife, ... like she would do everything to please her husband." Sahra agreed and added, "My priority is my home, my children, and my husband. This is my priority.... These are an ideal woman's priorities...."

Morooj's view was not unlike Eman's, Wafaa's, and Sahra's. She asserted that her view of an ideal woman is incredibly different from society's views:

> An ideal woman is capable of making use of her resources ... the woman that is capable in any and all fields. In her home, she is good with her husband, with her friends, and with her children; she is capable of making the best of her time ... educate herself because self-education is important too.... Though in society, staying at home, looking after the children, looking after the husband, and cooking is what a good wife does.... Personally, I was tired of staying at home and I could not continue living.... I felt like my thoughts and my vocabulary were limited, ... so I decided to go out and do something with my life.... When I worked outside, it was optional, it was not necessary financially.... People would say, "Her husband is good ... what else she does want, he is giving her everything—money and property." [laughter] ... This is what society wants. People kept bugging me with "How can you leave your children?" or "Now she wants to learn computers, now she wants to read or be an artist!" I do not pay attention to this kind of mentality because they are not going to control me.

As Morooj spoke about this part of her life, she seemed troubled, remembering those days when she was alone at home, unfulfilled and bored. I asked Morooj for more details:

Me: Now you are talking about outsiders like neighbours and acquaintances?

Morooj: Yes, outsiders and some friends. There was no acceptance of my decision to go out and learn.

Me: Did you find it difficult to continue?

Morooj: (Answering hastily) Only in the beginning. Then I didn't care that much, so it was not hard to ignore. I used to go to arts exhibitions, although it was not something women would do there.

Me: What about your in-laws? Did they interfere?

Morooj: No, they did not interfere because I was there if they needed help. I respected them and whenever they needed me around, I was there to support. I like them ... and they also like me as a real daughter for them and this is the least thing we could do for each other. Respect and love—love people and support them and they will be supportive of you, too.

Me: You found your decision to do something different hard in society at large?

Morooj: Yes, in society it is hard to overcome some barriers and it is hard to please people. It will be at your expense and they want you to be isolated and you will end up ill because seclusion and boredom can cause some psychological problems, even the woman who is relaxed and calm by nature, but because of too much pressure in society, she will be unhappy and she will struggle.... When I gather with home-staying mothers, I discover how they are struggling because no one understands them.... They are suffering alone and in silence, but society always wants women quiet, satisfied, content, not complaining, not getting ill, and not even feeling tired.... What do you think of Arabic society? It is devastating, their expectations of women "of and for women." Yes, unfortunately. Even in the educated circles, unfortunately, even educated families are like that. They try sometimes, but sometimes they tolerate it out of courtesy and only for a short time.

Morooj powerfully called attention to the other dilemma facing women. This was supported by Bourdieu (1999), who argued that some housewives suffer in silence: Ordinary women, staying at home or working, have so much hardship in their lives. Only a few make themselves heard by protesting and changing their lives like Morooj, while others remain locked in silence and despair.

As I reflect on Morooj's and Eman's comments, I contend that it is not only society that should be blamed. We, as women, should take responsibility for how we are influenced by our culture. Wafaa, Nahlaa, and others indicated that culture is not static; therefore, like Morooj, a woman is able to construct new models of realities unlike those imposed subtly and effectively by cultural traditions. As the women's narratives frequently reveal, here in Canada we are free from worrying about the reaction of kin or friends to decisions we make. I wondered if that would be an important factor in constructing a different gender perception. What are the implications of such a conclusion? Additionally, being away from home, there are no cultural or social expectations for us here when it comes to staying home or going to work, but there are other ways in which our gender as Arab Muslim women is constructed in Canadian society.

NOTE

1.   In Arabic this word means "big mouth."

Chapter Nine

A MUSLIM HYBRID IDENTITY

On many occasions during the interviews, I was intrigued by the women's continuous emphasis on their Islamic identity—a major theme that emerged within their narratives. Being a Muslim woman is a significant aspect of their identity. Islam, for the Arab Muslim women interviewed, is a source of inspiration. Perhaps the best terms to describe these women's identities would be "Muslim hybrid identity." As will be highlighted shortly, this became apparent through many critical choices they have made in their lives—choices that demonstrated their personal agency within their gendered identity construction. Being Arab Muslim Canadian women seems to mean that they have

> ... [forged] hybrid identities in response to their experiences and inter-
> actions with changing contextual realities within formal educational as
> well as community contexts. Using the margins as sites of resistance,
> these women deployed their hybrid identities and world-views to enact
> resistance against oppressive power relations in various contexts result-
> ing in empowerment.... (Chaudhry, 1997, p. 451)

In what follows, I highlight aspects of these hybrid identities.[1]

AUTONOMY AND CHOICE

Many critical life choices made by the participants have demonstrated their personal agency, which is a key in gendered identity construction. Manion (2003) argues that:

> Girls are socialized from a very early age to define themselves less
> in terms of autonomy and independence and more in terms of their

relationships with, and dependence upon, others. This defining sense of interdependence makes girls especially vulnerable to social pressures, especially those urging them to conform to traditional conceptions of femininity. (p. 24)

Is Manion's (2003) argument compatible with the perception expressed by Fadwa and the other women interviewed, and where does this fit within the spectrum? These women have asserted their capability for making choices, and their choices reflect their agency and personal autonomy.

Sahra, for instance, acknowledged that her choices—choosing to be an engineer, choosing her spouse, and choosing to live in Canada—reflect her personality. She said that being an engineer did not change the way she perceives herself as a woman, her abilities, or the world around her. Instead, she stated, "My point of view is what affected my choices, ... including engineering."

Eman chose to teach special-needs children. Currently, she is taking courses to achieve this goal: "I always wanted to be a teacher.... My father was a teacher and my mother is a teacher, ... and after having a son with special needs, ... I planned on becoming a teacher of special needs...."

Fadwa's narrative is exceptional. Although challenged by her parents and her extended family when she changed her career path from medicine to teaching, Fadwa was determined to pursue her dream: "It took me about two to three years to convince my parents that teaching is really for me. It wasn't something that I thought of before, ... but when I looked at all the things I have volunteered for and all the jobs that I have had, they were all teaching-related, so it only made sense and it was a very natural step for me."

Her parents objected to her plans, yet, for Fadwa, what was an even greater challenge was talking to the people in her village:

And the big problem wasn't even my parents.... It was trying to break the news to the people in the village.... They were all under the impression that I was gonna be a doctor.... I was still called "doctor." ... They said, "But we thought you were going into medicine." I had to explain to them that the process in Canada is different. If I was there, I would've graduated high school at age 16. I would have done five years of university at the end of which, by age 21, I would have been a doctor.... I explained that it is different in Canada since I need a degree in science prior to medical school.... And as soon as I put it to them in that kind of context, the concept of [women's] social role and gender role kicks in, ... and I know that's their reality and that's how they reason things out ... and they said "It's better that you chose the path that you did because this way you can come back and get married...."

Fadwa made her decision more palatable using her extended family's reasoning. She made plans for her future based on autonomous choices. Her choices were not compatible with the cultural values of the people in the village, yet Fadwa is self-assured that her goal is compatible with her faith.

OUTSTANDING ASPECTS OF THE PARTICIPANTS' IDENTITIES: A CREATION OF HYBRID IDENTITY

While my study explores how these Arab Muslim women's gender percep-tions may have been influenced by Canadian education, I must point out that the participants constantly emphasized the fact that their perceptions were greatly influenced by their Muslim identities. Shanaz Khan (2000) identified this hybridity as a "Third Space"[2] in Muslim women's identity, an ambiguous identity in which Muslim women create a space between the mainstream racism and discrimination they may face as Muslims in Canada, and any patriarchal religious dogmas that discriminate against them (Bullock, 2005, p. 291). Aminah Beverly McCloud (1995) perceives this so-called hybrid space as synthetic and as a space in which a fusion between two identities—Muslim and Canadian—occurs. I further argue that this "Third Space" highlights the women's involvement as citizens in Canadian society while also embracing their faith as Muslims. The narra-tives reveal that there are "no contradictions between the two allegiances" (Ramadan, 2004, p. 84).

I was intrigued by the women's continuous emphasis on their Islamic identity. A major theme that emerged from the women's narratives was that being a "Muslim" woman is a significant aspect of their identity. In other words, Islam, for the Arab Muslim women interviewed, is a source of inspi-ration. The women indicated that gender, as an unstable and unquestioned component of one's identity, should not be taken for granted. They agreed that "gender is constructed by individuals as well as by social forces, in-dividuals do not automatically adopt predetermined gender roles; they are continually active in building, negotiating, and maintaining perceptions of their gender. Gender is a relational construct" (Wesley, 2000, p. 156). The roles that women are expected to play as obedient wives, self-sacrificing mothers, and diligent housewives are constantly challenged in the participants' narratives. Greater equality, equal educational opportunities, and career aspirations represent values held by many Arab Muslim women. Camilla Gibb and Celia Rothenberg (2000) suggest that religious identity "becomes primary" (p. 234) for immigrant Palestinian and Harari[3] Muslim women in Canada. I therefore infer that being Muslim women is the foremost component of my participants' identities.

In a more general sense, Erikson (1968) indicates that,

> Identity can be seen as the complex relation between the physical, the cultural, and the social processes on one hand, and the self-image and self-esteem of the individual on the other hand. It refers to the area in which individual processes in the context of individual lives are "attuned." (as cited in Buitelaar, Ketner & Bosma, 2004, p. 147)

According to Erikson (1968), identity and ideology are two faces of the same coin: "An ideological system is a coherent body of shared images, ideas, and ideals that, on one hand, provides a way of life for the participants; and, on the other hand, provides a sense of solidarity that links individuals in collective identities" (as cited in Buitelaar, Ketner & Bosma, 2004, p. 154). Thus, the women interviewed, all of whom agree that Islam has provided them with a sense of identity, did not perceive Islam as merely a practical religion, but, more importantly, they have embraced it as a way of life.

Rayaprol (1997) suggests that "in the contemporary world of transnational culture exchanges, the movement of people between nations is no longer an exile in any complete sense. Identities and cultures get delocalized, but rarely detached from memories of past places and times" (p. 2), and this is clearly reflected in the women's narratives. Viewed from this perspective, Muslim identity is actively "produced, reproduced, and transformed, through a series of social processes" (Kahni-Hopkins & Hopkins, 2002, p. 289).

Recent studies of Muslim women in the United States have revealed that Muslim women creatively negotiate their gender, religion, and ethnic identities in light of dominant Western discourses, social norms, and modernist discourses that often define these women as the "other" (Read & Bartkowski, 2000, p. 397), a finding that correlates to my own study. The Arab Muslim women's narratives reveal how they have created for themselves a space in which they embrace their Islamic identity and transcend boundaries that have reduced them to subservient victims of their faith. Also, various studies (i.e., Ahmad, 2001; Basit, 1997; Gregg, 1996; Jacobson, 1998; Saroglou & Galand, 2004) illustrate that immigrant

Muslim women from different nationalities and backgrounds are active agents both in their communities and in wider society, while consistently stressing their Islamic identity.

Moreover, other studies also suggest that "Immigrants' integration into the adoptive country's culture does not necessarily lead to the abandonment of the original culture" (Saroglou & Galand, 2004, p. 125). The adoptive country may also provide a safe space for cultural reproduction for young Arab Muslim women, so that their religious identity may remain intact. This resonates with both my experience and that of the women. Intriguingly, Damji and Lee's (1995) study concludes that "Canadian attitudes toward women are more egalitarian than those of many countries from which Muslims have emigrated" (para. 11). As will be discussed in the following chapters, Canada has given Arab Muslim women, and immigrants in general, enormous opportunities for self-fulfillment while maintaining a space to live and practise their faith.

In short, like Buitelaar, Ketner, and Bosma (2004), I conclude that Muslim women possess

> *Asserted* [emphasis added] identity, an identity that is chosen. Because it is a matter of personal choice, the Islamic identity can be very meaningful. Stressing Islamic identity in a non-Muslim context can give minorities a feeling that at least in some ways they can be in command of their own lives; it can also provide a sense of belonging. (p. 154)

NOTES

1.   On hybridity, see Bhabha (1994).
2.   See Bhabha (1990) on hybridity and third space.
3.   Palestinian and Harari Muslim are minority groups in Canada. Harari refers to an ethnic group originally from Ethiopia.

Chapter Ten

ARAB MUSLIM WOMEN'S ACTIVISM

Through the theme of Arab Muslim women's activism, I explore how each of the women I interviewed perceives women's societal contribution. Do these women perceive and value a role for women in the public sphere? I explore ways in which these women have contributed to their societies. Also, I strive to understand how their social contributions influence the way they view themselves as women.

Yasmine, who is an activist in the local Canadian Muslim community, told me that "the way a woman and a man can contribute to society is by finding her or his inner strength." She explained that,

> A person needs to find his or her strength and work with it.... Individually, we can construct a better society.... Each of us can create better communities. Islam has influenced me greatly in thinking about my role in society. I do this in every step of the way to improve my work, to help my children succeed, and to help my community. This role applies to both men and women in helping build their community and the larger Canadian society as much as they can.... A woman or a man needs to start from the family because it is the smallest part of their society.... The woman should be looking after her home first, but if she has more time and energy to do other things, then she should look to the public sphere.

Nora's involvement in society started when she organized gymnastics classes in the Muslim community for women, something in which she took great pride. She was proud of helping people and believed that taking the initiative to fill a need leads to building a coherent society. For instance, when Nora took a course in nutrition in her faculty, she made notes and distributed them to people in the community.

Morooj emphasizes that "education is first and foremost." Like Yasmine and Nora, Morooj feels that societal contribution begins with educating oneself and one's family. She asserts that bringing up good citizens starts at home. She highly values volunteering:

> I have to give to my society.... One has to take the initiative without waiting for a give back [material profit to one's self].... If one instills in children the love of giving to their society, then one is raising a generation of good citizens.... Not necessarily ideals, but important things that we sometimes ignore or overlook how important they are....

Ruba, like Morooj, feels that societal contribution begins with contributing to oneself and one's family. Importantly, she adds:

> The youth need a positive influence in order to grow up stronger ... these days, in general, whether Western or Middle Eastern, because I think the boundaries are melting so much ... that it's so open. The problems they [youth] are facing there they are so much like the problems we are facing here, maybe not to the same extent, but they are facing a lot of the same problems.... Encourage them to be strong and outspoken.... As Arabs, ... we try to raise our children ... not speaking out against anything.... "Mama, be quiet, it's not your problem, don't worry about it." You speak out, you get into trouble.... This is our generation. It's very sad that we grew up this way ... to be very silent.... In our native society, ... if you speak out against something, there's a lot at stake, ... but here it is not the same society.... I see [a] second generation of people who are born in this country and have Arabic parents.... They are brought up to have the silent attitude which muzzles people, quiets them, [and] silences them.... It's very sad.... This is not a positive contribution to society, not at all....

Ruba rightly recognizes and names a real concern for the younger generation. An outspoken personality is invaluable for social contribution. Youth, men, and women can be instruments for positive change in their societies, especially with respect to gender issues, if they speak up and fully participate in society.

Fadwa agreed with Morooj, Ruba, and Yasmine's perceptions. Besides being good parents, Fadwa advocates the best ways for women and men to contribute to society:

> The Prophet [PBUH] says that the best people are the most useful to other people. I think this is something that refers to men and/or women. It's just a matter of how they go about doing it.... Women as social activists—I

really believe in the importance of that. Men have dominated the political arena for a long time.... Social activism is [needed], ... and women can really be excellent at it.

Also, Fadwa acknowledges that her endeavour to pursue a Master's degree is mainly to please her parents, but it is also to contribute to her society.

Therefore, all these narratives reflect the interviewees' positive outlook on women's societal contribution. They are all contributing or planning to be socially active. The women share a powerful belief in Islamic support of women's causes, and how Islam encourages them to obtain a higher education. Women are becoming catalysts for change and progress in any society. These women's perceptions of the meaning and means of social activism are inspirational. They support diverse ways in which a woman can contribute to her society. But is their society benefiting from their readiness for social activism?

143

THE QUESTION OF FEMINISM

In each interview I asked the participants about feminist issues, workshops, and conferences. I chose this question because some studies have revealed that the introduction to feminist ideologies in the West has influenced women from other cultural backgrounds. Moghissi (1999) agrees that "The exposure to feminist ideas and involvement in other new social movements, while influencing women's self-perception, has encouraged more critical thinking among many Iranian women [living in Canada]" (p. 215). However, because the word "feminism" has a negative connotation in some Arab Muslim societies, "Muslim women will be unlikely to subscribe to a Western notion of feminism, which would mean abandoning beliefs which they have a commitment to and which provide them with mechanisms to deal with and resist the oppression they face" (Hashim, 1999, p. 12).

When Arab Muslim female writers and academics highlight the position of women in their own societies, they usually become subject to criticism and denunciation from Arab Muslims, both the public and scholars, for attempting to follow Western feminist "nonsense" (Abdo, 2002). Other Muslim women try to "separate themselves from feminism as a movement because they identify [it] as Western and ethnocentric and non-responsive to their experience as non-European women of color" (Moghissi, 1999, p. 214). Some women argue that labelling themselves as "feminist" is confining and exclusive. Some also add that labelling themselves as "feminist" would overshadow other aspects of their identity. Others are fearful of the consequence of being labelled as feminists because of the negative conno- tation associated with the term in Arab Muslim societies. Mooney (1998) agrees that some women "fear the negative consequences of being associ- ated with feminism because of the family and societal pressure" (p. 95). Moreover, Awan asserted that,

> In some Muslim societies, European and American models of women's liberation have had a significant impact. In others, women have expressed a desire for a model of liberation that integrates more fully the structures of the traditional extended families and the assignment of role that this implies. At the same time, however, one can detect in many parts of the Islamic world a growing backlash against women in the women's move- ment. (as cited in Dangor, 2001, p. 11)

144

According to Esposito (1992), this growing backlash against women's movements in Arab Muslim societies can be attributed to the continued backlash between Islam and the West. Esposito (1992) claims that the his- tory between Islam and the West is best described as one of conflict and mistrust, stemming from the real and perceived economic, political, and theological threats that Islamic and Western social systems have posed to each other. This tense relationship has continued and even intensified in recent years, and has had an effect on feminism and women's liberation. Thus, some women in Arab Muslim societies who are pro-feminist do not identify openly with the label.

Pro-feminists, in Arab Muslim societies, are, according to Badran (1998):

> Women who typically are not concerned with ideology but are pragmatists who have carved out lives and careers for themselves and in the context of their profession tend to promote general interests of women ... [and] participate in public life through their work and their literary produc- tion. They are trying to confront what they see as a menacing, regressive environment for women and place their individual work within larger perspectives. Rather than debate feminism they address gender issues and explore new directions. (Badran, 1994, p. 217, as cited in Mooney, 1998, p. 95)

The same can be said of my participants. The social activism mentioned in Mooney (1998) resonates with that of the Arab Muslim women interviewed.

Some of the women did not consider themselves feminists, did not asso-ciate themselves with feminism, and did not want to be labelled as such. However, the majority of the participants embody feminism, embrace the advancement of women's causes, and work toward achieving women's goals. Many of these women, individually and/or collectively, work to change the lives of women in the local Muslim community, yet none are self-proclaimed feminists. For example, Wafaa stated that,

> I never liked feminism. I never liked the way they think. Like, I would agree on some things, some things make sense, but other things I wouldn't. They push it too far, ... they push it to the extreme. And I'm not an extremist.... I'm glad that I don't live in medieval times or the 18th century or the 16th century because of the way women were treated. I'm glad I live in such a society—that it's not completely perfect, but it is better....

145

Unlike Wafaa and Ruba, I feel comfortable identifying with the term "feminist." My definition of "feminism" is that it is a movement that aims to raise women's awareness of their rights. I do not associate "feminism" with the West or with the East, but with a concept that can be found and applied to all cultures. I perceive feminism as not merely dealing with choices we make, but as having the freedom to make these choices. Like Sophie Harding (2000), I feel that "[my] definition of feminism does not come from books or a particular movement. It comes from a society; it comes from an ancestry and a bloodline of women who are not children of the Western-feminist movement" (p. 11). My feminism originates from my experiences. I have lived within gender-specific boundaries. The way I was raised strengthened my curious and outspoken personality, yet school and wider cultural experiences in the worlds in which I have lived have emphasized me as female, and thus as secondary to males. When I lived in Saudi Arabia, other women's struggles led me to reflect deeply on the roots of inequality and male patriarchy. I did not even know or understand feminism before coming to Canada. Like Lubna Chaudhry (1997), "I did not detract from my realization of the value of the resistance enacted by me ... I just needed to figure out a way to talk about the contextual nature of re-sistance and oppression" (p. 449), which is found in feminism. However, I attribute my feminism mainly to the *Quranic* messages I have learned since childhood—that God is fair and just. How, then, could God treat women with injustice and unfairness? The teachings of Islam have strongly influenced my perceptions toward my role in life. I have never viewed my role as having less value than that of a man's. Also, I am indebted to my education in Canada, my exposure to feminist theories, and, first and foremost, to my reading of various literature of Islam and Muslim thinkers.

The women I interviewed are highly assertive, and some are peace activists in the Canadian context, yet some of them acknowledged the difficulties involved in gaining access to leadership positions. They claimed that in Arab Muslim culture, leadership is always a male enterprise, particularly as religious authority. Some of the Arab Muslim women interviewed argued that women are not necessarily suitable for political and religious leadership positions simply because they are women. Their argument is based on the same premise as that of some male and female traditional Muslim scholars:

> It is argued that women undergo menstruation, child bearing and labour—a fact which may hamper their performance in the council to which they are elected. But this can be refuted by saying that men also may be subject to misjudgment or illness which may impair their performance. (The Muslim Brotherhood, as cited in Mooney, 1998, p. 99)

This view is based on an interpretation of Islamic teaching—that women, during their menses, are excused from the required fasting during Ramadan and from performing physical prayers five times a day. Such lenience has caused some conservative religious scholars to view women as inferior to men. Therefore, some scholars explain that "a woman can never achieve the same level of faith or spirituality as men because they cannot fulfill their religious duties all the time" (Muslim Women's League, 1995, para. 23). Like many Muslim scholars, I oppose this view and agree that "The *Quran* clearly indicates and asserts that human creation comes from, or is made of a *single* [italics in original] soul and grants human trusteeship for all" (Barazangi, 2000, p. 24). Another scholar, Bouhdiba (1998), argues that "Islam rejects the notion of the impurity of women. The binary of 'pure and impure' is not synonymous with the opposition of the sexes" (p. 14). This notion of impurity, for many conservative Muslim scholars who support misogynistic interpretations of the *Quran* and *Sunna (Hadith and Seera)*, is related to menstrual blood, which is considered as evidence of women's natural impurity.[2] This alleged "impurity" has been, for many scholars, the reason behind the rationale of preventing women from holding leadership positions, particularly in the religious realm.

By advocating that it is not compatible with women's nature to be in leadership positions, traditional male and female Muslim scholars overlook many indisputable facts and examples depicting the status of women in early Islamic eras as leaders and active participants in different domains. There are many examples of Muslim women in leadership positions in the early Islamic era. However, this is continually ignored.

Very few of the women interviewed are demanding and re-establishing women's rights in the Muslim community, or in the rest of Canadian society. However, Nora is engaging in a form of gender activism by being the first Muslim woman to be nominated to the Islamic Mosque Board to further the rights of women within the Muslim community. In her own way, she advocates for women's rights to work and participate in politics. I argue that the feminism of these women "is understood better as the achievement of a space for themselves, for autonomy, and a career in a culture that inconsistently forbids and permits professional autonomy and women's caring role" (Vidyasagar & Rea, 2004, p. 265).

I also agree with Hill (2003) that,

> Feminism begins from the lives of women, and the lives of women are highly varied and highly contradictory. These variations and contradictions should be expected, given the diffuse modes of gender power and their equally diverse and fluid impact upon women. (p. 62)

Ruba, unlike the majority of the women interviewed, is opposed to feminism and does not perceive that there are "women's issues." She also holds a different view that rejects the binaries of male/female and sex/gender. She implies that this way of thinking may lead to competition between sexes—something she perceives as unhealthy and unnecessary—reflecting the notion that women and men are essentially different and suited for different activities and professions (Bjorklund & Olsson, 2005). Ruba's view reflects Hessini's (1994) proposition that the viewpoint of some Muslim women in Middle Eastern societies is that equality between sexes destabilizes and dehumanizes women and undermines the collaborative relations between men and women. The opponents of complete equality between the sexes usually advocate the complementarity between the sexes.[2]

BELIEF IN WOMEN'S ISSUES

How did the participants feel about the need to support women's causes in the community and in society at large? Some of the women did not provide a substantive comment to the question. Others rejected the focus on women's issues. Yasmine is enthusiastic in helping women. She explains:

> I wanted to do a subspecialty in women's health, but it is not offered at [the local university] ... and I was unable to travel.... Now I work hand in hand with other women in the community, organizing religious circles, even entertaining plays, and health evenings for families, which are open to everyone—Canadian Muslims and non-Muslims.

Although Sahra has been invited to many women's conferences and feminist issues workshops, she has never attended any. She said, "Women play big roles, so why should I talk about it? ... I'm doing whatever I want, and there is no limit to what I can do, ... so I didn't feel that I have to talk about it or prove anything to anyone." By saying this, Sahra is overlooking the fact that her own life and personal achievements might inspire other women. Sahra's statement also reflects a similar attitude to Ruba's with regard to women's issues. Ruba believes that, both in Canada and in the Arab Muslim world, women are able to do what they want. She argued that,

> To me, there is no issue for women.... I did not face anything, ... so I'm not gonna go support something I'm not part of. I was never treated unjustly. I don't know anything about woman's abuse.... Also, I always think it's a matter of personal choice. If you wanna be an engineer, be an engineer.... I think what we need to do is make ... students aware of the options they have in terms of careers and education, and what that entails ... and what they have to do to get through.... I never prescribe myself to the idea [that] we need to have more women in a certain field. I think we need to have better people in certain fields to serve the field.... I do not accept that we need to encourage more males to study nursing—I don't see the connection between the gender and the career or the education.... As a Muslim woman, I know what my rights are. I'm a free woman. I have all my rights and nobody has taken that away from me and nobody can question that. It's not something I fight for at all.

Furthermore, Ruba asserts that "affirmative action"—for example, supporting more females in engineering—is not progressive. Instead, it is useless and only affirms the struggle between men and women, which is unnecessary:

> I find this whole struggle between male and female just a little too much for me, and it's a waste. I don't need to prove to anybody that I'm good because I am a female. I need to prove it to myself.... If you wanna view me within that box of gender, then it's your problem, it's not my problem....

148

Ruba's response regarding attending conferences on women's issues does not differ: "I don't think I'll ever be interested in that." Ruba blamed women for their status: "Women in our community ... are holding themselves back.... Many women are not seeking to be a part of something that will help them or will help their children," yet she showed an interest in helping youth, both men and women:

> I get along very, very well with the youth. I am not close to women in general.... We've become very selfish people in general. We do not care about the causes of other people and sometimes I think when some people get into the cause of women, it's usually because it looks good on their resume and it makes them look a little bit more sophisticated, and to me, that's not the right thing to do....

In restating this conversation, it becomes obvious that Ruba contradicts herself. First, she asserts that she is unwilling to take part in advocating for women as there are no barriers to overcome, yet in the next breath, she concludes that people should not be self-interested. In effect, Ruba overlooks the fact that many women strive for support within the community and in society at large.

As a striking contrast, Eman acknowledged how beneficial and informative it was for her to attend conferences and women's issues workshops:

> I've gone to Islamic conferences and workshops, and, yes, they did deal with women's issues ... and they did revive the understanding of women's issues, ... of women's oppression in society.... Unfortunately, in most Muslim countries and Muslim societies, we have the understanding of a woman's role to be in her house and in her house only. Conferences and workshops are trying to bring people to Islamic essence.... Conferences opened my eyes more to the Islamic tenets and essence, especially with regard to women.... The conferences and workshops were pretty enlightening, I have to say.

Also, Morooj had begun to attend conferences and discussion groups on women's issues and is planning to continue to attend them because they are educating her about how other women live their lives:

> I started going with my friend to a feminist organization at [a local] college; they have a meeting every month.... I liked it because I became aware of how other women think and how they live their lives—other women who are coming from different societies and cultures....

This wide array of perspectives tells a great deal about the level of advocacy that the women interviewed are willing to do for women's causes. The perceptions these women have shown reflect their gender socialization. Gender issues are usually subordinated by other issues in Arab Muslim culture. This became clear in Ruba's response, which may also reflect a lack of consciousness regarding women's causes.

Fadwa acknowledges the need to discuss issues pertaining to women's status in Canada, yet she is opposed to certain discourses that pertain to Canadian Muslim women. These discourses were expressed through some conferences and women's workshops that Fadwa has attended. The theme of these conferences was delegitimizing some Muslim women's experiences and struggles. The prevalent trend in these conferences is to focus on "other" women who think differently from the majority. Unfortunately, this has been the case with some conferences in Canada, and in Fadwa's perspective, this has influenced women's status. She recounts:

> When I think of women's roles, I remember some workshops and conferences I have been to. For instance, the last one was at [Regional] University. I'm realizing that women's voices are varying.... [They] can be very different and very diverse, even if they're within the same tradition or claim to be from the same tradition.... Muslim women can be very different and I used to be under the impression that just because we're women, our voices, even though they're different, can be harmonious because we're women. I had that perception, and now I'm realizing that not only are they different, there are ones that are in conflict or in dispute with one another. And I went to that conference on Islam and gender roles, Muslim women, and their issues. Some of those speakers were speaking on behalf of all Muslim women in the Middle East, [yet] their experiences did not speak to my experiences one bit, and I consider myself a Middle Eastern woman, ... [but] because I choose to live a certain way or to hold a certain opinion based on my positive experiences that some other people might have experienced ... but very, very negatively, [that] doesn't mean that my voice shouldn't be heard.... Something that we, as a whole, in academic discourse have to be wary of ... is vilifying, slandering, delegitimizing other people's experiences.

While workshops and conferences are a good way to exchange ideas and form new perspectives, I agree with Fadwa that they can be overwhelmingly exclusionary to one's perspective. The overarching conflict between different perspectives surrounding women's roles in society in general, women's issues in Islam, and various cultural practices are noteworthy.

CANADIAN AND ARAB MUSLIM WOMEN'S ROLES

My research explores women's previous experiences and how their gender perceptions were constructed, since "the present is a product of the past," and, as Deirdre Beddoe (1983) points out, "we are moulded and conditioned by a past of which we are alarmingly ignorant" (p. 6). The way Arab Muslim women construct their gender roles now is a product of both their previous experience in their country of origin and in Canada.

Having female role models in leadership positions is significant, yet are the majority of women playing important roles in the advancement of their societies, in Canada or in their countries of origin, and what are the differences? How do the participants view women's roles in Canadian society and in the Arab Muslim world? Yasmine asserted that "Women have a vital role in every society. Even in Yemen, the system I criticize a lot for their treatment of women, ... they have women's role models ... and this is in every culture...." Yasmine also declares that everywhere in the world, women are subject to oppression in its various forms:

> Women are subject to oppression everywhere in the world, especially if they are not educated. Women are raped and abused in different ways in both worlds. There, they are taken out of school to get married and start a family. They are not allowed to inherit.... Women here are oppressed, too.... Sometimes girls who are 14 or even 11 years old have had multiple sexual partners and have been prescribed contraceptives.... This is oppression and this is happening in both worlds in very different ways.

I, too, agree that women are subject to different forms of patriarchy. Yasmine adds that "Here, it is subtle ..." then she follows with an example from our native society:

> A girl I know who lives in an Arab Muslim country told me her marriage story. Once she arrived from school, ... her father, who is a religious imam, asked her to enter the guest room, and she asked, "Why do I have to go there now?" And he said to her right that minute that she is married and she has now to go in so they could see each other....

While Yasmine argues that oppression is a woman's first enemy in the East and in West, Nora, with a growing involvement in Canadian society, has a different viewpoint on women's roles here. Nora's interaction with men and women in Egypt and in Canada allows her to draw a comparison between the level of women's confidence in Canadian and Egyptian societies:

> Confidence should be reflected in the way a woman treats a man. That level of confidence determines the woman's role in society and her ability to engage in the outside world. In Egypt, a woman may neglect the importance of attending conferences and workshops because it is mixed in that you have males and females. Woman there find it difficult to challenge men in the workplace because it is understood that that's the man's enterprise.... Women there rarely compete with men for scholarships.... They find it easier to give up ... unlike women in Canada.... Women here take on challenges and they are ready to confront men. Challenging men is not anti-Islamic.... This is how early women lived their lives.... When I read or listen to Amro Khalid,[3] I know how women were in the early days of Islam—very strong fighters for their rights.... Then I tell myself that I want to be like Somaya,[4] or I want to be like Aisha. Canadian women are strong and confident, and I like that.... I am influenced by that. I have to be like them in that respect and I am not ashamed to say that they are better than us in this point. If I do not criticize myself, I will not move forward. Women here are hard workers; they are focused and never give up.

Nonetheless, Nora acknowledges that the reality of many women's lives in both worlds is distracting. In Egypt, she says that "Both highly educated men and women are suffering financially because of not being paid enough for their jobs.... In Canada, sometimes men and women don't get paid the same even for doing the same job."

Nahlaa felt that the difference between women's status in Canada and women's status in Arab Muslim societies is related to each society's respective labour laws. For instance, many women in Arab Muslim societies work outside of the home.

Nahlaa pointed out that laws here protect women's rights if they stay home or work outside their homes. There are exceptions to the norms, but the norm is a woman practising her full rights. Wafaa concluded from her life and experience in Canada that the system here opens new possibilities for women. Women's realities here give Wafaa hope that there are no limits to what women can do:

> My perception of Canadian women is that they rock! I don't see women holding back, being pulled back, or backing off from certain things. They just do it. They just do what they want.... Before seeing Canadian women,

I used to believe that a woman can only do one thing; it's either work or home. But when I came here, she has a chance; she can do both. She can be a mother and work at the same time. Women here are given hope; they have potential, and they have options.

Eman viewed the difference between women's roles here and women's roles in Arab Muslim societies through the lens of a woman who holds a managerial position. She suggested that women have to take a stand by pushing for further rights and more decision-making positions. Women in managerial positions should not be the exception, but the norm:

Back home, I would like to see women more in the decision-making roles; see them on the boards of schools and universities.... The dean at the time I was in university was a female, and I think that was the only time where I saw a female in a decision-making profession, but I would like to see more, so I'm not saying that there aren't any at all in Libya, but I'd like to see more.

153

Morooj observes that the economic situation for women in Canada requires women to work long hours, whereas many women in our Arab Muslim Middle Eastern societies do not have to work full-time to earn a living. I perceive Morooj's argument as mainly a class issue. There are as many working-class families in Canada as in Arab Muslim societies. However, I contend that this is just one of the many faces of patriarchy. In many Arab Muslim societies, women's employment is obstructed by male patriarchy within the family and society. While both men and women in the workplace are encountering bureaucracy that hinders their progress, women are discouraged because they receive considerably lower pay than men. The central difference in Morooj's perception between women's work in Canada and women's work in Arab Muslim Middle Eastern societies is that men in Arab Muslim societies are still considered the central providers for the family. And even if a woman earns money, she is not required to support her family unless she agrees to do so. Morooj adds that,

Women here work very long hours from morning until late afternoon.... Then they need to have savings because money here controls everything. To afford a living and support a family, both spouses need to work.... Here they are under pressure. In Libya, women's work is more for luxury.... Life's rhythm here is fast and if you do not run to get money, then it is hard to fulfill your obligation....

Morooj may not realize that her views of women's employment are class-sensitive. However, she justifiably remarks that,

> A woman in Arab Muslim society has a secondary role.... She is not required to spend her earnings on the family. Here it is different because a woman, in most cases, helps to provide for the family. She has control and makes decisions.... A woman here is a first-class citizen and she can achieve high status, but at the expense of her health and inner peace....

Although I find that some of Morooj's statements are a generalization of the status of Arab Muslim and Canadian women, I agree that contributing to the family's income elevates a woman's status in the household. Likewise, if women in Arab Muslim societies become a significant part of the workforce, then it only makes sense that they will attain better social status than they now hold.

Morooj added, "The gap between the two cultures is huge and wide.... The progress with respect to women's roles there is still now secondary and minor." In light of Morooj's analyses, I contend that economic independence offers women great freedom that would also deter patriarchy, yet because of the new globalized economy, which threatens government support of familial needs and social welfare, working-class women everywhere are suffering.

Ruba stated that "I cannot even compare." Her hesitation to compare women's positions here with women's positions in Arab Muslim societies is a result of the huge difference between the two ways of living, not only among women's groups, but society at large. In both cultures, according to Ruba, there "are stories that we don't hear about: The women who have been successful, the women who have been great mothers, and the women who have been great doctors. But do we hear about the women who are oppressed or abused?" However, she emphasizes that "The spotlight is only on Muslim Middle Eastern women, and then when abuse happens, in our ... North American society, we feel blessed that we are women living in the West. No, ... I think women here are facing the same abuse."

Ruba relates these differences to superficial reasons, overlooking the root cause for such disparity. Wafaa, in contrast, recounts that the difference result from cultural, social, and political contexts. She distinguishes between women's positions in Canada and women's positions in Arab Muslim societies as a difference between democratic nations and hierarchal political systems. Further, Wafaa acknowledges that,

> Here, it's a free country. Women do whatever they want. They [people in society] don't expect anything of a boy and of a girl.... A girl can be a construction worker here. There [in Arab Muslim societies], no way! ... There, you're an English major. She's a girl. She's gonna be a teacher. It's not enough for a boy there to be a teacher. It's not enough because he's gonna be responsible for a family.... He's gonna be the main breadwinner.... The girl's just gonna be the secondary position.... She's gonna be dependent on her husband.

The women's narratives reflect the idea that women are subject to oppression and different forms of patriarchy in both Canada and in Arab Muslim societies. I found that some comments reveal optimism or superficiality about Canadian women's status because they overlook other factors such as class and race, and how these factors perform and intersect in different dynamics regardless of geographical location.

155

WOMEN'S ROLE AND STATUS IN SOCIETY

The traditional gender role ascribed to a woman as wife and mother may limit her perception of her public role. Thus, traditional ideology has significant ramifications on women's roles in society. As a result, a woman's gender identity is constructed partly through her understanding of her role in society. In Arab Muslim society's cultural context, many women would perceive that a public role is not suitable for them. The "woman's nature" argument, which is indoctrinated through different means, is used continuously to justify exclusion and impediment of women from the public sphere.

Knowing how women, in this study's context, perceive their roles in society tells a great deal of how they perceive themselves as women. In this section, I explore the gender roles that the participants were holding or looking forward to holding. Were they satisfied with the role that women play in their societies of origin and in Canada?

I first asked these women how they perceive women's roles in Canadian society. Morooj felt that many Canadian women achieve more powerful positions, while Yasmine argued that in both cultures, women's identity is constructed to be subordinate, but in different ways. Yasmine implied that women's participation in society does not truly reflect their status. She asserted that,

In both cultures, there are manipulating men and manipulating women. Only religious people make a difference.... We have abusers here in Canada, as well as there.... Only religion makes someone good or bad, no matter what the religion is.... The two cultures are the same.

Nahlaa prioritized a woman's role as that of a mother and wife. She attributed her reasoning to biological characteristics of women. Nahlaa argued that,

The woman's body is created so that they can have children and bring up children, but when society needs women and needs their jobs, then they have to co-operate and help, besides bringing up children and doing the housework. Women can balance these two things, but a woman's job outside of her home should not interfere with her role at home because it is the primary [role]....

156

In a similar vein, Sahra relied on cultural expressions to make her point: "There is a famous saying in Egypt: 'Women are one-half of society and they are raising and educating the other half.'" Although Sahra mentioned earlier that because of her busy day, her husband is the primary caregiver for their daughter, she perceives that a woman's primary role is raising her children and her participation in society could be achieved through fulfilling her responsibilities at home.

I asked Sahra if being an engineer has influenced the way she perceived women's role in society. She declared that it has not. Furthermore, she explained that being the eldest in a family where both parents are working had created a sense that women's participation in society is the norm. Growing up and experiencing her mother's accomplishments at home and at work allowed her to assert that "That's what I believe in, and that's how I still believe life should be." Moreover, Sahra added:

I don't see much difference between roles [women are playing] in Canada and in Egypt because most women here work and in Egypt work.... Probably the differences lie in social life... Canadian women struggle more than Egyptian women because Egyptian women, most likely at the age of 25 or 26, get married and probably have a child or two.... Here the problem is that some of them [women] are in their 40s and they want to get married, but they can't. Men here do not want to have long-term commitment.... Women here are under more pressure and are struggling in terms of their social life.... Also, women are encouraged or even pushed to leave home early....

Taking a completely different stand on women's status in Canada, Morooj states that she is amazed at women's achievements in Canadian society. She attributes this to girls' upbringing. Seeing female role models in leadership positions is contesting women's traditional roles and society's perception of women's capabilities. Although I argue that this is an optimistic view of Canadian society and the way female gender is constructed in Western culture, I argue that Canadian women have achieved significantly higher status than women in Arab Muslim societies. In fact, "Canada has one of the highest levels of participation of women in the workforce of any developed country" (Poy, 2004, para. 2). This is inspiring for many Arab Muslim Canadian women. Morooj stated assertively that "When I compare Libyan women's role with Canadian women's roles, I wish that Arab Muslim women would have a stronger role in building their society.... Women's roles in Arab Muslim societies are absent." Morooj pointed out that,

> In Canada, women's age does not hinder their pursuit.... In my art classes, women range from 50–70 years old. Libyan women of that age are interested in embroidery, knitting, and tailoring. This is mostly because these activities suit society's structure; a woman stays home while doing these things.

"And for us, the most important thing is that a woman stays home," I commented. Morooj replied, "Yes, the most important thing in our culture is that a woman stays home. Anything she is interested in doing, she will try to achieve from home."

I enquired, "How does this reality affect your view of yourself?" She replied:

> Let's take art as an example: Libyan women are hindered by social norms to think in that direction.... If it is a hobby, then women fight to prove it to society.... People oppose it because a woman artist will need to go out, interact with men, and also will have to arrange for exhibitions.... All this creates openness to different realms, which is discouraged by societal norms.

"Is this not preferable?" I asked. Morooj answered, "No, it is not preferable, but now things are changing. Many young Libyan women are directing their attention to arts." Morooj noted some issues that Libyan women artists have encountered: "It was more difficult in the past, ... not only with photography but also with writing, such as writing novels, poems,[5] or any form of art.... Very recently, we got the college of art and many women choose it...."

She concluded, "Here [in Canada] a woman's role is not limited by age...." Morooj's perception is unique in that, unlike Sahra and Nahlaa, who emphasized that a woman's role is in her home, she was able to separate women's achievement in public and private spheres.

Also, Fadwa is able to differentiate between the role women play here and in our native societies, yet again emphasizing woman's nurturing role:

> Women back home have a bigger nurturer role than women here.... Women
> [here] will put their kids in daycare when the kids are four months old
> and six months old, and people need to do that because they have to make
> a living, but back home they do not, yet people have less money there.
> Back home the mothers stay at home for a few years ... or they leave the
> children with sisters, mothers, aunts, relatives, [or] other families.

Fadwa related the differences between women's roles here and in Arab Muslim societies to the differences in these societies' structures:

> Here society is structured in a way that is individualistically oriented as
> opposed to collectively oriented, such as [in] Arab Muslim society.... This
> is a psychological perspective or sociological perspective.... Because of
> this orientation, you get different ways by which people seek support.
> [There are] different ways by which women are able to exercise their roles
> as mothers, as workers, as employers, or as employees.

As far as the differences between women here and there are concerned, Fadwa explained that the reality of women as managers and political leaders is far more difficult to achieve in Arab Muslim societies, though she uniquely states that "Society can't depend only on men." Only Eman and Morooj emphasized the major role a woman plays in society as a participant in public space. Furthermore, Eman argued that the traditional view of women's roles does not originate in Islam:

> That's not the understanding in Islam. Our religion encourages women to
> go out.... The Prophet [PBUH] followed his wife's political advice.... Women
> are certainly encouraged to work wherever they can in society, ... so women
> are important at home certainly and outside the home because they're need-
> ed.... Society needs women both as teachers in schools or in the battlefield....
> Wherever women see that they are needed and can contribute, then so be it.
> I grew up seeing women work and go to school. My Muslim roots encourage
> this, and certainly our Prophet's [PBUH] teaching and life prove it....

Eman and Morooj advocated and emphasized the need for women's contribution in society, and unlike the majority of the women interviewed, Eman did not concentrate on motherhood as the woman's road for social contribution. She offered a gender-specific explanation for how she views women's role and contribution to society. However, the overall remarks of some of the women show that the biological differences between women and men are used to reinforce the traditional notion of women's roles. In the matter of women's roles in both cultures, a few participants supported the conclusion that Canadian women's roles and achievements have motivated and inspired them.

NOTES

1. *Sunna* are the sayings and actions of the Prophet (PBUH), as reported in books of *Hadith*. *Seera* is a historical account of the life of the Prophet (PBUH), including his family and his companions.

2. For more on the impurity of women in Islam, I recommend Maghen, Z. (2005), *Virtues of the flesh: Passion and purity in early Islamic jurisprudence* (vol. 23), Leiden: E.J. Brill.

3. For more discussion on complementarity between a man and woman in Islam, read Badawi, J. (1995), *Gender equity in Islam: Basic principles*, Plainfield: American Trust Publications.

4. Amro Khalid is a progressive Muslim activist.

5. Somaya is one of the Prophet's [PBUH] granddaughters who was a well-known activist in the early days of Islam.

6. Today some Arab Muslim women still publish poems using pseudonyms for fear of prosecution from male relatives.

Chapter Eleven

DIVERSITY VERSUS HOMOGENEITY

Arab Muslim women were invited to reflect on their education and gender perceptions at various periods of their lives before coming to Canada, as well as after attending schools in Canada. During the process of exploration, I highlighted the diversity and multiplicity of their race, ethnicity, class, and experience. My analysis is not focused on finding ways to de-emphasize the characteristics of the women's lives or their gender perceptions, nor do I intend to generalize the experiences of these subjects and impose them on other Arab Muslim women. I attempt to discuss them as a diverse group shaped by their particular histories and culture—their experiences and thoughts cannot be reduced to a set of certain simple characteristics. Yet it is important to find general themes and to discuss them.

Historically, in general terms at least, women have been considered a cohesive group with a defined struggle and a sole solution. Also, Muslim women have been grouped together (Harding, 2000, p. 9) as having the same needs and struggles. As a result, I agree that "unifying politically around the category of 'woman' is problematic" (Forrest, 1993, p. 211). While women may share similar experiences, it is fundamental that women's issues are not characterized as universal.

The assumption of homogeneity among all the participants because they are all Arab Muslim women is questionable. This homogeneous sense was interrupted by the stress of heterogeneity evident in each individual's perspective. The women in my study are originally from predominantly Arab Muslim countries: Egypt, Libya, Lebanon, Sudan, Syria, and Palestine, and I am from Saudi Arabia. These countries represent an enormous geographical area comprised of many subcultures. Thus, it would be too simplistic and reductionistic to ascribe certain characteristics and personality traits to all the women in these countries simply because they are all Muslims or Arabs.

It is worth emphasizing that the Arab Muslim world is vast. It stretches from Morocco in the west to the Arab Gulf in the east. The Arab Muslim world is an area of considerable diversity in terms of geography, economic base, and social class. One of the challenges I faced in my research was to stress both cultural context and cultural specificity when talking about gender discourse in Arab Muslim societies:

> It is clear that women do not represent a homogeneous social category in the Middle East. They are differentiated by region, class, and education—educated women are further divided—politically and ideologically. Yet, the available evidence shows that socio-economic development and increasing rates of female education and employment have affected the structure and size of the family, as well as women's gender consciousness. (Moghadam, 2004, p. 157)

Like Nira Yuval-Davis (1993), for example, I maintain that,

> Assuming the commonality of experiences in a very one-dimensional way and with a historical anxiety ... [means that] anyone who claims to be a member of the particular grouping can claim to represent it to outside agencies, and may benefit from it, no matter how different s/he is in terms of class, power, gender, etc., from the majority of the people claimed to be represented. (Yuval-Davis 1993, p. 6, as cited in Burlet & Reid, 1998, p. 274)

The overlapping of similarities among the narratives does not negate the diversity of the women interviewed:

> Given this historic social and cultural fluidity and tremendous diversity, and the recent escalation of change [post-September 11, 2001], we have to be very careful before generalizing about gender issues or any other aspect of social organization, or assuming that these issues are the same across ethnic, religious, racial, national, regional, or linguistic groupings. With this caveat in mind, it is nevertheless possible to suggest a framework within which to understand broad patterns of gender in the region, even without asserting that they apply everywhere. (Josef & Slyomovics, 2001, p. 1)

In saying this, it is noteworthy that the personalities and activities of the women interviewed stood in contrast to the dominant media and literature discourses regarding Muslim women. Indeed, these women's stories are challenging to reductionist, racist, sexist, and orientalist portrayals of

Muslim women and Islam. The Arab Muslim women interviewed expressed diverse perspectives and experiences, and perhaps the only point that can be generalized is that they were neither silent nor devoid of opinion about their lives, culture, and religion.

This study represents Arab Muslim women as actors and subjects rather than as objects in their social context.

BEING A MUSLIM WOMAN IN CANADA

Although living as a Muslim in a non-Muslim society can sometimes be difficult, the participants expressed their appreciation for the space given in Canada's multicultural society to freely practise their faith:

> Whether indigenous or foreign-born, Muslims who have built their lives in America are growing appreciative of several factors of the quality of life they enjoy: that many aspects of American life are quite consistent with the Muslim belief system; that interactions among people are becoming increasingly global; that, while Muslim countries may show signs of degeneration in religious, economic and political life, Muslims in the United States and Canada strive to practice their faith in a purer form. (Nimer, 2002, p. 19)

The freedom of choice and expression that I enjoy in the Canadian context is most intriguing. In Arab Muslim societies, many people are controlled by social law and cultural traditions, as well as by the political agendas of the states they live in. Many Arab Muslim people in the Canadian context are free to practise their faith without the social pressure that dictates certain norms and introduces them as essential aspects of the Islamic faith.[1] In Canada, for instance, many Arab Muslim people choose to practise their faith—it is not forced upon them. This is what Eman clearly conveyed in the following statement: "Cultural traditions have nothing to do with Islam.... I mean, I live Islam here in Canada, and I lived Islam in the United States more than I lived it in Libya.... In Libya, they live tradition, they live their customs, and their customs are like the social law."

Having the space to question some patriarchal cultural norms without societal pressure is possible in Canada, but such questioning is difficult in our native societies. I presume that Islam is a lived and enjoyed reality for many Muslims in North America (Nimer, 2002).

Yet, it is not always easy for Arab Muslim women to practise their religion and live by their faith in a non-Muslim environment. It can be very challenging to reconcile religious values with one's participation in the cultural community of one's native Canadian peers (Buitelaar, Ketner & Bosma, 2004; Shahjahan, 2004). For instance:

Morooj: This is a free society. It is a more open society here.

Me: Did it bother you?

Morooj: No, it does not bother me.

Me: What about your daughters?

Morooj: To a large extent, I am religious and it was fine. I encourage my daughters to learn and engage to take the best if they could. There are negative aspects of freedom that we do not follow because they are incompatible with our religion; we avoid them, but we respect them, and do not get involved in the values that are not accepted within our religious values. Accepting others as they are is very important.

My move to Canada has helped me assert my Islamic identity, unlike Riyad Shahjahan (2004) who, after coming to Canada, felt that part of his self was being silenced, and he did not have a sense of belonging in Canadian academic discourse. I, as a Muslim woman observing the *hijab*, am easily identified as a Muslim. On many occasions people have asked me questions about my *hijab* and my faith, which I am delighted to talk about. Although the media continue to depict Muslims as "fanatical" and "dangerous," among other things, I am able to help create a different perspective about Muslims through my academic[2] and personal life. Being part of Canadian academic discourses where the opportunity to present one's voice is available, I am able to assert my world views. This opportunity, combined with my spirituality, though challenging at times, has helped me to overcome barriers in attaining my goals in challenging Orientalist portrayals of Muslim women.

Since moving to Canada, my faith has deepened. Although I was a practising Muslim in Saudi Arabia, my spirituality has grown because of the move. Away from my home country, which is predominantly Muslim, I began to question which aspects of my spiritual beliefs and practices were cultural, and which stemmed from my faith. For instance, I started to reflect and think about the gender question. Reading different interpretations of the *Quranic* verses, especially those by well-known male and female Muslim scholars pertaining to women,[3] influenced my belief that my faith is not rigid on the subject of women, but flexible. My deep knowledge of the religious texts, the Holy *Quran* and the authentic *Hadith*, and my faith allowed me to question and challenge certain regimented rules imposed on women. I feel that "it is only from a position of knowledge that women can claim their rights and contest patriarchal interpretations of Islam" (Hashim, 1999, p. 12). Some of this growth might also be personal, as I came to Canada in my early 20s.

Through my studies of the *Quran*, I agree with Iman Hashim (1999) that "I am now in a position to oppose patriarchal interpretations and to challenge others when debates are foreclosed on the basis of my gender, which is remarkably liberatory" (p. 13). Nonetheless, I, Eman, and other Muslim women who currently live outside of Arab Muslim societies must acknowledge our privilege in being untouched, to a larger extent, by strict interpretations of Islam that are prevalent, practised, and imposed in many Arab Muslim societies. Hashim (1999) continues:

> I can only imagine the constraints facing women in other socio-geographical locations. It is important to be aware of the problems of advocating the dissemination and adoption of egalitarian interpretations, and not to underestimate the dangers involved in contesting patriarchal interpretations of Islam. (p. 13)

Our opportunities as Muslim women to deepen our faith in a secular society are made salient through these narratives. That Canada allows the freedom and space for one to practise his or her own religion freely is advantageous. This freedom is a source of confidence for new immigrants. Having mosques[4] where Muslims in many Canadian provinces go to pray is empowering to Muslims who come from all parts of the world.

The women interviewed appeared untroubled by the contradictions between their religious teachings, cultural traditions, and values and Canadian cultural values. The women interviewed may have experienced or/are experiencing differences between the lifestyle of their native Arab Muslim nation and their Canadian lifestyle, especially with respect to gender identities. Ginsburg and Tsing (1990) state that,

> An individual's position in a web of intersecting inequalities has too often been interpreted, and experienced, as paralyzing; yet, an awareness of this complexity can also be politically empowering as it suggests new modes of self-respect and alliance ... that both women's and men's identities are not characterized by singularity and coherency,

but are, in fact, "fragmented, multi-faceted and shift in different contexts." (pp. 5–9)

Thus, I argue that for these individuals, "the concept of multicultural-ism encourages them to contribute to developing" (Markovic & Manderson, 2002, p. 313) a new hybrid[5] identity. The participants seem well able to over-come any contradiction that may arise between their values and Canadian values. Being Muslim and Arab in Canada seems to lead individuals to

> Have forged hybrid identities in response to their experiences and in-teractions with changing contextual realities within formal educational as well as community contexts. Using the margins as sites of resistance, these women deployed their hybrid identities and world views to enact resistance against oppressive power relations in various contexts result-ing in empowerment.... (Chaudhry, 1997, p. 451)

THE MUSLIM WOMEN'S *HIJAB*

The Islamic dress code, with all its differences in colour and style, is a ma-jor issue. "To veil or not to veil" is an ongoing debate among Muslims and non-Muslims, male and female, orthodox and progressive. I contend that the debate over the *hijab*[6] is at the heart of discourses on gender regarding Arab Muslim women. Stewart (1990) argues that by "wearing the *hijab* they [Muslim women] externalize their identity as a visible discourse" (p. 46) and state their identity as Muslim women. The social action of wearing the *hijab* is a means by which they construct a narrative space (Cayer, 1996). Wearing the *hijab* allows women to depersonalize and desexualize the body. In some cases, the *hijab* is a strategy to contest imposed gender and domi-nant ideologies, and to alter the view of what it means to be both a "Muslim" woman and a "Canadian" (Ginsburg & Tsing, 1990, p. 72).

The discourse on the *hijab* emerged in the interviews, although none of my interview questions focused on the matter. As a Muslim woman, I know that the *hijab* is a significant aspect of a Muslim woman's identity. When I was searching for participants, I noticed that many young Muslim women adhere to the *hijab*, which may be perceived by many as widening the gen-der gap. However, "by adopting a dress which is more international, sober, practical and uniform, they react to and challenge hierarchies" (Jansen, 1998, p. 91), whether they are gender or racial.

Observing the *hijab* was not a requirement for inclusion in my research of Arab Muslim women. It just so happened that all of the interviewed women are *hijabis*.[7] Amazingly enough, one of them, Morooj, did not observe the *hijab* in her country of origin.[8] After coming to Canada, however, she decided to wear it. When I asked her why, Morooj asserted that it provides her with a sense of belonging and identity in the midst of Canada's social and cultural milieu.

Some female Muslim immigrants to Canada wear the *hijab* because their fathers or spouses require them to do so; others see it as an easier option economically. Other Muslim women argue that it is an affirmation of a woman's dignity (Hoodfar & McDonough, 2005, p. 142). Still others, like Morooj, perceive it as a symbol of their identities as Muslim women:

> Some women view the *hijab* as a powerful statement about their identity. They are proud to be Muslim and they want the world to know it. To one woman, the *hijab* is her rebellion and resistance against the "commercialization" of women's bodies that is so prevalent in the West. (Abdo, 2002, p. 232)

I add that it is prevalent in the East, too.

The *hijab* has been worn by many Arab Muslim women, and Asian and African Muslim women in Canada as a form of resistance—to challenge "traditional" stereotyped identities of Muslim women.[9] Muslim women's motivations for covering vary dramatically. "Some Muslim women veil to express their strongly held convictions about gender difference, others are motivated to do so more as a means of critiquing Western colonialism in the Middle East" (Read & Bartkowski, 2000, p. 396). Western anthropologist Elizabeth Fernea (1993) rightly concluded that "*hijab* means different things to different people within [Muslim] society, and it means different things to Westerners than it does to Middle Easterners"[10] (p. 122). This became evident in my encounters with many Muslim and non-Muslims males and females throughout my years in Canada as a *hijabi* Muslim woman.

Personally, I have never questioned my decision to wear the *hijab* since coming to Canada. Like Hirschmann (1998), I agree that "Muslim women not only participate voluntarily in veiling, but defend it as well, indeed, claiming that it is a mark of agency, cultural membership, and resistance" (p. 346). One of the themes of my Master's thesis was the *hijab*. I made this choice when I moved to Canada because I discovered the centrality of the *hijab* in academic writing and its image in Western society as a symbol of Muslim women's oppression, yet for many Muslim women, it is "a tool of women's agency in that it allows women to negotiate the structures of patriarchal custom to gain what they want, to assert their independence, and to claim their own identity" (Hirschmann, 1998, p. 359). I felt the need to challenge the stereotype and raise awareness regarding Muslim women's choice in the matter.

The *hijab* makes it easy to identify a Muslim woman, so Muslim women may become subject to harassment in societies in which the *hijab* is equated with oppression and backwardness, as in North America. Only in Ruba's interview was the *hijab* mentioned as an issue in Canada: "I get mistreated by some people.... My faith has actually given me rights, and someone is actually trying to force me to think that it does not, so they are ... oppressing me and not my faith."

I asked Ruba, "Who are you referring to by 'they'?" She paused and then continued, "Anyone making me feel guilty, or the ones who are treating me differently than my faith does.... Islam does not treat me unjustly." Ruba continues:

> The issue of *hijab*, for example, and then the mistreatment afterwards, ... like if you're feeling sorry for me because I am a Muslim woman, why are you mistreating me? If you're feeling that I'm oppressed by my own religion, why are you looking at me as if I'm somehow diseased, ... not smart enough? If you don't think I'm a free woman and you want to liberate me, why are you treating me that way? Shouldn't you be doing something that makes me actually be interested in what you're saying and treat me better so I would know the difference so I would join you, versus my faith?

The *hijab* is no innocent "symbol" in a volatile context (Hoodfar, 1993). Historically, it has been a politically loaded marker. It has come to symbolize everything from Islamic fundamentalism, freedom of religious expression, and women's subordination, to women's empowerment and equality (Hoodfar, 1993; Ahmed, 1992; Mernissi, 1987; Bullock, 2002). The *hijab* is one of the reasons why "Islam is often represented as a religion which denigrates women and limits their freedom" (Hashim, 1999, p. 7), yet many women—myself included, as well as those interviewed here—believe it protects them from oppression and the objectification of women's bodies.

The Arab Muslim women interviewed in this book are educating non-Muslims that their observance of the *hijab* does not hinder their physical activity. Nora, the gymnastics instructor, was interviewed by a reporter from a local newspaper about how Muslim women exercise when restricted by their dress code (i.e., the *hijab*). Nora, who is passionate about educating

Muslim women on the advantages of exercise, asserted that Muslim women are able to combine their gender identities with their faith. Nora teaches an aerobic class to 40 local Muslim women twice a week and emphasizes that a woman's *hijab* does not prevent her from exercising her roles and achieving her goals. Read and Bartkowski (2000), in a study about Muslim women and the *hijab*, concluded that "Muslim women construct gender identities that are malleable and inclusive enough to navigate through the controversy surrounding the veil and Muslim women's issues in general."

THE SHIFT IN WOMEN'S PERSPECTIVES

Does Muslim women's education in Canada change the way they perceive their gender roles? What are the struggles they encounter as a result of living within a different culture? How was their gender construction negotiated? How might their education in Canada have affected their views of themselves?

After moving to Canada, I was able to learn and think outside the box regarding traditional gender ideologies that are prevalent in Saudi society. I was able to read alternative interpretations of the Holy *Quran*. Books written by scholars from various parts of the Islamic world were more accessible in Canada. The alternative interpretations of the *Quran* have reshaped my concept of gender in Islam: "Much of what I encountered was unfamiliar, yet, at the same time, not too strange" (El-Solh, 1988, p. 92). My engagement with feminist literature in Canada "led me to turn a critical eye to the social conditions of women" (p. 92) in my country, in the Canadian context, and in other parts of the Arab world.

Reading feminist and orientalist literature as part of Western academic discourse led me to question why Arab Muslim women, particularly those from the Middle East, are mentioned only "as objects rather than actors in society, in conflict cases as the victim of an honor crime, [as] a divorced woman, [as] the 'sexually threatened wife,' or [as] the 'self sacrificing mother' [which] are illustrated in proverbs and folk tales" (Shami, 1988, p. 117), or as generalized images of oppressed Muslim women in orientalist literature. These images "blurred the distinctions between the varieties of positions occupied by Middle Eastern women" (pp. 117–118). I researched this topic and ascertained that many Western anthropologists and historians' views and much of Western literature and Western scholarly views of Muslim women were based on an essentialized "representation of the East by those of imperial control and the prerogative of power" (Viswanathan,

2001, p. 237). Also, some of their views tend to incorporate the marginal position and personality of Middle Eastern Arab Muslim women uncritically in their writing. With only a few exceptions, many Western historians', missionaries', and anthropologists' writings (Ahmed, 1992; Minault, 1998; Said, 1978) were and are portraying Muslim women as exotic or submissive without drawing the line between cultural traditions (i.e., societal norms) and Islamic discourses of gender. These dominant, negative, stereotypical opinions of Muslim women are also prevalent in both Western popular minds and Western popular culture.

As an insider, I knew that these images of Arab Muslim women are essentialist ideals and merely a generalization of a highly diverse group (Alghamdi, 2002). In my Master's thesis, I deconstructed common myths based on common Western views of Muslim women.

Consequently, my gender identity in Canada has been constructed, and has been influenced and altered to challenge orientalist portrayals of Arab Muslim women as being submissive, exotic, slaves for men, as well as the traditional gender ideology in Arab culture that subordinates women and perpetuates women's inferiority outside the home.

In retrospect, I wonder how much of my own world view is modelled on being an Arab Muslim woman, and how much is based on my eight years as a graduate student in Canada. How much am I a part of what I am observing? Here, I have explored how the Arab Muslim participants' gender perceptions shifted or modified as a result of their education in Canada.

Sahra's view regarding women's roles did not change, shift, or modify while living in Canada. She affirmed that she comes "from a family where my mother works and has a PhD and is a university professor while my father doesn't have a PhD, … but they're both equal.…" Similarly, Yasmine observed, "My ideas since coming to Canada did not shift, but toned, especially with regard to my interaction with the opposite sex." Yasmine added that "I am now more able to see shortcomings in both cultures and try to avoid them, and I am also able to see the good things in both worlds and instill them in my children." Nora scrutinized many of her world views as a result of being in Canada. She explained that although it is a challenging venture, it helped her to grow personally.

Interestingly, Wafaa's experiences in Canada have led her to believe that a woman is able to master many responsibilities and handle multiple tasks. She acknowledged that in Arab Muslim society, there are many women who handle multiple tasks too, yet they are not regarded positively. She also came to believe that a woman could be a good wife and mother, as well as being outspoken: "When I was back home, I used to think the good wife was submissive to everything: Don't argue about anything.... Now, no...."

Since coming to Canada, Eman was able to put to rest the constraints placed on women and men to live by cultural and traditional norms. Also, she attributed the changes in her views to being older and wiser. For instance, Eman's perception of an ideal woman is one of the perceptions that shifted as a result of her life here:

> In Canada, I practised my world views *more freely*.... My views, for instance, of an ideal woman have *relaxed* since I came here.... If I was in Libya, I would be captive to the ideal woman in society, ... but here in Canada, *I'm free to live as I want to live* because we don't have the pressures of the extended family or even immediate family of how things should be according to society.... Here I can be different, and I'm happy to be different....

Eman emphasized again that her maturity is another reason for the shift in her thoughts:

> I matured and I experienced many changes in my personal life that have also made me realize that women's roles are lacking where I come from, and it's not due to the religion, to Islam.... It's more due to the culture and that there haven't been many opportunities given to women to prove their capability in that field of decision making or in any other field....

Unexpectedly, coming to Canada illuminated and strengthened Islam in Eman's soul. She explained how living here is enlightening because she has learned more about her religious values and the teachings of Islam than she had when she was in Libya. She asserted that she is living the essence of Islam in the West more than she ever lived it in the East:

> Unfortunately, I was a victim just as many other people are victims to the ... media.... Whatever I read in the magazines and read in the books ... and whatever I heard in the news, I thought conveying Islam. And I thought that in Islam, women ... must be dressed in a certain way and that they cannot go out of the house, ... but in Canada, when I learned more about my religion, I was very much surprised.... Coming to Canada, believe it or not, that's where I learned more about the roles of women in Islam ... because ... in Libya we were more subject to culture and customs and what society wanted.... Here in Canada, I feel that I can explore and live my life the way I want to live it without becoming a victim of, or subject to, all the rules and regulations created by culture and society.

Morooj, too, claimed that being here gave her the space and the freedom of choice that would not have been feasible in Libya or anywhere in Arab Muslim society. She added that being free from social dictates and pressures is a great advantage. For someone as open-minded as Morooj, who was raised with fewer gender stereotypes, the social pressure at the time from her extended family and her parents to conform to the gender norms was overwhelming. She said that her uncles continually questioned the "unexplainable freedom" that her father allowed his daughters.

Ruba did not foresee any issue with men's and women's gender construction. She felt that though she had travelled and lived in many cultures, her views have not changed:

> My views with regard to the male/female issues, ... or what is so-called gender issues, did not change completely. The fact that I am living here did not change them one bit. It just made me more appreciative of my religion because ... I did not have to fight like other people are fighting to be recognized. I have been recognized since the day I was born, and nobody can take that away from me, ... and because I was raised in a family that did not treat me any differently, ... I did not come here and say, "Oh my God, look at what I can do, and I'm missing all these opportunities that nobody has opened for me, and now I can do things." It's not like that at all....

As a counterpoint to Ruba's idea, Fadwa's thoughts on women's roles and what women can do has changed since she came to Canada:

> My ideas were there, but the ability to practise them has absolutely shifted in Canada. I've had the opportunity to do way more things than I would have been able or allowed to do in the Middle East, ... [for example], just being able to take the bus on my own.... Well, back home I'd probably be able to take the bus on my own, but ... to go from one city to another city alone without having to worry about harassment in public just because I'm a woman travelling alone? Or something like paying bills, renting cars.... Just these simple, simple, luxuries.... Going to the movies alone ... there is no way I can go watch a movie alone [where my parents live] or in [my native country]. It would just be impossible, so, yes, living in Canada is liberating....

Fadwa's open-minded and encouraging father has also greatly influenced her and her decision to be here in the first place. These are all factors that have formed her current views of women's roles and of the world. She pinpointed another significant factor:

> The message I received consistently throughout was that with education, I can achieve anything. With people like our mother, Aisha,[11] Allah bless her, and Margaret Thatcher—even though I do not agree with her political views right now—but with strong female leadership characteristics to look up to, I am able to sustain my views....

A more important factor for Fadwa was being far removed from immediate contact with cultural traditions and gender ideologies: "being so far removed from my culture ... and my extended family has sort of desensitized me. I used to be much *much* [emphasis] more aware, nervous, and cognizant of what people would say and what people would think in the family." Fadwa added assertively, "As a woman, I found that I have more norms to deal with, ... more rules to abide by." Fadwa's first marriage proposal[12] taught her that there were more norms to deal with than she ever expected, yet Fadwa attributes her abilities to debate and challenge her aunts about this marriage proposal directly to her life and education in Canada:

> I honestly believe that my life here gave me the sense of confidence and the ability to argue and articulate and reason, and I do not have to agree with everyone to be okay. Knowing that and having to go through that experience of being removed from my culture for a long period of time but still tied to it makes me realize that if I go back and they are not happy [with me], ... even if they choose to ostracize me, [then], well, I have lived away from my culture for so long that it is not the end of the world.... What also gives me courage is that I met so many girls who are like me. They are good Muslim women. They pray five times a day. They do what they are supposed to do Islamically.... They are God-fearing, yet they do not agree with cultural norms.... The interaction with these women has really empowered me.... Seeing them has made me realize that it is okay to be different from the societal norms back home.

Fadwa enthusiastically revealed that a major part of her ability to think critically is also credited to her education:

> A lot of it has to do with the education system here. Also, as a child I went to private schools and it was a little more challenging.... The critical thinking might have come from the process of education in Canada, but

173

the courage to actually continue to question, to reason, [to] say something and get myself into a point where I say I disagree instead of just
retreating—that comes ... from interaction with the girls that I know who
are strong Muslim women.

These conversations confirm that many Arab Muslim women's
world views have been influenced, to a certain degree, by their lives
in Canada. Meeting new people, education, maturity, and exposure to
different perspectives were all some of the factors that have influenced
their perceptions, yet some of the women's persisting traditional views,
particularly with respect to equality between the sexes, remained un-
challenged and were reproduced in the Canadian context.

LOOKING TO THE FUTURE: HOPES AND DREAMS

If there is one thing that all the interviewees share, it is their hope for the
future. Although they were asked to talk about their dreams with regard
to women's issues and gender discourse, each woman lays out hopes and
visions—not necessarily personal hopes, but hopes and dreams that include
men, women, and youth, as well as society at large.

When Yasmine recalled her first work experience with women in the
small Yemeni village where she had her first clinical practice, she sighed
and expressed her concerns for these women:

> The treatment of women in Yemen is pathetic. This was 14 years ago.... I
> was unable to pronounce my disagreement with such treatment.... I be-
> lieve that they needed more than my help—they need a great lift. It is a
> human rights issue.... The discrimination of women ... was overwhelm-
> ing.... The mistreatment was unbearable and unimaginable.... There
> was a sexist saying in Yemen that "Only two things can carry heavy loads
> without giving the farmer a problem: a donkey and a woman."

Yasmine is aware that a major part of the issue in the Yemeni village was
illiteracy. "Women's education makes a big different," she said. Recently,
Yasmine started taking part in raising awareness of women's issues there.
Also, she is helping newcomers to Canada to secure education for their
children.

At the local level, Yasmine and a group of other Muslim women started
an organization to help women in the local community. It is a social

collaborative group, an association to provide support for single-parent families, organize holy days celebrations, and facilitate an annual evening of multi-faith discussions.

Nora's excitement and hopes for progress crossed the Canadian border. She hopes that the positive aspects of the life she has enjoyed in Canada will one day become a reality in Egypt. She is amazed at even the smallest gestures when

> A woman or a man is respected as a human being, not for the degree she or he holds. In Egypt, we cannot use the first name for our profs, but here ... you could call him or her by his first name. My previous supervisor is well known in the field and I was shocked to hear some students calling him by his first name.... This is what I will do when I go back to Egypt.

Nora hopes that some day soon, people in Egypt will value all educational fields, especially kinesiology and physical education. These fields are neglected, not only in Egypt, but also in other Arab Muslim societies. There is no emphasis on the value of health science fields,[13] although, ironically, chronic illnesses such as high blood pressure and diabetes are widespread in Arab Muslim societies. Physical exercise designed by professionals helps greatly with these illnesses. Nora reflects that "Until recently, kinesiology and physical education were not taken seriously in Egypt and no one wanted his or her children to pursue them as a field of study.... I will try my best to change this perception...."

On a personal level, Nora's outstanding talent led her to be nominated to sit on the local Muslim organization board: "The board is 40 years old and this is the first time a woman is part of it.... Now my dreams are kind of funny. I am dreaming of being part of Parliament."

Sahra, who is also from Egypt, foresaw a great deal of opportunity for women in Egypt. She said, "there are lots of opportunities for women to do anything they want. The fact that there are not enough women having higher positions is not because of the society; it is probably because women don't want to, or because they have different priorities." Sahra is optimistic about women's status and contends that women are progressing, considering the responsibilities they have to handle. She exemplified her supervisor: "My supervisor is taking a year off.... She is having a baby and is very excited.... You can imagine what this year can give her in her career; she can do more than just have a child, ... but she chooses this over career success."

Eman's dreams are collective. She hopes that Arab Muslim societies will eventually encourage women to be aware of their rights and responsibilities. Also, Eman is interested in women's desires to explore and "accomplish what they want to accomplish." On a personal level, Eman hoped to offer the best education for her daughters. She asserted, "It opens many doors for women. Having my children grow up as Muslims, ... strong-willed and loving and considerate, is my greatest hope."

Wafaa's next path is taking her love of writing seriously. She wishes to be a writer of fiction and poetry. This was not something she had expected of herself. She said:

> I never thought that I could write, but I wrote a poem, and I copied it onto a paper and I started editing, ... and I have been writing poems since then, and that's when I decided to be an English teacher. And I always dreamed of ... writing my own book, especially children's books.

Fadwa, with an eye on further education—possibly a PhD—as well as starting a family, said with satisfaction: "I could always pursue a PhD, hopefully at home or somewhere else, so I can perhaps be a professor there if I want to be, or influence more change." Furthermore, Fadwa said:

> I see myself being a little more useful to society there than I am here.... In Sudan, there is a huge, huge need.... There's poverty, there are a lot of problems that we have socially and politically, financially, and economically.... I just want to make even a little difference.

Morooj, with an artist's view of the world, dreams of having her own art exhibit and she is trying to locate funding for that purpose: "I would like to do some exhibitions for the Libyan community, Arab Muslim community, and the larger Canadian society, especially to show photos from Libya for children who grew up in Canada and do not know about the nature, historical sites, and beautiful scenes in Libya." Morooj, who was saddened by the many stories she dealt with as a social worker in Libya, wishes that she could do something to help Libyan women, both her own generation and younger ones: "When I go back to Libya I want to encourage women my age who have hobbies like painting, knitting, and embroidery to teach the younger generation of women who are interested in making small projects."

Ruba's look at the future directs her to the youth: "My passion is just the younger people, in general—males and females—they are the ones in need of help and guidance." Nahlaa, the youngest of all women in this book, and the one who is just starting her adult life, knows that she wants to plan her courses carefully so that she has more opportunities for post-graduate plans.

Fadwa, Nora, Morooj, Yasmine, Wafaa, Eman, Nahlaa, Ruba, and Sahra were all enthusiastic to find ways to help Arab Muslim women and others. All the experiences of these nine Arab Muslim women and the ways in which their gender is counteracted are presented through their own voices. The majority of the women spoke of combining multiple commitments to children, partners, work, study, and/or active participation in the community. All these commitments are subject to conflict, overlap, and disruptions. Likewise, Bateson (1990), in *Composing a Life*, asserts that a common thread between her stories and those of her friends is dealing with multiple commitments. She also says that "Each of us had to search in ambiguity for her own kind of integrity, learning to adapt and improvise in a culture in which we could only partly be at home" (p. 13). As Arab Muslim women, we improvise in both cultures—Middle Eastern and Canadian. Our native culture teaches us early on in our lives that we should look favourably at staying at home, while our host culture views us through the orientalist perception of Muslim women.

SUMMARY

Common themes occurred in the narratives. Arab Muslim women face challenges that are similar, but they also have differing perceptions and measures to negotiate the challenges. These similarities and differences challenge homogeneous notions of what it means to be a Muslim woman. Three significant premises were constant throughout the narratives:

- the connection to the Islamic teaching about women as "The Authentic" source of guidance in Arab Muslim lives and, more specifically, to their gender perceptions
- the cultural construction of what it means to be a woman
- the way we, as Arab Muslim women, value our education and are enabled to negotiate gender discourses as a result of it

My analysis focuses on these premises, since they have appeared and reappeared as threads throughout the narratives. In addition, the points of discussion are connected to each another. There is a connection between patriarchy and women's sexuality and gender roles, which is evident in the discussion of these themes. I view these themes as connected entities that do not exist in a vacuum; they are interrelated and interconnected to one another. They differ in priority for Arab Muslim women according to race, class, gendered identity, and educational level: "Women have been specifically impacted by virtue of their locations in various classes, nationalities, ethnicities and races" (Hirschmann, 1998, p. 347).

Deborah Cameron (1985) suggests that gender should not be used as an explanation of issues because it is itself a social construction in need of an explanation. I did not use the women's gender roles and perceptions to explain social and cultural expectations; rather, I used the social and cultural traditions' expectations of women to explore the gender perceptions that some participants shared. Jarviluoma, Moisala, and Vilkko (2003) agree that "in addition to examining gender roles, we should ask what the mechanisms are which create/construct [and re-produce] such roles" (p. 2); this question is a pillar and mainstay of my analyses in this book. The mechanisms that create and construct gender roles manifest the significance of answering a number of other questions:

- How are the categories of women/men and masculine/feminine socially constructed in Arab Muslim societies?
- What ideas and judgments are attached to them?
- What are the mechanisms that maintain, support, or challenge the prevailing gender discourse in Arab Muslim societies?
- How is power negotiated in gender constructions? (Javiluoma, Moisala & Vilkko, 2003, p. 2)

As it appears throughout the book, Muslim women's lives are highly diverse according to their "country of origin, rural/urban background of households prior to migration, regional and linguistic background in the subcontinent, [and] class position in the subcontinent ..." (Rattansi & Phoenix, 2005, p. 109), as well as according to their perceptions.

While writing this book, I relived not only the interviews and conversations, but also the stories these women recounted. I will relive these each time I read their narratives. The powerful stories of Arab Muslim women presented here, which articulate their faith and "grapple with the complexity of claiming Muslim identities in different contexts" (Chaudhry, 1997, p. 444), contribute a meaningful and relevant context to the literature on Arab Muslim immigrant women. They have successfully "enacted resistance to dominant moods of thoughts" (Chaudhry, 1997, p. 443), and, because of their education, they were able both to engage in the "Islam and women" debate and to benefit from it. Like Mukudi (2002), I feel that the Arab Muslim women interviewed "do not visualize themselves challenging their culturally defined positions. Instead, they seek opportunities that would make their experiences better ones through education" (p. 239).

These women, who lived their lives in Arab Muslim societies in a particular socio-historical context and then moved to Canada, have powerfully "exercised their agency in crafting their gender identity in a new context" (Read & Bartkowski, 2000, p. 114).

The narratives reveal that certain aspects of cultural traditions and society may influence the way Arab Muslim women perceive themselves as women. The women in this study also represented how their faith heavily influences the way in which they perceive themselves as women, and how they view their role in their society.

NOTES

1. For more on Muslim experiences of freedom in North America, see Ramadan (2004).

2. In my Master's work, PhD research, conference presentations, and scholarly publications, I provide an alternative way to view Muslims, particularly women.

3. A tremendous number of books about Islam and the *Quranic* interpretations in both English and Arabic are accessible and available in the West.

4. Muslim places of worship.

5. According to Bhabha (1990), "All forms of culture are continually in a process of hybridity ... hybridity is the third space which enables other positions to emerge ... sets up new structures of authority, new political initiatives ... a new era of negotiation of meaning and representation" (p. 207).

6. *Hijab* (covering of the hair) is different from the veil (full covering of face) or *neqab* (the covering of the face except the eyes), yet *hijab* is often referred to as the veil in Western discourse.

7. Women who observe the *hijab*.

8. Only in Saudi Arabia is the *hijab* compulsory.

9. For more, see Alvi, S., Hoodfar, H. & McDonough, S. (Eds.), (2003), *The Muslim veil in North America: Issues and debates*, Toronto: Women's Press.

10. For more, see Walbridge (1997) and Abu-Lughod (1986).

11. The Prophet Mohammed's wife (PBUT).

12. Fadwa's marriage proposal was discussed earlier.

13. Only the position of physician is highly regarded for its prestigious status in society.

Chapter Twelve

CONCLUSION

I want to acknowledge that although other Arab Muslim Canadian women's lives are not presented in this book, their experiences and dreams are nonetheless equally important and deserve to be heard in order to confront the alienation and the silencing of Arab Muslim women's experiences.

The Arab Muslim Canadian women's narratives in this book do not speak for all Arab Muslim Canadian communities and their interpretations of Islam. The women here "are a microcosm for something larger. In some cases they may represent the general traditions or belief system but they also reveal their personal, fluid relationships with their creator, community, and one another" (Bhimani, 2003, p. 11). These women's narratives reflect the diversity of Arab Muslim women's lives and dreams.

As Edward Said's legacy asserts that it is indigenous people's responsibility to contest and challenge the perception of outsiders, I took it upon myself to represent Arab Muslim Canadian women's narratives, lives, and dreams. Although the women here would not refer to themselves as oppressed—and I, too, would not consider them as such—they would not deny the challenges they face in their own communities and in society at large.

REVISITING MY INSIDER/OUTSIDER STATUS

I acknowledge that my interests and beliefs may have influenced my analysis and interpretations. My research questions were certainly influenced by my situation as an Arab Muslim woman in Canada as "research on gender inevitably reflects the researcher's own identity, questions, assumptions, and agenda that she or he explicitly or implicitly covertly brings into the field" (Friedl, 1994, p. 91). But, with regard to my analysis, I agree with Harding (1987) and other feminist scholars that being self-reflective and introducing the subjective element into the analysis increases the credibility of the data.

Although I am an Arab Muslim woman raised in the Arabic Islamic country of Saudi Arabia, my lens has been "honed and shaped in the West [particularly in Canada] where I have been exposed to a largely Western model of feminism" (Abdo, 2002, p. 229). This exposure opens doors for me to search for Arab Muslim feminist ideologies. The ideologies, books, and publications of Arab Muslim feminist scholars (i.e., Ahmed, 1992, 1999; Barazangi, 2000; El Saadawi, 1999) and researchers were not accessible to me while growing up in Saudi Arabia. Upon revisiting my insider/outsider status, I acknowledge my privilege as an Arab Muslim woman studying other Arab women at a Canadian university in a predominantly White community. My insider/outsider status is simultaneously re-emphasized.

I am mindful that, as Amal Amireh observes, "inappropriate Western feminist paradigms are often applied to the Arab world, even by Arab women scholars themselves" (as cited in Abdo, 2002, p. 229). This includes Western colonial discourse, which some Western feminists use to "devalue local cultures by presuming that there is only one path for emancipating women [which is by] adopting Western Models" (Abu-Lughod, 1998, p. 14). I used my heightened awareness of these pitfalls to avoid imposing Western paradigms on this study. My inclusion of the diversity of Arab Muslim women's voices and narratives works to value—rather than devalue—local cultures as some Arab Muslim studies have done. My awareness of my privilege as an insider/outsider, which allows me to move flexibly between the two spaces, cautions me "not to *simplify* [italics added] any or all of the factors [affecting Arab Muslim women's lives] into clichés, such as the Arab woman's total oppression under Islam" (Abdo, 2002, p. 229).

This complex and privileged insider/outsider position led me to think of other scholars' research in a different way. I argue that being an insider to the researched group gave more value to my research. Having "insider knowledge" of Arab culture and Islamic teachings to women was of great significance to me, as I might have been hindered in the research had I not possessed these valuable elements. Being an insider made me aware of what sort of questions to ask and when to ask them, and how to interpret the answers.

The benefit to being an insider in the narratives of Arab Muslim women is that I was able to share a central component of my experience with these Arab Muslim women. For them and for me, "Spiritual life is an intimate part of everyday life, and everyday things" (Carbaugh, 2001, p. 108). I conclude that our spirituality and faith is one main theme in how we all—the participants and myself—have constructed our gender identities.

Writing for audiences different from Arab Muslims was challenging. In writing for a Western audience, I had to clarify many aspects of the religion and the culture, and avoid making assumptions about, or rely on, the previous background knowledge of my readers. "A reader who is not properly informed might easily perceive erroneously simple solutions [or meanings] to what are actually extremely complex sets of culture, religious, and historical circumstances" (Abdo, 2002, p. 230). I could not assume that Western audiences are as intimately acquainted with Arab Muslim cultural traditions as I am. I was also cautious that some intercultural expressions and values might "convey" negativity to outsiders.

I have to be clear that it is not my intention to cover any culture with a blanket of either condemnation or approval. I believe that every culture has imperfections and virtues, and it is the privilege of its people to critique their culture. This pertains to the Arab Muslim women participants and to me. As insiders and as outsiders, we have the privilege of seeing the advantages and shortcomings of our native cultures and of our new Canadian culture. This offers new possibilities for constructing a better world for ourselves and for others.

Another aspect of my insider status surfaced when I revisited the participants' transcripts. I was mesmerized by the tone of one of my participants in particular. Ruba overemphasized her refusal to define any issue of gender discourses as women's issues. She clearly felt uncomfortable and exhibited a lack of confidence in me and my endeavour, which questioned my insider status. She consistently questioned the aim of this kind of research. As a result, "I became aware that there are many more dimensions—advantageous as well as restrictive—to my researcher role in my own Arab Muslim community than I had at first been conscious of" (El-Solh, 1988, p. 93), yet I remain convinced that:

> Everyone, at some time in their life, must choose whether to stay with a ready-made world that may be safe—but is also limiting—or to push forward, often past the frontiers of common sense, into personal place, unknown and united. (Winterson, 1997, p. xiv)

Being an insider, an Arab Muslim woman, established enough motivation on my part to be involved in such research. I concur with Morsy (1988), who states that "as Arab women researchers, we no doubt have the opportunity to make important theoretical contributions toward the understanding of our own societies" (p. 90), yet it was a challenging task. I was not the only researcher who faced the challenge of researching his or her own people. Like Abdo (2002), I was aware that,

> In my own attempt to examine Arab women through their lives ... I must
> not engage in the "elaboration of a victim discourse that fetishizes [extrav-
> agant irrational devotion] Islam [and] reifies Arab women" (p. 186), such
> that they become "objects—of study, of pity, and of liberation" sans "agency
> and subjectivity" (p. 185). Such an approach would replicate the conde-
> scending stance that First World women frequently tend to adopt toward
> Third World women (p. 203). (Amireh, as cited in Abdo, 2002, p. 229)

Researching my own culture was a heavy responsibility. When the participants thanked me for my efforts, I wondered what they were expecting
of me. The appreciation some of them expressed regarding my research
was irrespective of whether they perceived any results in my research.
"Traditionally, researchers are to hide their feelings and their personal
observations in a diary, while publishing only the 'scholarly account' of
their work" (Cooper, 1991, p. 110); however, what I did in my research is
not at all traditional—"Voices in the culture are constructed voices that
mirror an integration of the individual voice and common cultural voices.
Finding a place in the culture is finding one's constructed voice" (Cooper,
1991, p. 110).

Perhaps I have been empowered by including some aspects of my autobiography and self-reflections and analyses from my insider/outsider
position. I revealed an aspect of my identity that was hidden in my traditionally conservative closet when I chose to speak of my experience. An
autobiography seeks to "reveal the self, what is hidden inside, just as it
tries to see the other.... The written word for me became an act of rebellion against injustice exercised in the name of religion, or morals, or love"
(El Saadawi, 1999, pp. 292–293). It is an act of rebellion for myself and for
others who are brought up to believe that a "good behaving" woman should
neither disturb nor critique her cultural traditions to tell their stories.

In my culture, Arab Muslim women and men are indoctrinated to
believe that all aspects of their cultural traditions are sacred and are not
subject to critique or change. I also understand how the idea of critiquing
patriarchal aspects of one's societal norms and cultural traditions can be
conflicting. Critiquing patriarchy and gender discourses in one's own culture can be seen as disloyalty. I used to feel compelled to defend all aspects
of Arab Muslim cultural traditions and societal norms and deny any of their
shortcomings. Also, I am cognizant of the way other male and female Arab
Muslims may perceive my critique and analysis in my research, particularly because I am currently living and studying in the West at a time when
relations between the West and the Arab Muslim world are at a low ebb.

184

Nonetheless, both my Arab Muslim values and Western education, particularly in Canada, have made me "unapologetic in criticizing and condemning any patriarchal, antidemocratic aspects of any culture, especially the ones we know firsthand" (Tohidi, 1998, p. 289). As Edward Said advocates, I, too, argue that self-knowledge is unattainable without an equal degree of self-criticism (Said, 2003).

A CRITIQUE WITHIN

As I have mentioned earlier, I advocate the importance of being self-critical as a primary measure in attaining self-knowledge and, hence, progress. A critical look within is another way to describe being self-reflexive. To look inside one's self and honestly determine one's shortcomings is the first cornerstone in constructing a better self. I argue that critiquing current practices for the purpose of restructuring, constructing, and advancing one's culture requires a meaningful look within.

Guillemin and Gillam (2004) support the need for a researcher to be self-reflexive. Moreover, I argue that not being able to engage analytically and critically with one's own culture is also potentially problematic and may lead to ethnocentrism[1] or cultural relativism.

I realize that some of the women interviewed in this study were perhaps "creating unwarranted loyalties and uncritical acceptance of male defined cultural norms and values ... this may reinforce sexist values and patriarchal power relations within a diasporic community ... some cultural values often embody gendered—if not overtly misogynist—beliefs, practices and relations" (Moghissi, 1999, p. 208). I argue that the reality of some sexist traditions and practices within one's own culture deserve to be examined and critically analyzed.

Fadwa was brought up to be an independent thinker. She crafted her path courageously and was able to ignore social norms. She is able to make decisions, whether it was choosing teaching as a profession or living alone in Canada. Her comments draw attention to many interesting points where cultural traditions intersect with religious viewpoints and practices, especially those related to gender discourses. Culturally embedded gender patriarchy and hierarchy have not suppressed Fadwa's independence—a very inspiring achievement. Fadwa, in most of her narratives, contested various cultural practices in her society and critiqued how they are being employed by her relatives. Living in Canada on her own was one aspect of Fadwa's refusal to conform to and abide by what is expected of a woman.

185

In saying this, Fadwa acknowledged that being away from her culture has allowed her to become more self-confident because this distance enabled her to think critically. My critical look within is best described by Marilyn Frye:

> Being outside a conceptual system puts one in a position to see things that cannot be seen from within; to assume that position, to dislocate oneself from the system, to dis-locate, dis-affiliate, or disengage one's attention from it, is to experience a reorientation of attention … a feeling of disengagement and re-engagement of one's power as a perceiver. (as cited in de Lauretis, 1990, p. 144)

Clearly, the women interviewed in my research, such as young Fadwa, were, to a large extent, able to contest traditional gender structure and refuse to bend to social pressures. Like Abou-Bakr (1999) I agree that "we do not want to be defensive and apologetic so that we end up defending passionately the wrong side of the culture or wrong perception and application of religion" (p. 15).

On the other hand, hooks (1989) concedes that not being analytical and critical of an experience because it is supposedly different from one's own can be as much a perpetuation of racism as cultural imperialism, which hooks has condemned (p. 47). Yasmine, for instance, asserted that the Western ideal of women and the excessive focus on the appearance of Western women devalues their role and position in Western society. She also argued that if a woman's beauty marks her value, then this is an objectification of her body and is disrespectful of her as an intellectual being. Yasmine added that women's beauty is in her personality and character. While I agree with Yasmine's view, I am aware that the objectification of women's bodies can be found in other cultures. In Arab Muslim societies, as well as in many others, there is an overemphasis on physical beauty.[2]

From Yasmine's readiness to critique Western cultural norms, I note that some of the Arab Muslim women I interviewed were extremely willing to share their perspectives on Western discourses of Muslim women and provide a critical and analytical account of women's disadvantages in Western culture of which they are also part of; nonetheless, they were reluctant to be critical of their native culture. In fact, some of them questioned how far I would be willing to take my own critique. Yet it is possible that,

> Western imperialism requires Islamic culture [adherents] to defend themselves so strongly against the West, and this makes Islamic women's

criticism of their own culture difficult, catching them between being ostracized as Western sympathizers, and thus left out of the community, and not having their concerns heard, thus being left out of the community in a different way. (Hirschmann, 1998, p. 363)

I draw an analogy between some of the Arab Muslim women's attitudes on overlooking patriarchal aspects of the Arab culture and societal norms and the African-American women's attitude in not critiquing the sexism in their own communities. Kimberle Crenshaw (1992) "observes that through their failure to break ranks with their men on the issue of misogyny, African-American women, historically, have contributed to 'the maintenance of sexist and debilitating gender practices' within the community" (as cited in Moghissi, 1999, p. 215).

Counter-hegemonic discourse was constructed when Arab Muslim women were willing to look critically at the Arab Muslim culture: Some were willing, while others were not. According to Kumashiro (2003), critiquing one's own culture might be considered as disloyalty to one's heritage and background. For some individuals, critiquing one's own world views can be an uncomfortable process.

In a similar vein, before I began interviewing the participants for this research, they asked me whether I was married or single and whether I was living in Canada alone or with my family. This question is worth exploring in relation to looking critically within. Did the women ask me these questions because sustaining family relationships in the diaspora is considered important to one's emotional well-being, as other researchers indicate, or were the women concerned with how "liberal" I may be in ignoring social dictates? Some of these women themselves were bothered by the constant interference of others in the community, yet they were not curbing their personal interest in inquiring about me and questioning the foundation of my critique of certain aspects of traditional cultural practices.

Therefore, I consider a critical look within to be important because I contend that "it must be recognized that there is always a danger that the sentimental treatment of one's own culture lends support to nationalism and, along with it, the glorification of the home country, even to racism in reverse" (Moghissi, 1999, p. 216).

My initial defensiveness with regard to my culture when I first moved to Canada changed as I trained myself to critically look within to construct a better world for myself and for other women:

> Questions and assertions about the oppression of women in the "Muslim East" sensitized me to female subjugation. Stereotypical characterizations of Arab women put me on the defensive and forced me to research the subject in order to present coherent arguments in defense of my cohorts. Consideration of various dimensions of Arab women's social roles led me to serious thinking that eventually transformed me from an apologist confronting Western devaluation of Arab women to an anthropologist focusing on a variety of theoretical issues concerning us. (Morsy, 1988, p. 74)

My reasons for contesting my own culture stem from the belief that culture is not static. There is room for improvement in all cultures and this is how humanity could move forward instead of denying flaws. Being raised and exposed to different cultures is enriching to one's personality; the personal dislocation gives a fuller view and has many advantages. As a result of living within the margins, one can appreciate what has been taken for granted. In short, I wholeheartedly agree with Moghissi (1999) that,

> Being away from "home" sometimes may be the only way one can look at "home" critically, dispassionately and with reason. Indeed, as Said (2000, p. 365) argues, "in a secular and contingent" world, homes are always provisional. Borders and barriers, which enclose us within safety of familiar territory, can also become prisons, and are often defended beyond reason or necessity. (p. 216)

Additionally, after moving to the "free democratic world," I became both more critical of my earlier assumptions as well as increasingly aware of the implicit hierarchies that still exist within Canadian society. For instance, women still hold relatively few positions in government—provincially and federally—and in the fields of science and law.

CHALLENGES WITHIN THE INTERVIEWS

The most enjoyable aspect of my research has been interviewing Arab Muslim women who presented various views about women, gender, Islam, and cultural traditions. For those who expressed interest in sharing their world views, I dedicated my time to listen to what they had to say.

In many instances, the women had not thought about some of the issues I raised in my questionnaire, as some of the participants had explained to me, and therefore they had to construct a position on certain issues on the spot. Subsequently, I found that some of the participants frequently repeated or contradicted themselves. As Bassey (1999) explained, "most of us in speech repeat ourselves, get sidetracked and 'delete' sentences by leaving them unfinished" (p. 81). This was not an issue while I was interviewing—unless the thought was discontinued—but it became an issue while reading the transcripts. Painstaking and careful editing to maintain content was performed with the English transcripts for clarity and readability.

Another view is supported by Gergen (2004):

> The mutual gaze, subtle signs of agreement or disagreement, silence, smiles, frowns, and comments related to shared or diverse experiences all lend shape to the story being told [by the participants] ... if the story teller [narrator] is the same age, race, and/or gender as the listener, certain assumptions of similarity may lead to embellishments in themes that might be avoided were the listener someone completely different and vice versa. (p. 279)

Most of the interviews were freewheeling conversations with women with whom I have both commonalities and differences. Some of them chose to share a great deal of information and told me things of their own accord; others chose to be brief and concise. The women also have emotional contradictions. For instance, the emotional tone of Ruba's interviews escalated. Other women were happy, according to what they said, to finally be able to represent themselves and have the opportunity to oppose the discourses constructed around their lives and experiences. Some women were excited and could not wait to answer all of my questions, while others were awkward and hesitant in answering certain questions.

As a researcher, I was careful not to agree or disagree with the opinions of those being interviewed. I was also careful not to mention what others have said about the same issue in their own interviews. Nonetheless, people are sometimes apt to follow the predominant viewpoint to avoid being criticized. I expected that some of the participants would respond conservatively to questions related to men's and women's interactions. It is possible that some gave responses they believed, either consciously or unconsciously, reflected the acceptable viewpoint in their native culture rather than the view they personally held. It is also possible that they gave answers they thought I wanted to hear. Jack Douglas, in *Investigative Social Research* (1976), asserts that,

> People have devised immensely complex ways to avoid saying exactly
> what they see or grasp, of rationalizing and valuing these activities and
> even to avoid thinking symbolically of what they are doing in terms that
> would make them feel dishonest, cheap.... (p. 17)

According to this view, one cannot expect to reveal a completely reliable picture of what people truly think and believe. Sometimes individual conservatism would dictate answers that are desired by society. I believe that being an insider, a member of the Arab Muslim society, has an effect on how an interviewee wants to conform to societal and cultural norms in her answers to certain questions. Peter Berger (1963) observes that there is a human tendency to conform to society in order to be accepted by one's group: "What lies at the bottom of this apparently inevitable pressure towards consensus is probably a profound human desire to be accepted, presumably by whatever group is around to do the accepting" (p. 72).

Another point that needs to be considered here is what Douglas (1976) calls "problematic meanings" or perceptions that differ from one person to another that depend on social settings and gender perceptions. Douglas (1976) contends that "it is easy for a researcher to overlook these problematic meanings, to assume that the same terms always mean the same thing, and to present false pictures of the complex, problematic setting" (p. 88).

CONCLUSIONS

Although researching Arab Muslim women immigrants is still a rich and new area of research, little scholarly focus has been committed to the intersections of issues that pertain to Arab Muslim women in Canada, issues such as education, culture, historical origins, and adjustments to Canadian values and belief systems. Arab Muslim feminist scholars of women's and gender studies, policy-makers, and educators have largely overlooked the education and gender construction of Arab Muslim women immigrants in Canada. Fewer still have included narratives from the lives and experiences of Muslim women. My book contributes to the growing, but limited, literature on Arab Muslim women's lives in North America and, more specifically, in Canada. I contend that this book will add to the discourses that focus on women and gender, ethnicity, education, and identity. Indeed, by using multiple lenses to analyze long-standing assumptions with regard to the status of Muslim women, I present opportunities for researchers to understand gender from a Muslim woman's perspective, and gender and education from the experiences of Arab Muslim women in Canada.

AN EYE ON FUTURE ENDEAVOURS

While seeking participants for my research, I visited the prayer room at the University of Western Ontario's main campus and interacted with many young Arab Muslim women. These young women were pursuing their Bachelor's, Master's, and medical degrees at the university. They were also active agents in their own communities. Their involvement in attending the local Muslim community's occasions, fundraising for the mosque and the local Islamic school, organizing cross-faith and/or cross-cultural gatherings with other religious and cultural groups in Canadian society, and organizing gatherings for Muslim holiday celebrations[3] make them key figures for understanding the dynamics of immigrant identity formation in the Diaspora. The first and second generation of Canadian Arab Muslims expressed their interest in my research and similar endeavours in which their experiences are the backbone. According to them, this kind of research gives them a chance to formally engage in presenting their views about gender identity and about other aspects of their identity.

In my brief meetings with first-, second-, and third-generation Muslim women who were born, raised, and currently live in Canada with their families, I learned that they model firm values and opinions about principles of Islam and Arab cultural traditions. What was fascinating was that many of them who were raised in Canada speak Arabic fluently and had a perfect Arabic dialect (e.g., Sudanese, Iraqi, and Syrian). This made me more interested in knowing how they connect with their culture and roots. In my future work, I propose to focus on first- and second-generation Arab Muslim female youth and the socialization they have experienced in Canada, especially related to gender discourse. It would be significant, though, to study how they have dealt with issues of identity conflict between being Arab Muslim and Canadian. Additionally, it would be interesting to explore intergenerational conflict and tensions with respect to gender discourses.

Comparative studies between immigrants—first- and second-generation Arab Muslim women—could highlight differences between generations both in terms of education and gender perceptions. Generational contexts, ethnicity, gender, colour, religion, historical and cultural origin, and how these contexts overlap and intersect need to be examined (Cayer, 1996, p. 180).

Also, comparing female Arab Muslim immigrants in Canada with their peers of the same age living in Arab Muslim societies would provide interesting viewpoints about the interrelation between religion, minority/majority status, and cultural traditions. Such a comparison may reveal interesting connections between immigration dynamics and gender discourses. Furthermore, comparative studies of Arab females of differing religious affiliations (e.g., Arab Christian or Muslim Shii) and nationalities (e.g., Muslim Indian, Muslim Pakistani) would shed light on the various ways in which cultural traditions and religion contribute to the gender aspects of one's identity. These are all suggestions and possibilities for qualitative researchers who are interested in providing specific, detailed, and descriptive data to compare their findings with existing studies.

Although this research explores the narratives of nine Arab Muslim women, more in-depth research that takes a biographical approach is needed to reveal how individual Arab Muslim women understand their gender and how this might be affected as a result of living in two distinct cultures. These narratives may emerge in and through conflicting cultural narratives that reveal diversity and variability, as demonstrated here.

The state of Arab Muslim women's organizations in Canada is another area for further research.

FINAL THOUGHTS: PERSONAL REFLECTIONS

My aim in conducting this research was to explore how Arab Muslim women perceive themselves as women and view their gender roles after attending Canadian academic institutions. As the research unfolded, some myths surrounding Arab Muslim women's realities were unravelled. The Arab Muslim women's narratives highlight the heterogeneity of their perceptions, their abilities to create diverse models of realities, their competency to make decisions, and, moreover, influence courses of action that entail significant consequences in their lives. What is more fascinating is their strong commitment to their faith and their abilities to distinguish between Islamic teachings and cultural traditions and practices.

I describe this research as a quilt, a patchwork, a tapestry of Arab Muslim women's stories. To me, it is a piece of art that is colourful and rich. Through quilting the pieces of Arab Muslim women's rich narratives, a few personal lessons were learned, not as a researcher, but as a woman listening to other women with whom I share a religious background, common language, and cultural traditions. Although the Arabic culture intersecting with political, social, economic, and patriarchal forces generated more conflicting platforms for women than those offered by Islam, almost all of the women interviewed were inclined to challenge and resist, and not to live passively in a seemingly fixed world.

By far, this research endeavour has been one of my most enriching life experiences. This experience informed me of what it means to "engage with a more open notion of Muslim, [a notion] that is informed not only by religion and notions of static stereotypical culture" (Khan, 2000, p. 130), but also by women who are subjects of their history. I learned a great deal from these women. In knowing and listening to these women, I have gained a better understanding of issues that even I, as an Arab Muslim woman raised in an Arab society, did not fully appreciate. Their stories had a profound impact on my personal perspective. I will fondly remember the looks in their eyes, their gestures, and their words, not because they are necessarily documented in the book, but because of their enriching viewpoints, interesting stories, and uniqueness as characters on a personal level.

The sense of confidence and self-assertion in Morooj's tone is inspiring. Whatever the question I asked of her, Morooj answered eloquently, revealing inner peace and personal strength. While others struggled with some doubts, which were reflected in the way they responded to some questions, Morooj utilized and modelled what she believes makes a Muslim woman who she is. Her assured self-representation was manifested in her answers, posture, and looks.

Nora's narrative inspires me with the notion that nothing is an obstacle for a determined woman. Attending national exams and purposefully skipping science-related questions in order to improve the likelihood of fulfilling her dream of becoming a gymnastics teacher and health science researcher reveals how capable and confident Nora is.

Fadwa, inspired by early Muslim women, is able to challenge patriarchal aspects of social and cultural gender construction in Arab Muslim societies and in Canadian society. This was possible through the process of a Canadian education, which encourages questioning and reasoning instead of mere memorization. Also, having a network of confident, tough, and outspoken Arab Muslim women made this possible.

While reading, rereading, writing, and editing the narratives, I revisited every aspect of the women's narratives numerous times. Morooj and Fadwa clearly indicated that their education in Canada had greatly influenced their outspoken and unique personalities. Nora, Eman, and I are extremely fascinated by the abundance of informational resources that are available to students in Canada. The unique perspective of gender discourses the women presented is influenced by various factors. The main factor is their commitment to their faith. Other factors include their abilities to negotiate traditional boundaries that dictate specific gender norms, the freedom of speech and choice that is uniquely enjoyed within the Canadian context, their education in Canada, and, most importantly, their personal motivations and self-realizations. The women's knowledge of their faith and their education, though, are what I highlight as playing a significant part in their self-realization process.

Yet, as a result of these various factors, the women in my study became independent and influential whether they chose to stay at home or to be part of the public domain. These women are becoming catalysts of progress within their families, communities, and societies. Also, these women may become catalysts of feminist and liberal movements in their native societies by supporting existing activists and taking part in developmental processes. Fadwa and Wafaa are considering moving back permanently, or perhaps on a temporary basis, to their native societies, and thus may take part in the progression of women's issues. Indeed, Fadwa explicitly indicated that her plan is to return and become actively engaged in social activism, which is long-standing and flourishing in Arab Muslim societies. Their stories offered me personal growth. More importantly, all these narratives make sense of the belief in education "as a necessary liberalizing force" (Afshar, 1989, p. 269). Also, Bruner (2003) poses the question: "Does education make the spirit more generous by broadening the mind?" (p. 213).

My answer to this is *yes*.

Education is freeing and liberating.

NOTES

1. The *Sociology Dictionary* defines ethnocentrism as "the assumption that the culture of one's own group is moral, right, and rational and that other cultures are inferior" (Parkinson & Drislane, 1998, n.p.).

2. For more discussion on physical beauty in Arab Muslim culture, see Mernissi, *Doing Daily Battles* (1988).

3. Muslims celebrate two holy days every year—*Feast Eid* after fasting the month of Ramadan and *Eid Al-Hajj* when Muslims go on a pilgrimage to Mecca.

Epilogue

Thousands of stitches ... Intricate work ... But it didn't seem like work when they were together talking and laughing ... As the design became clear, so did all the stories, the bits of family history.... They'd told each other those stories all the time working and stitching. Watching how it fits together, becoming something other than the pieces they held in their hands. (Smyth, 1982)

The passage above evokes an image of how I have envisioned my participants' mosaic and patchwork. I draw an analogy between my research and my grandmother's stitched Bedouin quilt....

While I was selecting parts of these narratives, I felt it was as though I were selecting pieces of colourful and diverse material and stitching them together to make them meaningful again.... The process resembled what my grandmother did to make her powerful, Bedouin patchwork. My book became a quilt—a patchwork, a tapestry of stories.

The hues and textures of the multifaceted lives of nine Arab Muslim women who pieced together a quilt of narratives....
I shared the stories of women who opened their hearts to me, ...
who crafted their paths of freedom and personal agency....
Each gave me a piece of colourful tapestry that I will use to make this rich, personal, vivid narrative tapestry....

It is a journey I started but will never end.... It ends where it began ... with collecting stories of inspiring women, ... and it begins where it ends, ... where I am searching for more ideas that are awakened in me and I only want them to grow ... with passion and commitment to explore more ... and understand more....

A plethora of unanswered potential questions still remain for a new journey.

Over the years I became more politically aware and "I realized the difficulty of attaining the condition that would unleash the potentially liberating force" (Morsy, 1988, p. 73).

I am empowered that I articulated my position as an Arab Muslim woman ... this belief has sustained me through difficult moments....

Appendix A

GROUNDWORK

The theories that inform my work are wide-ranging: I have included an overview of Islamic perspectives on gender issues; an investigation of the theories of prominent Western gender theorists; a brief discussion on Arab feminists who have investigated gender issues in Arab Muslim societies, especially with respect to women; and an exploration of Muslim feminists' and scholars' perspectives of gender issues in Islam. I stress that theories and discourses that generalize women based on their cultural and religious backgrounds, or that isolate any one facet of identity while ignoring others (Cayer, 1996), fail to grasp the complexity of women's lives. Therefore, my theoretical framework is drawn from a wide range of perspectives.

The construction of female gender identity through parents, culture, and schooling is explained by Amira Proweller (1998). She suggests that "Girls fold in expectations about their bodies, their minds, and their future roles from a recipe of cultural forms that signify and position them as girls" (p. 207). In my research, I note that gender is largely a matter of how femininity is imprinted in both adolescence and childhood within a culture. How are gender inequities formed socially, religiously, and culturally? How do certain roles become prescribed for girls and women as "natural roles"? Beginning in elementary school, girls are given certain "knowledge, skills, and attitudes" (Proweller, 1998, p. 207) that later translate into restricted access to wider opportunities in schooling and employment.

ISLAMIC PERSPECTIVES ON GENDER

As an Arab Muslim woman researching educated Arab Muslim women's narratives, particularly their gender perceptions, I decided that the literature review should include an overview of the Islamic perception of gender discourse and women's roles and status. My acknowledgment of the need to engage in a brief conceptual framework of Islamic teachings to women encompasses an understanding of the Islamic perspective of gender. This necessitates a brief explanation of the foundational sources of Islam with respect to women—the Quran[1] and Sunna.[2] Both Quranic and Hadith[3] texts have been translated into English.[4]

Before I delve into Islamic teachings on women's roles, I give a brief and general explanation of the significance of the Quran and Hadith with respect to Islam.

THE HOLY QURAN

The Quran is what all Muslims accept as the primary source, or highest authority, in Islam. It is what all Muslims believe to be the word of Allah conveyed and revealed thorough the agency of the angel Gabriel to the Prophet Mohammed (PBUH) in the 7th century (Hoot, Szecsi & Moosa, 2003, p. 86). It is believed to have been transmitted without change or error by those who heard him (Hassan, 1999, p. 464). Accordingly, for the majority of Muslims, the Quran is believed to be without equal (Daniel, 1960). Norman Daniel further suggests that "The Quran in Islam is very nearly what Christ is in Christianity: the word of God, [and] the whole expression of revelation" (p. 53). The Quran is the revealed source—the primary source, chronologically and ontologically, and the ultimate source for Muslim consciousness (Bouhdiba, 1998, p. viii). Maysam Al-Faruqi (2000) explains:

> The Quran constitutes the one and only reference for anyone who wants to identify himself or herself as Muslim ... it is the context of the text that defines all Islamic beliefs, including the divine authorship, God's nature, His unity and transcendence, and His relation to the world and to humankind. (pp. 76–77)

The Quran is considered Kalamu Allah, the Arabic translation for "the Word of God." Thus, all teaching in the Quran is a practical guide for all Muslim believers. As such, it is important to shed some light on a few of the Quranic verses that explicitly discuss women's gender roles.

The Quran improved the status of women from that in Judeo-Christian traditions by raising them to the same spiritual dignity as men (Arkoun, 1994). In fact, the Quran never ascribes the downfall of the first couple, Adam and Eve, to Eve as Christian and Judaic texts do (Hassan, 1999). The

Quran never describes (nor mentions) Eve, who is presented as the first created woman, as having been created inferior or secondary to Adam (Baden, 1992, p. 7; Kvam et al., 1999). Also, the creation of Adam is mentioned in reference to humankind in general and not to Adam as a male nor to the prophet Adam (Barazangi, 2004).Many progressive Muslims argue that "the *Quran* even-handedly used both feminine and masculine terms and imagery to describe the creation of humanity from a single source. Allah's original creation was undifferentiated and not either man or woman" (Hassan, 1999, p. 470).

The *Quran* mentions and praises prominent women across history such as "Eve, Bilqis, the Queen of Sheba, Mary's daughters of Imran, the Virgin of Immaculate Conception to whom two verses are almost exclusively devoted" (Bouhdiba, 1998, p. 19). Islam, through the *Quran* and the *Hadith*, "addresses all issues of women's status, role and gender relations as well, and has done so since the first Islamic community" (Cayer, 1996, p. 148).

The *Quranic* revelations mention women as often as men in terms of ordinances and accommodation: "I waste not the labour of any that labours among you, be you male or female ..." (*Quran*, 3:195). The *Quran*, as a divine text and as the source of "Islam, offers to woman, besides absolute equality before God, inalienable rights that all societies must respect" (Ramadan, 2001, p. 339).

Most importantly, the *Quran* bans female infanticide (which was widely practised in pre-Islamic Arabia) and entitles women to contract their own marriage, receive dowries, retain control of wealth, and receive maintenance and shares in inheritances. In the early centuries of Islam, various legal schools of thought were established, and within the framework of the *Sharia*,[5] norms and laws were formulated to meet a woman's needs in a society where her largely domestic, child-bearing role rendered her sheltered and dependent upon her father, her husband, and close male relations (Badawi, 1995; Jawad, 1998).

The following are two texts from the *Quran* that emphasize the equality of humans, regardless of their gender:

> Each human being shall face the consequences of his or her deeds. And their Lord has accepted them and answered them: Never will I suffer to lose the work of any of you, be he or she male or female: you are members one of another. (*Quran* 3:195)

> If any do deeds of righteousness, be they male or female, and have faith, they will enter paradise and not the least injustice will be done to them. (*Quran* 4:124)

The *Quran*'s verses have received varying interpretations. The most conservative scholars assert that women's complementarity, which is mentioned in the *Quran*, means staying at home and taking care of the family. Moreover, some misogynist extremists Muslim scholars assert that,

> Woman proceeds from man. Woman is chronologically secondary. She finds her finality in man. She is made for his pleasure, his repose, his fulfillment ... married life, then, is hierarchized. The Islamic family was to be essentially man worshipping.... (Bouhdiba, 1998, p. 11)

In progressive Muslim views, complementarity does not preclude higher levels of education for women, even though they are still seen as the companions of men rather than as autonomous individuals. "Some Arab feminists find themselves arriving at new definitions over time" (Stromquist, 1989, p. 156).

The *Quran* addresses all inequalities, not just gender inequality. The superiority of men over women, which has been profoundly embedded in Arab cultural traditions since pre-Islamic Arabian society, is not supported by the *Quran*. Islam eradicated such a hierarchal structure by instilling in its followers the doctrine that there are no differences between a man and a woman. Regardless of class, gender, or skin colour, all are considered equal in rights and responsibilities. Islam singles out *taqwa* (piety) as that which differentiates human beings—male and male, female and female, and male and female—from each other, not gender or sexuality (Wadud, 1999, as cited in Leo, 2005, p. 138).

The *Quran* and *Sunna* (*Hadith* and *Seera*) place great value on women's education as it encourages all humans to acquire knowledge. The *Quran* quotes Allah as saying, "Say, O my lord, Advance me in Knowledge"[6] and in another verse, "God will raise up, to ranks, those of you who believe and who have been granted knowledge."[7] Women and men are commanded by God to achieve social responsibility, uphold morality, and combat vice.

Moreover, the verse "believers, men and women, are protectors, one of another: they enjoin what is just, and forbid what is evil"[8] indicates that women must acquire knowledge to be eligible for active leadership. The knowledge encouraged by Islamic texts is not only religious, but also secular and scientific. Muslim scholars have quoted the Prophet (PBUH) as recommending that his followers seek knowledge of religious matters from Aisha, his wife, a renowned scholar in her time. The Prophet (PBUH) said, "half the knowledge of my revelation should be acquired from all of my companions and the other half from Aisha" (as cited in Syed, 2004, p.

24). This is vivid evidence that the Prophet (PBUH) regarded women both as eligible students and as trusted teachers (Al-Manea, 1984).

In addition, the value placed on male offspring also has no basis in Islam; indeed, it contradicts what the *Quran* presents Allah as saying:

> Indeed lost are they who have killed their children, foolishly, without knowledge, and have forbidden that which Allah has provided for them, inventing a lie against Allah. They have indeed gone astray and were not guided. (*Quran* 6:140)

This brief introduction gives an overview of the *Quran*ic gender discourse and how women are positioned in that discourse.

SUNNA

Sunna is believed to comprise the sayings and actions of the Prophet (PBUH) (Badawi, 1995b; Baden, 1992). *Hadith* contains the sayings while *Seera*, as biography, contains all the actions of the Prophet (PBUH), including his interactions with his family and his companions: "It is not because of the Prophet [PBUH] that Muslims accept the *Quran* but because of the *Quran* that they accept the authority of the Prophet [PBUH]" (Al-Faruqi, 2000, p. 76). The *Quran*'s and *Hadith*'s value emerges from the fact that they are eternal discourses. They establish the model that God has chosen for his community, and this divine choice cannot change (Ali, 2000; Badawi, 1995a; McCloud, 2000). While the *Quran* is the divine Word—*kalamu Allah*—the universal logos, the pure idea, the *Sunna* of the Prophet [PBUH] is the practical model—the ideal behaviour embodied in a living being, which, through history, is nevertheless the privileged echo of transcendence (Bouhdiba, 1998, p. 2). Carl Ernst (2003) noted that Mohammed's (PBUH) "prophetic experience provided the basis of fervent ritual practice, ethical ideals, and social structures that are deeply etched ..." (p. 92). Thus, it is widely accepted among Muslims that,

> *Hadith* are reports, narrations of the saying and acts of the Prophet Mohammed [PBUH]. They comprise two parts: the *matn* (content) and the *isnad* (chain of reporters). It has long been recognized that either part may be poorly reported or false, so their authenticity may be suspect. Early scholars compiled [*sic*] collections of the most trustworthy *Hadith*. The most widely reconsidered compilations are these of *Bukahari*,

Muslim, Abu Da'ud, Tirmidh, Ibn Maja, and Nisa'i. These collections are
used as an addition to the *Quran* for understanding Islam. The extent to
which these are to be used in guidance for Muslims is somewhat difficult to ascertain but they are still frequently used and the *Sharia* could
not have been developed without them. (Vidyasagar & Rea, 2004, p. 278)

Additionally, the development of a Muslim lifestyle and theology has
probably been built upon the *Hadith* as much as upon the *Quran*, but the
Hadith does not have the same weight and symbolic value as does the *Quran*
to most Muslims (Vidyasagar & Rea, 2004, p. 278).

In the authentic *Hadith*, many incidents of the early Islamic era are documented. Two of them are in the context of the "occasions for revelation."
Within two particular *Quranic* verses specifically related to women:

202

(a) It was related that Um Salama, a wife of the Prophet [PBUH], was in her
room with her maid combing her hair, when she heard the Prophet [PBUH]
calling for a community gathering for an announcement in the mosque: "O
people!" Her maid says, "You don't have to go; he is calling for the men, not
the women." *Um Salama* replies: "Indeed, I am one of the people."

(b) *Um Salama* went to the Prophet [PBUH] and wondered: why are the
men being praised for their sacrifices in the *hijra*[9] and not the women?
Hence, the revelation of verse 195 of chapter 3: "And God has heard them
and responded: verily, I suffer not the work of any worker of you, male or
female, to be lost, you are one of another...."

(c) The incident is narrated of a group of women complaining to the Prophet
[PBUH] that the *Quran* only mentions the wives of the Prophet [PBUH] and
not women in general: "Men are mentioned in everything and we are not; is
there any goodness in us to be mentioned and commended?" Hence, verse
35: "Verily, Muslims, men and women, believers, men and women, dutiful
men and women, truthful men and women, patient men and women, hum-
ble men and women, charitable men and women, fasting men and women,
chaste men and women, those who mention and remember God—men and
women—, for all those God has prepared forgiveness and a great reward. (as
cited in Abou-Bakr, 2001, para. 2-6)

All these narrations signify women's status in the *Hadith* and *Seera* and
in the early days of Islam. Historical documents reveal that women in the
first Islamic community, such as the ancient warrior *Nusyabah*, were ardent

feminists. Not only did *Um Salama*, as documented above, protest the exclusive mention of men in the Godly revelation, but so too did *Nusyabah* ask the Prophet (PBUH) why, in the *Quran*, God always addressed himself to men and never to women (Bouhdiba, 1998, p. 19). Afterward, God recognized the validity of her question for thereafter revelations referred to "believers" in both genders.

The *Quran* states:

> For Muslim men and women, for believing men and women, for devout men and women, for true men and women. For men and women who are patient and constant, for men and women who give charity, for men and women who fast (and deny themselves), for men and women who guard their chastity, and for men and women who engage in Allah's praise, for them has Allah prepared forgiveness and a great reward. (*Quran*, 33:35)

This verse maintains equality between the sexes. Women's opinions in the Prophet's (PBUH) lifetime were respected and even sought. Aisha, the Prophet's (PBUH) wife, was consulted during the completion of the *Hadith*. Umm Salamah was considered one of the best authorities on the Prophet's (PBUH) life and teachings. Aysha's knowledge of *Hadith* was also thought to have challenged some of the falsified *Hadith* that diminished the role of women (Baden, 1992, p. 4). Muslim men travelled all the way from Iraq, Syria, and Egypt to seek guidance from Aisha (Al-Asqalani, 1328, as cited in Al-Manea, 1984). Women also sought the Prophet's (PBUH) guidance on matters even while men were present (Al-Qaradawi, n.d.). Fatima, the Prophet's (PBUH) daughter, whose knowledge of poetry, history, and theology was acclaimed, delivered lectures on ethical and moral issues to the Prophet's (PBUH) companions. *Sukainah* bint *Al-Hussain's* house—the Prophet's (PBUH) granddaughter's house—was a meeting place for famous Arab poets and scholars. The history of the Prophet's (PBUH) time and of the early days of Islam reported names of Muslim women physicians, including *Zaynab*, *Rafidah*, *Umm Muta*, and *Umm Kabsha*, who were known experts in medicine and surgery (Al Munajjed, 1997; Dangor, 2001; Engineer, 1992). Muslim women have always played an active and important role in the shaping of early Islamic society. The Prophet's (PBUH) wives were "feminists" in that their agency and activism were integral to the foundation and growth of the first Islamic community and of Islam itself (Bullock, 2002).

Moreover, the *Quranic* stance on women's political participation is relatively clear. The *Quran* has not particularly prohibited women from having positions of leadership; in fact, the *Quran* presents Bilqis, the Queen of Sheba, as a female holding political power (Al-Tabari, 1964, as cited in Nashat &

Tucker, 1999). Thus, the idea that women could seek political or religious leadership is embedded in Islamic teachings to women.

During the early days of Islam, women worked in trade, medicine, and animal husbandry, and also participated in Islamic battles (Al-Manea, 1984). Historian Ibn Saad, in *At-Tabaqat*, included the biographies of many remarkable women of the Prophet Mohammed's (PBUH) time, some of whom fought in Muslim armies and demonstrated remarkable courage. In the battle of *Uhud*, for instance, *Umm Umara* fought in the defence of the Prophet (PBUH), and lost her arm in the fray (Ibn-Saad, 1958, p.18). These legends serve as a platform for opposing what seems to be a dominant theme in the work of many Muslim scholars who claim that, according to Islam, a woman's place is the home.

Prophet Mohammed's (PBUH) views on women's education are evident in statements such as "The search of knowledge is a duty for every Muslim male and female" and "Seek knowledge from the cradle to the grave."[10] The Prophet Mohammed (PBUH) is presented as a messenger who delivered God's message and as someone who is followed by all Muslims.

Both the *Quran* and *Sunna* mention women as active participants in public life. Differences of opinion among Muslim scholars have led many to interpret the sacred texts differently:

> Although Muslims accept the *Quran* as the primary and authoritative textual source containing the word of God, and *Hadith* as an inspired secondary source that sheds light on the interpretation of the verses of the *Quran*, when it comes to deriving laws from these sources, serious differences of opinion between the various schools of juristic thought arise. (Ali, 2000, p. 80)

I argue, as do many progressive Muslims, that the *Quran* is specific about many issues related to women, including their status vis-à-vis men. Islam is frequently interpreted by men, however, to the detriment of women (El-Nahhas, 1999). It is worth mentioning that the differences in scholarly opinion have become evident in, for instance, gender matters and family laws. This juristic thought is known as *Ijtehad*.

IJTEHAD

Ijtehad is the third source of Islamic laws. Based on the *Quran* and *Sunna*, *Ijtehad* is what Muslim religious scholars perceive to be appropriate in many matters pertaining to life. For instance, if Muslim scholars cannot extract a law from the *Quran* or the *Sunna*, they conclude an opinion based on this sacred text. The meaning of the word *Ijtehad*, in this context, follows:

> *Ijtihad* is a judgment on a legal or theological question, based on the text in *Al-Quran* or *Sunna*. Contrary to what many think, *Ijtihad* is a painstaking work based initially on Al-*Quran* and *Hadith*. It is considered one of the sources of Islamic *Shari'ah*. (Sakr & Al-Hussein, n.d.)

Many Muslim religious scholars, the majority of whom are male, have formed social rules based on their *Ijtehad* (consensus of opinion) (Afkhami, 1997; Alghamdi, 2002; Ask & Tjomsland, 1998; Basarudin, 2002; Hassan, 1999; Wadud, 1999). These highly conservative religious scholars—male, and from different Muslim backgrounds— "often act as interpretative authorities who are formally charged with distilling insights from the *Quran* and *Sunna* and with disseminating these scriptural interpretations to the Muslim laity" (Mason, 1988, as cited in Read & Bartkowski, 2000, p. 398). Also, Basarudin (2002) eloquently explains that "different systems of male dominance, and their internal variations according to class and ethnicity, exercise an influence that inflicts and modifies the actual practice of Islam as well as the ideological construction of what may be regarded as properly Islamic" (para. 8). Indeed, there is a divergence between theory and the practice of Islamic teachings to women. Moreover, Basarudin (2002), Hassan (1999), and Wadud (1999) agree that the negative attitudes pertaining to women that prevail in Muslim societies are rooted in theology (Ask & Tjomsland, 1998, p. 26). Theology is not born of divine revelation alone but conditioned by social circumstances and traditions prevalent in society. Hassan also stresses that the male-dominated interpretations have succeeded in manipulating the ontological, theological, sociological, and eschatological status of Muslim women to empower men and disempower women (Sharma & Young, 1999, p. 250). Further, Hassan claims that religion is being used as an instrument of oppression rather than as means of liberation (Basarudin, 2002, para. 9).

I argue that a major component of theology is *Ijtehad*. It is the *Ijtehad* that is used to conclude that a woman's duty is exclusively in her home. Thus, although in both the *Quran* and the *Sunna* women's role and status is highlighted as significant, many traditional Muslim scholars use the *Ijtehad* to provide an opposite view.

The conclusion to be drawn from a thorough reading of the thousands of reference works on Islamic jurisprudence is that it is a human science that was initially established by great thinkers. These were followed by the strict traditionalists who spurned deductive reasoning altogether and insisted on a dogmatic adherence to Scripture (Hassan, 1999). With their limited knowledge and lack of intellectual abilities, these so-called "expositers" invested the purely human field of Islamic jurisprudence with a divine character (Heggy, 2004, para. 21).

Misogynistic interpretations of the *Quranic* verses, Prophetic (PBUH) narrations, and Islamic philosophical and theological literature have been imposed for centuries (Altorki, 1988): "Women have been taught that the law of God orders them to stay close to their homes and unreservedly to obey their husbands" (Al-Manea, 1984, p. 25). Thus, mapping the conceptual framework of how women are portrayed and positioned in the sacred texts is a significant context for this research.

Although the *Quran* and the *Sunna* are foundational resources of the Islamic tenets, there is no single definitive interpretation of each or of both. Muslims do not have a single, divine interpretation of these sacred texts, and I argue that this lack of a sole divine interpretation is attributed to the flexibility of Islam as a faith. In other words, the absence of a definite interpretation of the Islamic divine texts means that Muslims are encouraged to interpret the *Quran* and *Hadith* texts in light of contemporary contexts. Many Muslim scholars argue that "the *Quran* and *Hadith* are translated [interpreted] within textual and historical contexts" (Nimer, 2002, p. 3). Indeed, Ali (2000) stated that "rights, duties, and obligations are reflective of culture, traditions, and customs of society as well as economic and political factors, and, in the Islamic traditions" (p. 5). In other words, any interpretation of the sacred texts is inclusive of the present context. Therefore, the interpretations provided by progressive Muslim scholars during this century are valid because they are inclusive of historical and contextual aspects other than those during the life of the Prophet (PBUH) and his companions.

In the past three decades, Arab Muslim feminists argued that any description of women's status, rights, and roles in Islam is ideological and based on an interpretation of the *Quran* and *Sunna* (Noor, 2005; Hassan, 1999). My research lays the groundwork for stressing the importance of progressive interpretations of the *Quran* and of Islamic teachings to women in general, and may also provide a role model for young Arab Muslim women. I argue that "Islam's universal message of equality and egalitarianism was delivered 15 centuries ago, but countless generations of Muslim women have yet to see the final and necessary culmination of that aspect of Islamic project" (Noor, 2003, p. 330).

Today, many educated Arab Muslim women legitimize their arguments regarding Islamic teachings to women by situating them within the
framework of Islam (Badran, 1994; Yamani, 1996). Many feminist Muslim
scholars argue that the restoration of Muslim women's status, especially
in the public sphere, would entail the need to refer to women's rights and
responsibilities in the early Islamic era. Among Muslim feminists, "Haleh
Afshar claims that the 'Islamist' women's return to the 'source' is the desire
to return to the golden age of Islam" (Afshar & Maynard, 2000; Hendessi &
Shafi, 2004, para. 24). Dangor (2001) rightly argues that changes in Arab
Muslim women's attitudes toward their roles, however, can be attributed to
new opportunities that education and work outside the home have provided
them "beyond the traditional confinement of marriage and motherhood"
(p. 127). Educated Arab Muslim women are now able to negotiate the existing inequalities and gender hierarchies within their cultural milieu
(Ali, 2000; Baden, 1992). More progressive Muslims, both women and
men, are addressing the need to reinstitute the Islamic laws and practices
set in the discourses of early Islam (Afshari, 1994), and are attempting
to develop feminism within Islam as they examine scriptural sources
and religious history to produce an Islamic theory of women's liberation
(Ghadbian, 1997).

In *Gender and Human Rights in Islam and International Law: Equal before
Allah, Unequal before Man?*, Shaheen Ali (2000) argues that Muslim women
can and are pursuing feminist goals by challenging and redefining their
cultural heritage, but this does not mean setting aside all cultural norms.
I contend that Muslim women need to redefine gender discourses without
abandoning all aspects of their culture by scrutinizing and critiquing aspects of cultural traditions that have no basis, that contradict the sacred
texts, and that are patriarchal in nature. Through her book, Ali (2000)
provides an exceptional illustration of the revival of Islamic law of women's
rights by a woman, for women. Her work—and the work of other Muslim
women—is a significant contribution which strives to ensure that Islam is
presented in a way other than as a restrictive and retrogressive tradition
(Ali, 2000).

Fazlur Rahman's *Themes of the Quran* (1980) outlines the important
themes in the *Quran* and clarifies the differences between modernist and
traditionalist interpretations of women's status in the *Quran* and the *Sunna*
(*Hadith* and *Seera*). Other input that has provided an analysis of the female
characters in the *Quran*, the *Hadith*, and in Islamic history includes *Women
in the Quran: Traditions and Interpretation* (1994) by Barbara Stowasser. D.A.
Spellberg's *Politics, Gender, and Islamic Past* (1994) is also important because

it looks at the early history of Islam. However, the most recent and significant contribution in this field is the work of Amina Wadud, the author of the groundbreaking *Quran and Women* (1999).

Part of understanding the achievements of Muslim women throughout early Islamic history is delineating aspects of that history relevant to Muslim women's role in society. For many centuries, however, in Arab Muslim societies, gender differences have been used as a tool for male domination and female oppression. Thus, Arab Muslim women's gender perceptions are not a result of individual, conscious choices, but are historically, socially, and culturally constructed. Cultural and patriarchal practices play a role in many aspects. For instance, Muslim women's legal and religious right to inherit, own, and dispose of property has often been circumvented by male relatives, including brothers, uncles, or husbands (Moghadam, 2003, 2004). Another traditional view of women's roles held by many Muslim religious scholars and based on rigid interpretations is that a woman's main and only role is as a wife and mother. This view prescribes that a woman holding any public role is a threat to the social order. Therefore, Muslim women are encouraged to value traditional roles such as that of housewife and mother, and careers outside the home have traditionally been considered a male domain (Al-Smadoni, 1991; Jawad, 1998; Mernissi, 1987; Schvaneveldt, Kerpelman & Schvaneveldt, 2005; Walther, 1993).

BRIEF HISTORY OF EARLY PROGRESSIVE ISLAMIC THOUGHT

Among early activist Islamic leaders were Mohammed Al-Ghazali (1058–1111) and Mohammed Abdu (1865–1905). Mohammed Abdu posited that Islam was the first community to recognize the full equality of women. "This argument places the foundation for most feminist arguments today in support of a 'pure' Islam to be found in the distant past to which women must return to regain their proper place beside their male counterparts in modern times" (Leo, 2005, p. 130).

Another prominent contemporary Arab Muslim journalist Safinaz Kazim argues that Islam granted women the right to work, vote, and participate in any productive way in the construction of society. She argues that Islam "view[s] men and women as Muslims, not as gendered beings" (as cited in Mooney, 1998, p. 100). Any perusal of Islamic history indicates that women played a prominent role in government, education, and politics. After reviewing progressive Muslim views of gender issues with regard to women's roles, one can conclude that Islam is an exceptionally dynamic religion.

While the *Quran* has been, as I have shown, interpreted by progressive Muslims as supportive of women's equality (Roded, 1999), and while political participation of women and equality between genders are all significant aspects of Islam, suggestions that women should not be subordinated and that Muslim women's rights should be enhanced are still frequently considered an overwhelming threat to Islam (Vidyasagar & Rea, 2004).

Unfortunately, these misogynistic, narrow views of women's roles and status prevail and are thoroughly embedded through different means, and Islam is persistently used to justify these views.

The following highlights two major factors that have shaped Arab Muslim feminists' perspectives: Patriarchy, and Colonialism and Imperialism.

Patriarchy

The term "patriarchy," traditionally defined by Greek and Roman law, refers to the role of the father, who, as the male household head, held ultimate legal and economic power over young males and all females. The basis of this law was the belief that women are not only different from men, who are used as the standard, but they are inferior based on their biology (Doumato, 1991; Gill, 2003; Moghadam, 2004). Women are generally physically weaker than men, and on this basis have been thought incapable of rationality; therefore, they were to be ruled and subordinated. An outstanding analysis provided by Simone de Beauvoir in *The Second Sex* was that "one is not born but rather becomes a woman" (Gill, 2003, p. 210). Simone de Beauvoir speaks to my experiences as I have learned and believed that the superior human being is always male and that woman is defined in relation to man. Gill continues: "To express what she perceived as women's immanence and men's transcendence, de Beauvoir coined the concept of woman as the 'other'" (Gill, 2003, p. 211). De Beauvoir explains:

> Humanity is male and man defines woman not in herself but as relative to him; she is not regarded as an autonomous being … she is the inessential as opposed to the essential. He is the subject, he is the absolute. She is the 'Other.'" (as cited in Gill, 2003, p. 211)

Feminist scholars across disciplines have maintained that the gender hierarchy in patriarchal societies places women in subordinate positions. Historically, gender roles and family relationships in Middle Eastern culture have been steeped in patriarchy (Walther, 1993; Schvaneveldt,

Kerpelman & Schvaneveldt, 2005). I argue that "traditional norms and patriarchal values have shaped the role [and status] of women in Muslim society" (Dangor, 2001, p. 126). Also, in Western culture, "patriarchy is alive and well. Men throughout the world continue to control politics and the economy while girls and women are disadvantaged and exploited in a variety of ways" (Weiler, 2001, p. 11).

Colonialism and Imperialism

> Women and women's bodies have become the central locus of tensions among internal and external discourses; Islamist and secularists persuasions; progressive and repressive forces. In some parts of Arab Muslim societies, the postcolonial period has produced a "neopatriarchy." While patriarchies obviously predate colonialism, contemporary patriarchies are products of the intersection between the colonial and indigenous domains of state and political processes. (Josef & Slyomovics, 2001, p. 10)

This passage needs to be thoroughly explained. In the late 18th to early 19th century, some Arabic Islamic states experienced a deep-seated transformation in all aspects of life—economic, political, and social—as a result of European colonial power. According to Ahmed (1992), the European political and cultural encroachments were complex and negative. The outcomes, however, of the process of change were positive, particularly for women. Unlike the Mongols' and the Turks' influence, the influence of British colonial power was constructive in some aspects mainly because it encouraged women to participate and engage in public domains of society, including the revolt against colonial power, such as the one that occurred in Algeria (Ahmed, 1999, as cited in Perkins, 2002). Yet many scholars, including Ahmed (1992, 1999) and Said (1983, 1989), argue that such advantages were not premeditated and colonial influence was used to control the colonized minds and lands. Others, like Fadwa El-Guindi (1999), an Egyptian feminist, argue that colonial contact and interference in Arab Muslim women's issues (e.g., Egypt and Algeria) have had negative repercussions on the colonized East.

Ahmed (1992) claims that "The subject of women first surfaced as a topic of consequence in the writing of Muslim men intellectuals in Egypt[11] and Turkey" (p. 128). Then, a new discourse on women emerged, overlapping old cultural traditions and religious beliefs on gender and linking issues of women, nationalism, national development, and cultural change. The social institutions and mechanisms that excluded women from traditionally male professions were slowly but surely dismantled (Ahmed, 1992; Zuhur, 1992). One of the goals of the colonial powers in that context was to abandon native cultures in colonized societies. The plan to discard native cultural traditions was considered by some as the most effective and quickest way to emancipate women, according to Ahmed (1992). However, Ahmed (1992) claims that there is no intrinsic connection between the issue of women's oppression and the issues of culture; Ahmed supports her argument with an example from Western feminist history. She states: "Western feminists do not therefore call for the abandonment of the entire Western heritage and the wholesale adoption of some other cultures as the only resource for Western women; rather they engage critically and constructively with that heritage in its own terms" (Ahmed, 1992, p. 128). Complex discussions of women's issues in colonial Arabic and Islamic states (e.g., Egypt and Algeria) became significant in the changes to the social construction of gender and political and cultural meaning.

The notion of disregarding native traditions and adopting Western ones became insistent and pronounced with colonial domination. It was in this context that the links between women's issues and issues of nationalism and culture were enduringly forged (Ahmed, 1992). The *hijab*, for instance, especially in the colonial era, connoted not a social but a political meaning. It was during that period of the British colonization of Egypt, when Huda Sharwai, an Egyptian activist, became well known for her march to abolish all Egyptian women's head covering, blaming it for the oppression of women (Ahmed, 1992; El Guindi, 1999). However, El-Guindi (1999) credits the strong emergence of the Islamic dress in Egypt in the late 19th century "as an expression to resistance to the West, an inversion of the Western value systems, and even as a partial acceptance of Western mores" (as cited in Perkins, 2002, p. 70). I hypothesize that in that historical context, the *hijab* became a political symbol.

At that time, all women's issues (e.g., the *hijab* and education) were used as links to the nationalism, culture, and politics of the region: "Progress or regress in the position and rights of women has often directly depended on which side of the debates over nationalism and culture the men holding or gaining political power espoused" (Ahmed, 1992, p. 129). By the end of the 19th century, Arab Muslim women in Egypt were pursuing a wide range of professions and activities such as teaching and nursing (L. Ahmed, 1999; El Saadawi, 1980). Some were observing the *hijab* while others were not.

Although colonialism opened the door to women's engagement in social life and made the topic of women's rights in Arab nations a central issue of national debates, it launched an ongoing struggle that prevails today between Muslim religious scholars and Western colonialist and imperialist powers. Since the 18th century with the colonialism of Arab Muslim Middle Eastern and North African societies by French and British colonial powers, the depiction in the Western discourses of "oppressive Arab men and powerless submissive women" has been predominant (Ahmed, 1992, 1999). Many orientalist narratives (Ahmed, 1992; Kandiyoti, 1991) are used to discredit Islam and native cultures. Women were positioned in these stories as either submissive or as exotic *harems* and this became the colonial "proof of the inferiority of Islam and the justification of their effort to undermine the Muslim religion and society" (Esposito, 1998; Hashim, 1999, p. 8). As a result, intensive tension prevails. Hashim (1999) continues:

> The result has been that as a defensive reaction, the Islamist position regarding women has become even more retrogressive and reactionary, to the extent that Afkhami, an academic and political activist, goes so far as to suggest that "contemporary Islamist regimes are most lucidly identified, and differentiated from other regimes, by the position they assign to women in the family and in society" (Afkhami 1995, p. 1). Any intervention targeted at women, or any attempt by feminists to change the position of Muslim women from a position which totally rejects Islam, results in accusations of cultural imperialism or neo-imperialism. (Kandiyoti, 1991, as cited in Hashim, 1999, p. 8)

The Arab post-colonial theorist Edward Said's (1978) study, *Orientalism*, suggests that the relation between "West" and "non-West" has been characterized by conflict, division, and dichotomies as an unavoidable consequence of and reaction to colonialism, but how have these concepts reconstructed gender issues in the Arab world? I argue that women's issues since the colonialist period of Arab Muslim societies have been situated between colonialist—currently imperialist—discourses that manipulate the public by prorating women's "liberation" and women's issues and religious extremists' discourses, which are also using women's issues to fulfill their own political agenda.

The discourse of patriarchal colonialism used feminism and the issue of Arab women's status to lead a colonial attack on the colonized societies. For instance, ironically, prominent men who were well known as the enemies of feminism in their own societies, such as Lord Cromer, the British consul general, advocated against the oppression of Arab Muslim women in Arab society. Yet this only legitimizes Western domination (Ahmed, 1992).

According to Ahmed (1992), this justified "colonial policies of actively trying to subvert the cultures and the religions of the colonized people" (Ahmed, 1992, p. 243).

With the British occupation of Egypt, which began in 1882, upper-middle-class Egyptian men were educated in Westernized secular schools, which applied the British educational system. Upper-class Egyptians, therefore, rejected their own cultural and traditional ways and favoured the Western lifestyle, creating a division between themselves and the middle class. Ahmed (1992) continues: "Issues of culture and attitudes toward Western ways were intertwined with issues of class and access to economic resources, positions and status" (p. 147). For instance, the concept of the *harem* is perpetuated by Western colonies in the Middle Eastern countries, especially in Egypt. Said (1978) addresses how frequently Western orientalism was concurrently symbolizing Muslim Arab women's oppression and eroticism. The word *harem* literally means holy or forbidden, and the word is originally[12] used in reference to the part of a house preserved for female members of the family. The *harem* is a system that exists in Arab and Muslim societies and still prevails. It does not necessarily reflect a negative connotation. The *harem* illustrates a physical distance between men and women in public and private spheres. Yet the concept of the *harem*, as presented by Western historians in the colonial era, symbolizes eroticism and exoticism (Afshar, 2000). This association influenced the construction of women's gender in Arab Muslim society as well as abroad with increasing immigration to North America and Europe. I argue that the *harem* and other Arab Muslim concepts are "culturally and contextually specific" (Doumato, 1996), and one cannot appreciate the multiplicity of its meanings in that context. Thus, with cultural specific concepts, I concur with Haleh Afshar (2000) that "feminism [needs] to respect the deep cultural and historical differences that have existed in the lived and remembered lives of women the world over" (p. 914).

During the British colonialism of Egypt, the Egyptian scholar and thinker Qasim Amin wrote *The Emancipation for Women* (1899) in which he attacked the poor treatment of women, which he saw as a violation of Islamic principles. He sought to demonstrate that the freedom and emancipation of women was the intention of Islamic teaching. Traditionalist scholars furiously disputed that Amin was speaking in the name of Islam; however, not being a graduate of an Islamic university led him to avoid the religious aspect of Egyptian women's issues in his second contribution. *The New Women*, (1901) Amin's second book, avoids discussing Islamic teaching to women; in fact, this book is believed by some to promote Western perceptions of women (Mooney, 1998). This exemplifies how the tension is persistent between progressive and traditional scholars.

The period following colonialism gave intellectuals hope for the realization of a new reality without the oppression of colonialists and imperialists on the one hand and religious extremists on the other (El-Nahhas, 1999; Mooney, 1998). However, since the late 1980s, a new wave of cultural and economic domination appeared; this one operated from a distance and became a new ruling force—so-called neo-colonialism. This new power is a dominant force in the Middle East and utilizes many tools, including the media. According to Perkins (2002), Ahmed (1992) employed imagery to gender the European West and Arab East. The European West and the Arab East have been conventionally gendered throughout colonialist discourses as the West (the male) copulating with the East (the female) to produce a progeny—the Islamic resistance (L. Ahmed, 1999; Perkins, 2002). Yet Perkins (2002), in her analyses, assumes that Ahmed does not employ these terms naively; rather, that Ahmed uses this language to voice the irony inherent in her claim of the tension between Islamic and colonial—currently imperialist—powers (p. 70) that constantly manipulates women's issues and gender discourse.

From the discussion above, I provide a conceptual framework on "how 'modernist' looking West and 'traditionalist looking' East each constructed an essentially new vision of feminism and its relation to new constructions of faith, culture, and femininity, and the analysis of religious meanings" (Moghissi, 2000, as cited in Afshar & Maynard, 2000, p. 811). This made forming an Islamic identity for Muslim women, myself included, as well as gender discourse, a complex matter.

My book focuses on educated Arab Muslim women's gender perceptions and roles, and the ways in which they perceive these roles. The brief overview of the socio-cultural context is significant because "people can never be regarded simply as individuals standing before society or as independent human beings" (Gilmore, 1987, p. 24, in Harris, 2004, p. 24). In Arab Muslim societies, "gender roles depend entirely on society's perception of men's and women's roles at a given time and place. The meaning given to gender identity is also subject to change" (Tohidi & Bodman, 1998, p. 165).

Gender roles, social meanings given to differences between men and women, are distinguished from sexual functions that are based on biological differences. However, "many Muslim women in the Middle East and North Africa are unwilling to accept the notion of 'differences' that translates into unequal rights and second class citizenship" (Moghadam, 2003, p. 19).

It is of great importance to include the conceptual frameworks around Islam and the Arabic culture, both in their socio-historical contexts and with regard to their connection to gender relations. I have attempted to convey my perception, and the perceptions of the Arab Muslim women interviewed: "there is a significant gap between what the *Quran* says and the manner in which its teachings are practiced" (Ali, 1993, as cited in Hashim, 1999, p. 9).

THE METHODOLOGY THAT HAS INFORMED MY WORK: BRIEF OVERVIEW

I employed narrative inquiry as a method and a methodology because I contend that knowledge is found in the ordinary thinking of people in everyday life (Smith, 1987a, 1987b), particularly when indigenous people are researching their own lives. This concurs with Said (1987), who said that it is the responsibility of indigenous people to provide their narratives to counter the vision of outsiders. The narratives of Arab Muslim women allowed me to untangle women's perceptions and counter the Orientalist portrayal of Muslim women.

I have used narrative in this research as a lens and a means to explore Arab Muslim women's gender perceptions, particularly in a changing socio-historical context. Being a part of Arab Muslim society, and now a part of a new and distinct culture as a Canadian, may change these women's perceptions. Additionally, "narrating is a form of social positioning" (Daiute, 2004, p. 113)—one is positioned by one's narratives.

In my decision to use narrative inquiry as a method, "I needed a methodology that would not just seek facts and events, but would look for ways in which such narrated facts and events suggest a woman's relationship with the society in which she lives, and her current construction of self" (Mann, 1998, p. 81). Like Atkinson (1998), I contend that if we want to know the unique experience and perspectives of an individual, there is no better way to get this than in the person's own voice (p. 5).

Narrative can be used as a method of inquiry to examine gender inequalities evidenced through people's stories. Erika Friedl (1994) argues that,

> When people think and talk about themselves, about their lives, they do so in *stories* [italics added]. Things and people and relationships are understood, structured, and remembered in narratives. The construction of gender and the revelation of identities happen in accounts of what

people think and do, in the stories they tell about themselves and about each other. (p. 91)

Stories from childhood and one's upbringing may reveal many aspects of one's life and one's perceptions of gender. In some cases, "to remember what it was like to be a child, being prepared for traditional roles in [a] society, and then to violate those roles by analytic discussion was too painful" (Bateson, 1990, p. 33), and that pain needed to be explored and shared. Additionally, narrative inquiry allows everyday experience, often taken for granted, to gain further importance and prominence. Prus (1996) suggests that,

> Our everyday lived experience is so taken for granted as to go unnoticed, it is often through breakdown that the researcher achieves flashes of insight into the lived world, although it is important to note that the taken-for-granted, everyday world can never be made completely explicit. (p. 59)

A significant characteristic of narrative is that it can allow for new meanings and diverse ways of knowing to emerge. Narrative becomes a vehicle for the "'story of origin,' the accommodating and hospitable space for new stories to evolve, and the fertile grounds for unrealized potential and possibility" (DeLuca, 1996, p. 53). In narrative inquiry, particularly in my research, stories told by a participant are of great importance. The stories are the backbone of this endeavour, which is to provide for a better understanding of the lives and dreams of Arab Muslim women.

I used open-ended questions, given before the interviews, since they offer a wide range of perspectives and provide more details of the participants' experiences. Indeed, choosing open-ended questions for narrative inquiry allowed the Arab Muslim women's lived experiences to be shared and appreciated. In my research, I combined open-ended questions that probed for narrative with questions that probed for demographic information.[13] I started my interviews with a demographic questionnaire that posed questions about participants' location, date of birth, education, profession, marital status, number of children, and details about their educational background.

NARRATIVE ANALYSIS: BRIEF OVERVIEW

Once the data were collected, tapes were transcribed. I transcribed the interview narrations exactly as spoken, including notations for non-verbal information, such as pauses, laughs, sighs, and utterances such as "hmmm" and "mmmm." I printed the transcripts in a narrative text format for data analysis. As Didion (1961) suggests, narrative fills the space between "what happens" and "what it means" (as cited in Kramp, 2004, p. 107). Yet a detailed analysis is a necessary next step. "Narrative analysis allows for systematic study of personal experience and meaning: how events have been constructed by active participants" (Riessman, 1993, p. 70).

Aristotle said that every story has a beginning, a middle, and an end. My open-ended questions and my analysis follow the same framework. I begin by providing a biographical account of each participant, addressing the women's experiences of schooling in their societies of origin and their effects on their construction of gender perceptions and identities. These perceptions are then examined in terms of whether or not they have varied as a result of attending Canadian academic institutions.

During the analysis stage, I read, reread, and searched for themes. Thematic and content analyses were used to analyze the women's narratives. In the thematic analyses, different streams of data were analyzed for recurring topics and themes regarding the participants' social position, self-understanding, and experiences (Smith, 1992; Winter & McClelland, 1978). According to this method, the women's narratives were examined for thematic content that might reveal the ideological, motivational, and idiosyncratic meanings of individuals and groups, relationships, symbols, and institutions.

Thematic analysis of content involves noticing recurring themes and patterns of association in content (i.e., themes that co-occur), in a single text, and comparing participants' narrations or sections of texts to detect particularized meanings by contrast. These two procedures—interpretive analyses of association and of contrast—sometimes yield a codified set of categories that enables the systematic content analysis of many texts (Stewart & Malley, 2004, p. 225). When thematic analysis is itself the goal, the systematic coding of texts is always secondary to an initial thematic analysis in which patterns of association and contrast are uncovered (Stewart & Malley, 2004, p. 225; Winter, 1973). In this research, I have used thematic analysis to explore how the participants have narrated their gender perceptions and educational achievements.

NOTES

1. The Muslim holy book, which is the primary source for knowing God's intentions (Kvam, Schearing & Ziegler, 1999).

2. The Prophet Mohammed's (PBUH) words and practices.
3. The collection of the Prophet's (PBUH) sayings.
4. Some literature was reviewed to provide an interpretation of the *Quran* and the *Hadith*.
5. *Sharia* refers to Islamic law and is based on the *Quran, Hadith*, and *Ijtehad*.
6. *Quran*, translated by Abdullah Yousef Ali: verse, XX, 114, p. 814.
7. *Quran*, translated by Abdullah Yousef Ali: verse, LVIII, 11, p. 15.
8. *Quran*, translated by Abdullah Yousef Ali: verse, IX, 71, p. 461.
9. An Arabic word meaning "immigration," and in this context refers to the Prophet Mohammed's (PBUH) and his companions' immigration from Mecca to Madinah.
10. These phrases are attributed to the Prophet Mohammed (PBUH).
11. Qasim Amin is one of the early progressive Egyptian intellectuals.
12. This is the meaning of the word *harem* in the Arab Muslim social context.
13. In the appendices, I provide both demographic questions and open-ended questions.

Appendix B

LETTER OF INFORMATION

QUILTED NARRATIVES OF ARAB MUSLIM WOMEN'S TAPESTRY: INTERSECTING EDUCATIONAL EXPERIENCES AND GENDER PERCEPTIONS

My name is Amani Alghamdi, and I am a PhD student at the Faculty of Education at the University of Western Ontario. I am currently conducting a research about change, if any, in gender perception in educated Arab Muslim women after their education in Canada. I would like to invite you to participate in this research.

The aim of the research is to explore how living and attending a Canadian educational institution might have influenced Arab Muslim women's gender perceptions.

Demographic and identification information for the study will be collected through a written demographic survey. Once the survey has been completed, you are invited to participate in semi-structured interviews (one to two hours for the initial interview). The interview will be audio-recorded. A 30-minute follow-up will be arranged to allow you to respond to the transcripts. If the conversations in the interviews divulge information about unreported abuse, then anonymity cannot be guaranteed and the researcher will report that to the authorities.

Should you consent to participate in this research, please be aware that you have the right to withdraw at any time. You may also decline to answer any specific question that you prefer not to answer. If you agree to participate in this project, please sign the consent form on the next page.

If you have any question about this research, or any comments to make now or at a later date, please contact Amani Alghamdi (661-2111, ext 88577) or my supervisor, Dr. Sharon Rich (661-2111, ext. 88551).

Sincerely,

Amani K. Hamdan Alghamdi
PhD candidate

Appendix C

IDENTIFICATION QUESTIONS (BACKGROUND QUESTIONS)[1]

Date of Birth/ Place of Birth	Total Years of Schooling and Field of Study	Profession	Marital Status (S/M)	Year of Coming to Canada	Number of Children (if any)

I. EDUCATIONAL HISTORY

Level of Education	Age: Entering School/ Leaving School	Location Urban/Rural	School Type
a. Primary			
Comments			
b. Junior			
Comments			
c. High School			
Comments			
d. University/ College			
Comments			
e. Graduate			
Comments			

NOTE

1. Some of these questions were adapted from other studies (Qin, 2000; Cao, 1997; El-Nahhas, 1999).

Appendix D

ARAB MUSLIM WOMEN INTERVIEW GUIDE [1]

Key questions and potential probes (not all questions will be asked):

1. Tell me about your *family* in which you were born.
Probes
   (a) What was expected of you as a daughter?
   (b) If you have (a) brother(s), to what extent were you treated differently
        from him (them)?
   (c) To what extent does religion (Islam) and/or culture (Arab and Middle
        Eastern) influence the way boys and girls were treated in the family?
   (d) If you have children, tell me more about them (i.e., age, sex, educa-
        tional level).
   (e) When you were pregnant, did it make any difference to you whether you
        had a boy or a girl? What was your husband's and family's attitude?

2. Tell me about your *educational experiences* in your own society.
Probes
   (a) Where was the school located (rural/urban)?
   (b) Which of your school experiences influenced you the most?
   (c) Was the school you attended a sex-segregated school? To what extent
        did that influence you?
   (d) What was expected of you as a "good" student?
   (e) To what extent were your parents interested in your schooling?
   (f) To what extent did your parents encourage/discourage your school-
        ing (i.e., excused you from household chores, assisted you with your
        studies, offered you special awards, embarrassed you when you did
        well in school, expressed pride in your success in school, other)?
   (g) What were your favourite school subjects? Why?
   (h) How did you happen to decide on a field of study? Were you advised or
        assigned?

(i) What made you decide to quit or continue school at this point?

(j) If you went to a mixed school (boys with girls), were there differences in the expectations for the boys and the girls?

(k) To what extent did the cultural beliefs and or religious beliefs hinder or support your educational pursuit (i.e., a belief that women are not as smart as men, a belief that it is more important to educate sons than daughters, a belief that women should be educated only up to a certain age or degree).

3. Tell me about your educational experiences in Canada.
Probes

(a) What is new about your educational experiences here?

(b) What is the male/female ratio between faculty and students where you study? How does this compare to your country of origin? In what ways has this affected the way you experience school?

(c) How has your field of study affected the way you think of women's role in any society?

(d) What kinds of women's issues events, workshops, conferences, lectures, and/or courses have you attended since you came to Canada? In what ways have they influenced your thoughts on women's roles?

4. Tell me about your *work experiences*, if any, in your country of origin.
Probes

(a) What was expected of you as a "good" worker?

(b) If you were working in a mixed or sex-segregated workplace, how were you treated compared to your male colleagues? In your view, were there differences in the expectations of male and female workers?

(c) To what extent does the religion (Islam) and/or the culture (Arab and Middle Eastern) influence the treatment of men and women in the workplace?

(d) What are your thoughts on the idea that women are naturally better at some activities than men, and men are naturally better than women at other activities?

(e) In your opinion, what are the best ways women can contribute to society? A man?

5. If married, in what ways has *your marriage* had an impact on your perception of your gender role?
Probes

(a) How did you meet and choose your husband?

(b) How did you decide to pursue your education when you got married?

(c) In what ways does having university education influence a woman's (man's) choice for a partner?

(d) Some people believe that it is bad for the marriage if a woman has more education than her husband. Other people think that it is fine for a woman to have more education than her husband. How do you feel about this?

(e) Suppose a woman has to choose between either marriage or pursuing her educational dreams (i.e., a PhD). What do you think she should do? Why?

(f) If you worked in your country of origin, how did you manage your work and family responsibilities? Who took care of housework and family responsibilities? How much help did you have from others (husband, in-laws, maids, parents)?

(g) What was expected of a "good" wife and a "good" mother in your family?

(h) Who is considered an ideal woman in your society? To what extent, if any, has this changed for you?

(i) If you live in Canada with your family (husband and children), how do you manage combining studies or work and family responsibilities?

(j) How do you share your family responsibilities (housework, child care, household decisions, bills management, children's education, and family planning) with your husband? How did that change since you came to Canada?

(k) To what extent does your religion (Islam) and/or culture (Arab and Middle Eastern) influence the sharing of family responsibilities?

6. In your experience, do people in your country of origin believe that *women and men are equal*?

Probes

(a) To what extent does your religion (Islam) and/or culture (Arabic and Middle Eastern) influence the way you think *of the equality of men and women*?

(b) To what extent do your family (your parents, your husband) and your close friends share your opinion on this matter?

(c) How has your idea about equality between the sexes changed, shifted, or modified since you came to Canada?

(d) Some people believe that a university and/or higher education are equally important for both men and women. Other people believe that it is more important for men to have a university and/or a higher degree. What is your opinion on this?

    (e) When choosing your field of study in Canada, what issue or problem did you face?

    (f) Who encouraged or discouraged you?

    (g) If you were not married, to what extent would it be harder to immigrate or study abroad? To what extent is it hard for a single woman to immigrate and study in Canada?

7. Tell me about your *social life* before and after coming to Canada.
Probes

    (a) Before coming to Canada, did you have any kind of contact with unrelated men (i.e., men other than relatives)?

    (b) How has your social life changed since coming to Canada?

    (c) How has the change, if any, in your social life changed the ways you think of women's roles?

    (d) To what extent does your religion (Islam) and/or culture (Arab and Middle Eastern) influenced the way you thought of women's role?

    (e) Describe the types of interaction that you would have with men in your home country.

    (f) Describe the relationship you had with women in your society.

    (g) To what extent have your interactions with men changed since you came to Canada?

    (h) What kind of contact do you have with Canadian female friends and how do they influence you?

    (i) How have your views of men's and women's interactions changed since you came to Canada and went to Canadian schools?

    (j) What do you think of women's role in Canadian society? How do you compare women's roles here, based on your contacts with Canadian women, with women's roles in your country of origin? How do you explain the similarities and/or differences?

    (k) How have your thoughts of women's roles changed since you came here?

NOTES

1.   Some of these questions were adapted from other studies (Qin, 2000; Cao, 1997; El-Nahhas, 1999).

References

Abdo, D. (2002). Uncovering the harem in the classroom. *Women's Studies Quarterly, 30*(1/2), 227–238.

Abou-Bakr, O. (2001). Islamic feminism? What's in the name? Preliminary reflections. *Association for Middle East Women's Studies, 15*(4)–16(1), 1–4.

Abu-Laban, B. (1980). *An olive branch on the family tree: The Arabs in Canada.* Toronto: McClelland & Stewart Ltd. in association with the Multiculturalism Directorate, Department of the Secretary of State and the Canadian Government Publishing Centre, Supply and Services Canada.

Abu-Laban, S.M. (1991). Family and religion among Muslim immigrants and their descendants. In E. Waugh, S.M. Abu-Laban & R.B. Qureshi (Eds.), *Muslim families in North America* (pp. 6–31). Edmonton: University of Alberta Press.

Abu-Lughod, L. (1986). *Veiled sentiments: Honor and poetry in a Bedouin society.* Berkeley: University of California Press.

Abu-Lughod, L. (Ed.). (1998). *Remaking women: Feminism and modernity in the Middle East.* Princeton: Princeton University Press.

Afkhami, M. (1997). Promoting women's rights in the Muslim world. *Journal of Democracy, 8*(1), 157–166.

Afshar, H. (1989). Education: Hopes, expectations, and achievements of Muslim women in West Yorkshire. *Gender and Education, 1*(3), 261–272.

Afshar, H. & Maynard, M. (2000). Gender and ethnicity at the millennium: From margin to center. *Ethnic and Racial Studies, 23*(5), 805–819.

Afshari, R. (1994). Egalitarian Islam and misogynist Islamic tradition: A critique of the feminist reinterpretation of Islamic history and heritage. *Critique: Journal of Critical Studies of Iran and the Middle East, 4*(Spring), 13–34.

Agnew, V. (2002). *Gender, Migration, and Citizenship Resources Project. Part II: A literature review and bibliography on health.* A research project of the Centre for Feminist Research no. II. Toronto: York University.

Ahmad, F. (2001). Modern traditions? British Muslim women and academic achievement. *Gender and Education, 13*(2), 137–152.

Ahmed, L. (1989). Feminism and cross cultural inquiry: The terms of discourse in Islam. In E. Weed (Ed.), *Coming to terms: Feminism, theory, politics* (pp. 145–151). New York: Routledge.

Ahmed, L. (1992). *Women and gender in Islam: Historical roots of modern debate*. New Haven: Yale University Press.

Ahmed, L. (1999). *A border passage: From Cairo to America—a woman's journey*. New York: Farrar, Straus, and Giroux.

Ahmed, S. (1999). Islam and development: Opportunities and constraints for Somali women. *Gender and Development, 7*(1), 69–72.

Aisenberg, N. & Harrington, M. (1988). *Women of academe: Outsiders in the sacred grove*. Amherst: University of Massachusetts Press.

Al-Adib, A. (1967). *Manhaj at-Tarbihah 'ind al-imam Ali'*. An-Najaf: al-Matba'ah al-Hadiariyyah.

Al-Faruqi, M. (2000). Women's self-identity in the Qur'an and Islamic law. In G. Webb (Ed.), *Windows of faith: Muslim women scholar-activists in North America* (pp. 72–101). Syracuse: Syracuse University Press.

Alghamdi, A. (2002). *Bringing a global education perspective to understand the "other": A case study of Western myths of Muslim women*. Unpublished MA thesis, Mount Saint Vincent University, Halifax.

Al-Hibri, A. (1982). *Women and Islam*. Toronto: Pergamon Press.

Al-Hibri, A. (2000). An introduction to Muslim women's rights. In G. Webb (Ed.), *Windows of faith: Muslim women scholar-activists in North America* (pp. 51–71). Syracuse: Syracuse University Press.

Ali, K. (2006). *Sexual ethics and Islam: Feminist reflections on Qur'an, Hadith, and jurisprudence*. Oxford: Oneworld.

Ali, S. (2000). *Gender and human rights in Islam and international law: Equal before Allah, unequal before man?* The Hague & Boston: Kluwer Law International.

Al-Manea, A. (1984). *Historical and contemporary policies of women's education in Saudi Arabia*. Unpublished PhD thesis, University of Michigan, Ann Arbor.

Al Munajjed, M. (1997). *Women in Saudi Arabia today*. New York: St. Martin's Press.

Al-Qaradawi, Y. (n.d.). *The voice of a woman in Islam*. Retrieved June 1, 2005, from http://www.albany.edu/~ha4934/qaradawi.html

Al-Smadoni, A.E. (1991). Parents' expectations in raising their preschool children and its relation with some family factors. *Educational Studies, 35*, 207–233.

Althaus, F. (1997). Female circumcision: Rite of passage or violation of rights? *International Family Planning Perspectives, 23*(3).

Altorki, S. (1988). At home in the field. In S. Altorki & C. El-Solh (Eds.), *Arab women in the field: Studying your own society* (pp. 49–68). Syracuse: Syracuse University Press.

Alvi, S., Hoodfar, H. & McDonough, S. (Eds.). (2003). *The Muslim veil in North America: Issues and debates*. Toronto: Women's Press.

Amawi, A. (1996). Women and property rights in Islam. In S. Sabbagh (Ed.), *Arab women between defiance and restraint* (pp. 151–158). New York: Olive Branch Press.

Apple, M. (1999). *Power, meaning, and identity: Essays in critical educational studies.* New York: P. Lang.

Arab Women: Out of the shadows, into the world. (2004, June 17). Retrieved July 3, 2005, from http://www.religiousconsultation.org/News

Arebi, S. (1994). *Women & words in Saudi Arabia: The politics of literary discourse.* New York: Columbia University Press.

Arkoun, M. (1994). *Rethinking Islam: Common questions, uncommon answers.* Boulder: Westview Press.

Ask, K. & Tjomsland, M. (Eds.). (1998). *Women and Islamization: Contemporary dimensions of discourse on gender relations.* New York & Oxford: Berg.

Athar, S. (Ed.). (1996). *Sex education: An Islamic perspective.* Chicago: Kazi Publications.

Atkinson, R. (1998). *The life story interview.* Thousand Oaks: Sage Publications.

Awan, S. (1989). *People of the Indus Valley: Pakistani-Canadians.* Ottawa: Sadiq Noor Alan Awan.

Azmi, S. (2001). Muslim educational institutions in Toronto, Canada. *Journal of Muslim Minority Affairs, 21*(2), 259–272.

Badawi, J. (1995). *Gender equity in Islam: Basic principles.* Plainfield: American Trust Publications.

Baden, S. (1992). *The position for women in Islamic countries: Possibilities, constraints, and strategies for change* (Report no. 4). Brighton: Institute of Development Studies.

Badran, M. (1994). Gender activism: Feminists and Islamists in Egypt. In V. Moghadam (Ed.), *Identity politics and women: Cultural reassertions and feminisms in international perspective* (pp. 202–217). Boulder: Westview Press.

Badran, M. (2005). Between secular and Islamic feminism/s: Reflections on the Middle East and beyond. *Journal of Middle East Women's Studies, 1*(1), 6–29.

Badran, M. & Cooke, M. (1990). *Opening the gates: A century of Arab feminist writing.* London: Virago Press.

Bailey, K. (1993). *The girls are the ones with the pointy nails: An exploration of children's conceptions of gender.* London: Althouse Press.

Bainton, R. (1957). *What Christianity says about sex, love, and marriage.* New York: Association Press.

Baksh, N. (2005). *Waking up to progressive Muslims.* Retrieved May 15, 2005, from http://www.ihyafoundation.com/index.php?page=nazim_baksh/15

Barazangi, N. (2000). Muslim women's Islamic higher learning as a human right: Theory and practice. In G. Webb (Ed.), *Windows of faith: Muslim women scholar-activists in North America* (pp. 22–47). Syracuse: Syracuse University Press.

Barazangi, N. (2004). *Woman's identity and the Qur'an: A new reading.* Florida: University of Florida Press.

Bardach, A. (1993, August). Tearing off the veil. *Vanity Fair, 122–158.*

Barlas, A. (2002). *"Believing women" in Islam: Unreading patriarchal interpretations of the Quran.* Austin: University of Texas Press.

Basarudin, A. (2002). *Are Islam and human rights compatible? Revisiting Muslim women's rights.* Retrieved June 1, 2005, from the website of the Islamic Institute for Human Rights (website no longer active).

Basit, T. (1997). *Eastern values, Western milieu: Identities and aspirations of adolescents British Muslim girls.* Aldershot: Ashgate.

Bassey, M. (1999). *Case study research in educational settings.* Buckingham: Open University Press.

Bateson, M. (1990). *Composing a life.* New York: Atlantic Monthly Press.

Beddoe, D. (1983). *Discovering women's history: A practical manual.* London & Boston: Pandora Press.

Berger, P. (1963). *Invitation to sociology.* Garden City: Doubleday.

Berkey, J. (1996). Circumcision circumscribed: Female excision and cultural accommodation. *International Journal of Middle East Studies, 28,* 19–38.

Bhabha, H. (1990). The third space: Interview with Homi Bhabha. In J. Rutherford (Ed.), *Identity* (pp. 206–221). London: Lawrence & Wishart.

Bhabha, H. (1994). *The location of culture.* New York: Routledge.

Bhimani, S. (2003). *Majalis al-ilm: Sessions of knowledge.* Toronto: TSAR.

Bjorklund, K. & Olsson, A. (2005). *Glass ceiling for women in academia.* Retrieved April, 4, 2005, from http://www.esib.org/project/equality/EQhandbook/ch2.html.

Booth, M. (2001). Woman in Islam: Men and the "women's press" in turn of the 20th century Egypt. *International Journal of Middle East Studies, 33*(2), 171–201.

Bouhdiba, A. (1998). *Sexuality in Islam* (2nd ed.), A. Sheridan (Trans.). London: Saqi Books.

Bourdieu, P.E.A. (1999). *The weight of the world: Social suffering in contemporary society,* P. Ferguson (Trans.). Cambridge: Polity Press.

Bruner, J. (2003). Self-making narratives. In R. Fivush & C. Haden (Eds.), *Autobiographical memory and the construction of a narrative self: Developmental and cultural perspectives* (pp. 209–226). Mahwah: L. Erlbaum.

Buitelaar, M., Ketner, S. & Bosma, H. (2004). Identity strategies of adolescent girls of Moroccan descent in the Netherlands. *Identity: A Journal of Theory and Research, 4*(2), 145–169.

Bullock, K. (2002). *Rethinking Muslim women and the veil: Challenging historical and modern stereotypes.* Herndon: The International Institute of Islamic Thought.

Bullock, K. (Ed.). (2005). *Muslim women activists in North America: Speaking for ourselves.* Texas: University of Texas Press.

Burlet, S. & Reid, H. (1998). A gendered uprising: Political representation and minority ethnic communities. *Ethnic and Racial Studies, 21*(2), 270–287.

Camarota, S. (2002). *The Muslim wave: Dealing with immigration from the Middle East.* Retrieved June 12, 2005, from http://www.cis.org/articles/2002/sac830.htm

Cameron, D. (1985). *Feminism and linguistic theory.* New York: St. Martin's Press.

Cao, L. (1997). *Dreams and dilemmas: Chinese female students' experiences of overseas education in the United States.* Unpublished PhD dissertation, Teachers College, Columbia University, Columbia.

Carbaugh, D. (2001). "The people will come to you": Black feet narrative as a resource for contemporary living. In J. Brockmeier & D. Carbaugh (Eds.), *Narrative and identity: Studies in autobiography, self, and culture* (pp. 103–128). Amsterdam: John Benjamins.

Cayer, C. (1996). *Hijab, narrative, and production of gender among second-generation, Indo-Pakistani, Muslim women in Greater Toronto.* Unpublished MA thesis, York University, Toronto.

Chaudhry, L. (1997). Researching "my people," researching myself: Fragments of reflexive tale. *Qualitative Studies in Education, 10*(4), 441–453.

Chodorow, N. (1978). *The reproduction of mothering: psychoanalysis and the sociology of gender.* Berkeley: University of California Press.

Clandinin, J. & Connelly, M. (2000). *Narrative inquiry: Experience and story in qualitative research.* San Francisco: John Wiley & Sons.

Cook, S. (n.d.). *The myth of the hymen continues.* Retrieved January 5, 2005, from http://www.islamicgarden.com/mythhymen.html

Cooper, J. (1991). Telling our own stories. In C. Witherell & N. Noddings (Eds.), *Stories lives tell: Narrative and dialogue in education* (pp. 96–112). New York: Teachers College Press.

Czarniawska, B. (2004). *Narratives in social science research.* New Delhi: Sage Publications.

Dahl, T. (1997). *Muslim family law: Study of women's rights in Islam.* Oslo & Oxford: Scandinavian University Press.

Daiute, C. (2004). Creative uses of cultural genres. In C. Daiute & C. Lightfoot (Eds.), *Narrative analysis: Studying the development of individuals in society* (pp. 111–133). Thousand Oaks & London: Sage Publications.

Damji, T. & Lee, C.M. (1995). Gender role identity and perceptions of Ismaili Muslim men and women. *Journal of Social Psychology, 135,* 215–223.

Dangor, S. (2001). Historical perspective, current literature, and an opinion survey among Muslim women in contemporary South Africa: A case study. *Journal of Muslim Minority Affairs, 21*(1), 109–129.

Daniel, N. (1993). *Islam and the West: The making of an image.* Oxford: Oneworld.

231

Deak, J. (2003). *Girls will be girls: raising confident and courageous daughters*. New York: Hyperion.

Dei, G. (1997). Race and production of identity in schooling experiences of African Canadian youth. *Discourse: Studies in the Central Politics of Education, 18*(2).

de Lauretis, T. (1990). Upping the anti (sic) in feminist theory. In M. Hirsch and E. Fox Keller (Eds.), Conflicts in feminism. New York: Routledge.

DeLuca, S. (1996). *Uncovering the passion: The reclaiming of self in the teaching lives of nurse educators*. Unpublished MA thesis, University of Western Ontario, London.

Dickerson, A., & Taylor, M. (2000). Self-limiting behaviour in women: Self-esteem and self-efficacy as predictors. *Group and Organization Management, 25*(2), 191–210.

Didion, J. (1961). *Slouching toward Bethlehem*. New York: Dell.

Douglas, J. (1976). *Investigative social research: Individual and team field research* (vol. 29). Beverly Hills: Sage Publications.

Doumato, E. (1991). Hearing other voices: Christian women and the coming of Islam. *International Journal of Middle East Studies, 23*(2), 177–199.

Doumato, E. (1996). Am I "part of the problem?" A college teacher wonders whether teaching about Muslim women promotes positive understanding, or just more manifestation. *Middle East Women's Studies Review, 11*(2), 11–13.

El Guindi, F. (1999). *Veil: modesty, privacy, and resistance*. New York: Berg.

El-Nahhas, S. (1999). *Egyptian women (in Cairo): Struggle for identity and citizenship*. Unpublished PhD thesis, University of Alberta, Edmonton.

El Saadawi, N. (1980). *The hidden face of Eve: Women in the Arab world*, S. Hetata (Trans.). London: Zed Press.

El Saadawi, N. (1997). *The Nawal El Saadawi reader*. London & New York: Zed Books.

El Saadawi, N. (1999). *A daughter of Isis: The autobiography of Nawal El Saadawi*, S. Hetata (Trans.). London & New York: Zed Books.

El Saadawi, N. (2002). *Walking through fire: A life of Nawal El Saadawi*. London: Zed Books.

El-Solh, C. (1988). Gender, class, and origin: Aspects of role during fieldwork in Arab society. In S. Altorki & C. El-Solh (Eds.), *Arab women in the field: Studying your own society* (pp. 91–114). Syracuse: Syracuse University Press.

Engineer, A. (1992). *The rights of women in Islam*. New York: St. Martin's Press.

Epstein, C. (1970). *Woman's place: Options and limits in professional careers*. Berkeley: University of California Press.

Erikson, E.H. (1968). *Identity: Youth and crisis*. New York: Norton.

Ernst, C. (2003). *Following Muhammad: Rethinking Islam in the contemporary world*. Chapel Hill: University of North Carolina Press.

Esposito, J. (1988). *Islam: The straight path*. New York: Oxford University Press.

Esposito, J. (1992). *The Islamic threat: Myth or reality?* Oxford: Oxford University Press.

Esposito, J. (1998). Introduction: Women in Islam and Muslim societies. In Y. Haddad & J. Esposito (Eds.), *Islam, gender & social change* (pp. 1–3). New York: Oxford University Press.

Farmer, L. (1996). *Informing young women: Gender equity through literacy skills.* Jefferson: McFarland.

Fenton, J. (1988). *Transplanting religious traditions: Asian Indians in America.* New York & London: Praeger Publishers.

Fernea, E. (1993). The veiled revolution. In D. Bowen & E. Early (Eds.), *Everyday life in the Muslim Middle East* (pp. 119–125). Bloomington: Indiana University Press.

Forrest, L. (1993). Feminist and friendship in a college education. *Gender & Education, 5*(2), 211.

Foucault, M. (1991). *Discipline and punish: The birth of the prison*, A. Sheridan (Trans.). London: Penguin.

Freire, P. (2003). *Pedagogy of the oppressed.* New York & London: Continuum.

Friedl, E. (1994). Notes from the village: On the ethnographic construction of women in Iran. In F. Müge & S. Balaghi (Eds.), *Reconstructing gender in the Middle East: Tradition, identity, and power* (pp. 85–99). New York: Columbia University Press.

Frontline. (2005). *Amina Wadud interview.* Retrieved July 31, 2005, from http://www.pbs.org/wgbh/pages/frontline/shows/muslims/interviews/wadud.html

Gaskell, J. & McLaren, A. (Eds.). (1991). *Women and education* (2nd ed.). Calgary: Detselig Enterprises Limited.

Gerami, S. (1996). *Women and fundamentalism: Islam and Christianity.* New York: Garland Publishing.

Gergen, M. (2004). Once upon a time: A narratologist's tale. In C. Daiute & C. Lightfoot (Eds.), *Narrative analysis: Studying the development of individuals in society* (pp. 267–285). Thousand Oaks & London: Sage Publications.

Ghadbian, N. (1997). Islamists and women in the Arab world: From reaction to reform? *The American Journal of Islamic Social Sciences, 12*(1), 19–35.

Gibb, C. & Rothenberg, C. (2000). Believing women: Harari and Palestinian women at home and in the Canadian diaspora. *Journal of Muslim Minority Affairs, 20*(2), 234–259.

Gill, M. (2003). Feminist literary theories and literary discourse in two George Lamming texts. In E. Barriteau (Ed.), *Confronting power, theorizing gender: Interdisciplinary perspectives in the Caribbean.* Kingston, Jamaica: University of the West Indies Press.

Ginsburg, F. & Tsing, A. (1990). *Uncertain terms: Negotiating gender in American culture.* Boston: Beacon Press.

Gocek, F. & Balaghi, S. (Eds.). (1994). *Reconstructing gender in the Middle East*. New York: Columbia University Press.

Goldziher, I. (1971). *Muslim studies*, S. Stren & C. Barber (Trans.). Chicago: Aldine.

Graham-Brown, S. (2001). Women's activism in the Middle East: A historical perspective. In S. Josef & S. Slyomovics (Eds.), *Women and power in the Middle East* (pp. 23–33). Philadelphia: University of Pennsylvania Press.

Green, E. (1998). "Women doing friendship": An analysis of women's leisure as a site of identity construction, empowerment, and resistance. *Leisure Studies*, *17*, 171–185.

Gregg, G. (1996). Themes of authority in life histories of young Moroccans. In S. Miller & R. Bourgia (Eds.), *Representations of power in Morocco*. Cambridge: Harvard University Press.

Guillemin, M., & Gillam, L. (2004). Ethics, reflexivity, and "ethically important moments" in research. *Qualitative Inquiry, 10*(2), 261–280.

Haddad, Y. (1978). Muslims in Canada: A preliminary study. In H. Coward & L. Kawamura (Eds.), *Religion and ethnicity: Essays* (pp. 71–100). Waterloo: Wilfred Laurier University Press.

Haddad, Y. (1991a). American foreign policy in the Middle East and its impact on the identity of Arab Muslims in the United States. In Y. Haddad (Ed.), *The Muslims of America*. Oxford: Oxford University Press.

Haddad, Y. (1991b). Introduction. In Y. Haddad (Ed.), *The Muslims of America*. Oxford: Oxford University Press.

Haddad, Y. & Lummis, A. (1987). *Islamic values in the United States: A comparative study*. New York: Oxford University Press.

Hamdani, D. (1991). *The Muslims of America*. Oxford: Oxford University Press.

Harding, G. (2000). *Our words, our revolutions: Di/Verse voices of Black women, First Nations women, and women of colour in Canada*. Toronto: Inanna Publications and Education.

Harding, S. (Ed.). (1987). *Feminism and methodology: Social science issues*. Bloomington: Indiana University Press.

Harding, S.G. (2000). *Our words, our revolutions: Di/verse voices of Black women, First Nations women, and women of colour in Canada*. Toronto: Inanna Publications and Education.

Harris, C. (2004). *Control and supervision: Gender relation in Tajakistan*. London & Sterling: Pluto Press.

Hashim, I. (1999). Reconciling Islam and feminism. *Gender and Development, 7*(1), 7–14.

Hassan, R. (1991). The issue of woman-man equality in the Islamic tradition (1993 CE). In L. Gorb, R. Hassan & H. Gordon (Eds.), *Women's and men's liberation: Testimonies of spirit* (pp. 65–82). New York: Greenwood Press.

Hassan, R. (1999). Feminism in Islam. In A. Sharma & K. Young (Eds.), *Feminism and world religions* (pp. 248–278). Electronic resource. Albany: State University of New York Press.

Hatem, M. (1993). Toward the development of post-Islamist and post-nationalist feminist discourses in the Middle East. In J. Tucker (Ed.), *Arab women: Old boundaries, new frontiers* (pp. 29–48). Bloomington: Indiana University Press.

Heggy, T. (2004). *Women and progress.* Retrieved May 18, 2005, from http://me-transparent.com/texts/tarek_heggy_women_and_progress.htm

Hendessi, M. & Shafi, R. (2004). *A response to Haleh Afshar's article in WAF journal no. 5.* Retrieved November 28, 2004, from http://waf.gn.apc.org

Hertz-Lazarowitz, R. & Shapira, T. (2005). Muslim women's life stories: Building leadership. *Anthropology and Education Quarterly, 36*(2), 165.

Hessini, L. (1994). Wearing the *hijab* in contemporary Morocco: Choice and identity. In F. Göçek & S. Balaghi (Eds.), *Reconstructing gender in the Middle East: Tradition, identity, and power* (pp. 40–56). New York: Columbia University Press.

Hill, D. (2003). Women and difference in Caribbean gender theory: Notes towards a strategic universalist feminism. In E. Barriteau (Ed.), *Confronting power, theorizing gender: Interdisciplinary perspectives in the Caribbean* (pp. 46–74). Kingston: University of the West Indies Press.

Hirschmann, N. (1998). Western feminism, Eastern veiling, and the question of free agency. *Constellations, 5*(3), 345–368.

Holland, D. & Eisenhart, M. (1988). Women's ways of going to school: Cultural production of women's identities as workers. In L. Weis (Ed.), *Class, race, and gender in American education* (pp. 266–301). Albany: State University of New York Press.

Hoodfar, H. (1993). The veil in their minds and on our heads: The persistence of colonial images of Muslim women. *Resources for Feminist Research, 22*(3/4), 5–18.

Hoodfar, H. & McDonough, S. (2005). Muslims in Canada: From ethnic groups to religious community. In P. Bramadat & D. Seljak (Eds.), *Religion and ethnicity in Canada* (pp. 133–152). Toronto: Pearson Longman.

hooks, b. (1989). *Talking back: Thinking feminist, thinking black.* Boston: South End Press.

hooks, b. (1994). *Teaching to transgress: Education as the practice of freedom.* New York: Routledge.

Hoot, J., Szecsi, T. & Moosa, S. (2003). What teachers of young children should know about Islam. *Early Childhood Education Journal, 31*(2), 85–90.

Ibn-Hisham, A. (1978). *Sirat an-Nabi.* Cairo: al-Maktabah at-Tawfiqiyyah.

Ibn-Saad, M. (1958). *at-Tabbaqat al-Kubra*. Beirut: Dar Sadir.

IRIN. (2005). *Razor's edge: The controversy of female genital mutilation*. Retrieved June 18, 2005, from http://www.irinnews.org/webspecials/FGM/45980.asp

Jacobson, J. (1998). *Islam in transition: Religion and identity among British Pakistani youth*. London: Routledge.

Jansen, W. (1998). Contested identities: Women and religion in Algeria and Jordan. In K. Ask & M. Tjomsland (Eds.), *Women and Islamization* (pp. 73–102). Oxford: Berg.

Jarviluoma, H., Moisala, P. & Vilkko, A. (2003). *Gender and qualitative methods*. London: Sage Publications.

Jawad, H. (1998). *The rights of women in Islam: An authentic approach*. London: Macmillan Press Ltd.

Josef, S. & Slyomovics, S. (Eds.). (2001). *Women and power in the Middle East*. Philadelphia: University of Pennsylvania Press.

Kahni-Hopkins, V. & Hopkins, N. (2002). "Representing" British Muslims: The strategic dimension to identity construction. *Ethnic and Racial Studies, 25*(2), 288–309.

Kandiyoti, D. (Ed.). (1996). *Gendering the Middle East: Emerging perspectives*. New York: Syracuse University Press.

Keddie, N. (1991). Introduction: Deciphering Middle Eastern women's history. In N. Keddie & B. Baron (Eds.), *Women in Middle Eastern history: Shifting boundaries in sex and gender* (pp. 1–22). New Haven: Yale University Press.

Kelly, P. (1999). Integration and identity in Muslim schools: Britain, United States, and Montreal. *Islam and Christian-Muslim Relations, 10*(2), 197–217.

Khalidi, R. & Tucker, J. (1996). Women's rights in the Arab world. In S. Sabbagh (Ed.), *Arab women between defiance and restraint* (pp. 9–21). New York: Olive Branch Press.

Khan, S. (2000). *Muslim women: Crafting a North American identity*. Gainseville: University of Florida Press.

Knobeloch, L., Salna, B., Hogan, A., Postle, J. & Anderson, H. (2000). Blue babies and nitrate-contaminated well water. *Environmental Health Perspectives, 108*(7), 657–678.

Kopping, L. (1993). *Gender and education: An analysis of factors influencing the academic participation of Chinese women*. Unpublished PhD dissertation, University of Iowa, Iowa City.

Kramp, M. (2004). Exploring life and experience through narrative inquiry. In K. deMarrais & S. Lapan (Eds.), *Foundations for research: Methods of inquiry in education and the social sciences* (pp. 101–121). Mahwah & London: L. Erlbaum Associates.

Kumashiro, K. (2003). Against repetition: Addressing resistance to anti-oppressive change in the practices of learning, teaching, supervising, and researching.

In A. Howell & F. Tuitt (Eds.). *Race and higher education: Rethinking pedagogy in diverse college classrooms.* Cambridge, MA: Harvard Educational Review.

Kvam, K., Schearing, L. & Ziegler, V. (Eds.). (1999). *Eve & Adam: Jewish, Christian, and Muslim readings on Genesis and gender.* Bloomington: Indiana University Press.

Leo, E. (2005). Islamic female sexuality and gender in modern feminist interpretation. *Islam and Christian-Muslim Relations, 16*(2), 129–140.

Lerner, G. (1986). *The creation of patriarchy.* Oxford: Oxford University Press.

Lewis, B. (1994). *Islam and the West.* New York: Oxford University Press.

Lewis, B. (1997). *The Middle East: A brief history of the last 2,000 years.* New York: Scribner.

Lewis, B. (2001). *Islam in History: Ideas, people, and events in the Middle East.* Chicago: Open Court Publishing Company.

Lightfoot, S. (1983). *The good high school: Portraits of character and culture.* New York: Basic Books.

Limon, J. (1989). Carne, carnales, and the carnivalesque. *American Ethnologist, 16*(3), 471–486.

Long, J. (1989). Telling women's lives: "Slant," "straight," and "messy." *Current Perspectives on Aging and the Life Cycle, 3,* 191–223.

Mabro, J. (1991). *Veiled half-truths: Western traveler's perceptions of Middle Eastern women.* London: I.B. Tauris & Co., Ltd.

Mani, L. (1990). Multiple mediations: Feminist scholarship in the age of multinational reception. *Feminist Review, 35,* 24–41.

Mani, L. (1992). Cultural theory, colonial texts: Reading eyewitness accounts of widow burning. In L. Grossberg, C. Nelson, P. Treichler, L. Baughman & J. Wise (Eds.), *Cultural studies* (pp. 392–408). New York: Routledge.

Manion, J. (2003). Girls blush, sometimes: Gender, moral agency, and the problem of shame. *Hypatia, 18*(3), 21–41.

Mann, C. (1998). Family fables. In M. Chamberlain & P. Thompson (Eds.), *Narrative and genre* (pp. 81–98). London & New York: Routledge.

Marcotte, R. (2003). How far have reforms gone in Islam? *Women's Studies International Forum, 26*(2), 153–166.

Markovic, M. & Manderson, L. (2002). Crossing national boundaries: Social identity formation among recent immigrant women in Australia from former Yugoslavia. *Identity: An International Journal of Theory and Research, 2*(4), 303–316.

Matsui, M. (1991). *A case study of female foreign students from Japan and the People's Republic of China at an American university: Change in their gender role perceptions.* Unpublished PhD thesis, State University of New York at Buffalo, Buffalo.

McCloud, A. (1995). *African American Islam.* New York: Routledge

McCloud, A. (2000). The scholar and the fatwa: Legal issues facing African American and immigrant Muslim communities in the United States. In

G. Webb (Ed.), *Windows of faith: Muslim women scholar-activists in North America* (pp. 136–144). Syracuse: Syracuse University Press.

McMurtire, B. (2001). For many Muslim students, college is a balancing act. *The Chronicle of Higher Education, 49*(11), A55.

McPeck, J. (1981). *Critical thinking and education.* Oxford: M. Robertson.

McQuillan, J., & Pfeiffer, J. (2001). Why Anne makes us dizzy: Reading Anne of Green Gables from a gender perspective. *Mosaic: A Journal for the Interdisciplinary Study of Literature, 34*(2), 17–32.

McTaggart, S. (n.d.). *The differences of being an Arab in a Jewish state: Case study on Palestinian women.* Retrieved May 30, 2005, from www.ittijah.org/pdf/mctaggart.pdf

Mehdid, M. (1993). The Western invention of Arab womanhood: The "oriental" female. In H. Afshar (Ed.), *Women in the Middle East: Perceptions, realities, and struggles for liberation* (pp. 18–58). Houndmills: Macmillan.

Mensch, B., Ibrahim, B., Lee, S. & El-Gibaly, O. (2000). *Socialization to gender roles and marriage among Egyptian adolescents.* Paper presented at the Annual Meeting for the Population Association of America, Los Angeles.

Mernissi, F. (1987). *Beyond the veil: Male-female dynamics in modern Muslim society.* Bloomington: Indiana University Press.

Mernissi, F. (1991). *The veil and the male elite: A feminist interpretation of women's rights in Islam,* M.J. Lakeland (Trans.). Reading & Don Mills: Addison-Wesley Publishing Co.

Merriam, K. (1979). Women, education, and profession in Egypt. *Comparative Education Review, 23,* 256–270.

Minault, G. (1998). Women, legal reform, and Muslim identity. In M. Hasan (Ed.), *Islam, communities, and the nation* (pp. 139–158). New Delhi: Manohar.

Moghadam, V. (2003). *Global feminism and women's citizenship in the Muslim world: The cases of Iran, Algeria, and Afghanistan.* Paper presented at the "Citizenship, Borders, and Gender: Mobility and Immobility" conference, Yale University.

Moghadam, V. (2004). Patriarchy in transition: Women and the changing family in the Middle East. *Journal of Comparative Family Studies, 35*(2), 137.

Moghissi, H. (1999). Away from home: Iranian women, displacement cultural resistance, and change. *Journal of Comparative Family Studies, 30,* 207–217.

Mohammed, P. (2003). A symbiotic visiting relationship: Caribbean feminist historiography and Caribbean feminist theory. In E. Barriteau (Ed.), *Confronting power, theorizing gender: Interdisciplinary perspectives in the Caribbean* (pp. 101–125). Kingston: University of the West Indies Press.

Mohanty, C. (1991a). Cartographies of struggle: Third world women and the politics of feminism. In C. Mohanty, A. Russo & L. Torres (Eds.), *Third World women and the politics of feminism* (pp. 28–47). Bloomington: Indiana University Press.

Mohanty, C. (1991b). Under Western eyes: Feminist scholarship and colonial discourses. In C. Mohanty, A. Russo & L. Torres (Eds.), *Third world women and the politics of feminism* (pp. 51–80). Bloomington & Indianapolis: Indiana University Press.

Mooney, S. (1998). *Women's activism: A case study of Egypt.* Unpublished MA thesis, University of Alberta, Edmonton.

Morsy, S. (1988). Fieldwork in my Egyptian homeland: Toward the demise of anthropology's distinctive other hegemonic tradition. In S. Altorki & C. El-Solh (Eds.), *Arab women in the field: Studying your own society* (pp. 69–90). Syracuse: Syracuse University Press.

Mukudi, E. (2002). Gender and education in Africa (essay review). *Comparative Education Review, 46*(2), 234–241.

Muslim Women's League. (1995). *Gender equity in Islam.* Retrieved May 20, 2005, from http://www.mwlusa.org/publications/positionpapers/gender.html

Nader, L. (1994). Comparative consciousness. In R. Borofsky (Ed.), *In assessing cultural anthropology* (pp. 84–96). New York: McGraw-Hill.

Nagel, C. (2002). Constructing difference and sameness: The politics of assimilation in London's Arab communities. *Ethnic and Racial Studies, 25*(2), 258–287.

Naseef, F. (1999). *Women in Islam: A discourse in rights and obligations,* S. Abedin (Trans.). Cairo: International Islamic Committee for Woman & Child.

Nashat, C. & Tucker, J. (1999). *Women in the Middle East and North Africa: Restoring women to history.* Bloomington: Indiana University Press.

Nimer, M. (2002). *The North American Muslim resource guide: Muslim community life in the United States and Canada.* New York: Routledge.

Noor, F. (2003). What is the victory of Islam? Towards a different understanding of the Ummah and political success in the contemporary world. In O. Safi (Ed.), *Progressive Muslims* (pp. 320–332). Oxford: Oneworld.

Omran, A. (1992). *Family planning in the legacy of Islam.* London & New York: Routledge.

Pai, Y. (1990). Cultural pluralism, democracy, and multicultural education. In B. Cassara (Ed.), *Adult education in a multicultural society* (pp. 11–27). New York: Routledge.

Perkins, A. (2002). Veil of tradition, veil of resistance: Islamic dress in contemporary Egypt. *Text, Practice, Performance, 4,* 65–84.

Poy, V. (2004). *The gender gap.* Retrieved July 22, 2005, from http://www.sen.parl.gc.ca/vpoy/english/Special_Interests/speeches/Speech%20-%20Zonta%20Club%2024104.htm

Proweller, A. (1998). *Constructing female identities: Meaning making in an upper middle-class youth culture.* New York: State University of New York Press.

Prus, R. (1996). *Symbolic interaction and ethnographic research: Intersubjectivity and the study of human lived experience*. Albany: State University of New York Press.

Qin, D. (2000). *Reweaving self: Changes in self-understanding among Chinese women graduate students in the United States*. Unpublished PhD thesis, Boston College, Boston.

Rahman, F. (1980). *Major themes of the Quran*. Chicago: Bibliotheca Islamica.

Ramadan, T. (2001). *Islam, the West, and the challenges of modernity*. Markfield & Leicester: The Islamic Foundation.

Ramadan, T. (2004). *Western Muslims and the future of Islam*. New York: Oxford University Press.

Rattansi, A. & Phoenix, A. (2005). Rethinking youth identities: Modernist and postmodernist frameworks. *Identity: An International Journal of Theory and Research, 5*(2), 97–123.

Rayaprol, A. (1997). *Negotiating identities: Women in the Indian diaspora*. Delhi & New York: Oxford University Press.

Read, J. & Bartkowski, J. (2000). To veil or not to veil? A case study of identity negotiation among Muslim women in Austin, Texas. *Gender and Society, 14*(3), 395–417.

Richardson, L. & Taylor, V. (1983). *Feminist frontiers: Rethinking sex, gender, and society*. Reading: Addison-Wesley Publishing Co.

Riessman, C.K. (1993). *Narrative analysis* (vol. 30). London: Sage Publications.

Roald, A. (2001). *Women in Islam: The Western experience*. London & New York: Routledge.

Roded, R. (Ed.). (1999). *Women in Islam and the Middle East: A reader*. London & New York: I.B. Tauris.

Sahgal, G. (1992). Secular spaces: The experience of Asian women organizing. In N. Yuval-Davis (Ed.), *Refusing holy orders: Women and fundamentalism in Britain* (pp. 163–197). London: Virago Press.

Said, E. (1978). *Orientalism*. New York: Pantheon Books.

Said, E. (1993). *Culture and imperialism*. New York: Alfred A. Knopf.

Said, E. (1997). *Covering Islam: How the media and the experts determine how we see the rest of the world*. New York: Vintage.

Sakr, A. & Al-Hussein, H. (n.d.). *Introducing Islam to non-Muslims*. Retrieved May 14, 2004, from http://bubl.ac.uk/link/linkbrowse.cfm?menuid=2616

Saroglou, V. & Galand, P. (2004). Identities, values, and religion: A study among Muslim, other immigrant, and native Belgian young adults after the 9/11 attacks. *Identity: An International Journal of Theory and Research, 4*, 97–132.

Sarroub, L. (2005). *All American Yemeni girls: Being a Muslim in a public school*. Philadelphia: University of Pennsylvania Press.

Schvaneveldt, P., Kerpelman, J. & Schvaneveldt, J. (2005). Generational and cultural changes in family life in the United Arab Emirates: A comparison of mothers and daughters. *Journal of Comparative Family Studies, 36*(1), 77–91.

Scott, J. (1999). *Gender and the politics of history.* New York: Columbia University Press.

Shabaan, B. (1995). The muted voice of women's interpreters. In M. Afkhami (Ed.), *Title, faith, and freedom: Women's human rights in the Muslim world* (pp. 61–77). London: I.B. Tauris.

Shahjahan, R.A. (2004). Reclaiming and reconnecting to our spirituality in the academy. *International Journal of Children's Spirituality, 9*(1), 81–95.

Shaikh, S. (2004). Knowledge, women, and gender in the *Hadith*: A feminist interpretation. *Islam and Christian-Muslim Relations, 15*(1), 99–108.

Shalhoub-Kevorkian, N. (2002). Growing from within: The de-colonization of the mind. In R. Lentin & N. Abdo (Eds.), *Women and the politics of military confrontation: Palestinian and Israeli gendered narratives of dislocation* (pp. 176–194). New York & Oxford: Berghahn Books.

Shami, S. (1988). Studying your own: The complexities of a shared culture. In S. Altorki & C. El-Solh (Eds.), *Arab women in the field: Studying your own society* (pp. 115–138). Syracuse: Syracuse University Press.

Sharma, A., & Young, K. (Eds.). (1999). *Feminism and world religions.* New York: State University of New York.

Shaull, R. (2003). Introduction. In P. Freire, *Pedagogy of the oppressed.* New York and London: Continuum.

Shilling, N. (1980). The social and political roles of Arab women: A study of conflict. In J. Smith (Ed.), *Women in contemporary Muslim societies* (pp. 100–145). Cranbury: Associated University Press.

Siddiqi, D. (1998). Taslima Nasreen and others: The contest over gender in Bangladesh. In H. Bodman & N. Tohidi (Eds.), *Women in Muslim societies: Diversity within unity* (pp. 205–228). Boulder: Lynne Rienner Publishers.

Siddiqi, M. (1991). *The modest status of women in Islam.* Lahore: Kazi Publications.

Simmons, G. (2003). Are we up to the challenge? The need for a radical re-ordering of the Islamic discourse on women. In O. Safi (Ed.), *Progressive Muslims: On justice, gender, and pluralism* (pp. 235–250). Oxford: Oneworld.

Smick, E. (2006). *Canada's immigration policy.* Retrieved April 2006, from http://www.cfr.org/publication/11047/canadas_immigration_policy.html?breadcrumb=%2Fbios%2F12310%2Felisabeth_smick

Smith, D. (1987a). *The everyday world as problematic: A feminist sociology.* Boston: Northeastern University Press.

Smith, D. (1987b). Women's perspective as a radical critique of sociology. In S. Harding (Ed.), *Feminism and methodology* (pp. 84–96). Bloomington: Indiana University Press.

Smith, D. (1992). Sociology from women's experience: A reaffirmation. *Sociological Theory, 10*(1), 88–98.

Smith, L. (1999). *Decolonizing methodologies: Research and indigenous peoples.* London: Zed Books.

Smyth, D. (1982). *Quilt.* Toronto: Women's Educational Press.

Solis, J. (2004). Narrating and counternarrating illegality as an identity. In C. Daiute & C. Lightfoot (Eds.), *Narrative analysis: Studying the development of individuals in society* (pp. 181–200). Thousand Oaks & London: Sage Publications.

Spellberg, D. (1994). *Politics, gender, and the Islamic past: The legacy of 'A'isha Bint ABI Bakr.* New York: Columbia University Press.

Stewart, A. & Malley, J. (2004). Women of "the greatest generation": Feeling on the margin of social history. In C. Daiute & C. Lightfoot (Eds.), *Narrative analysis: Studying the development of individuals in society* (pp. 223–244). Thousand Oaks & London: Sage Publications.

Stewart, K. (1990). Backtalking the wilderness: "Appalachain" en-genderings. In F. Ginsburg & A. Tsing (Eds.), *Uncertain terms: Negotiating gender in American culture* (pp. 43–58). Boston: Beacon Press.

Stowasser, B. (1993). Women's issues in modern Islamic thought. In J. Tucker (Ed.), *Arab women: Old boundaries, new frontiers* (pp. 3–28). Bloomington: Indiana University Press.

Stowasser, B. (1994). *Women in the Qur'an, traditions, and interpretation.* New York: Oxford University Press.

Strickland, D. (1994). Educating African American learners at risk: Finding a better way. *Language Arts, 71*(5), 328–336.

Stromquist, N. (1989). Determinants of educational participation and achievement of women in the Third World: A review of the evidence and a theoretical critique. *Review of Educational Research, 59*(2), 143–183.

Syed, M. (2004). *The position of women in Islam: A progressive view.* New York: State University of New York Press.

Tett, G. (1994). Guardians of the faith: Gender and religion in an (ex) Soviet Tajik village. In C. El-Solh & J. Mabro (Eds.), *Muslim women's choices* (pp. 128–151). London: Berg.

Tohidi, N. (1998). The issues at hand. In H. Bodman & N. Tohidi (Eds.), *Women in Muslim societies: Diversity within unity* (pp. 277–294). Boulder: Lynne Rienner Publishers.

Tohidi, N. & Bodman, H. (Eds.). (1998). *Women in Muslim societies: Diversity within unity.* Boulder: Lynne Rienner Publishers.

Toress, L. (1991). The construction of self in U.S. Latina autobiographies. In C. Mohanty, A. Russo & L. Torres (Eds.), *Third World women and the politics of feminism* (pp. 127–144). Bloomington: Indiana University Press.

Tsing, A. (1993). *In the realm of the diamond queen: Marginality in an out-of-the-way place.* Princeton: Princeton University Press.

Tucker, J. (Ed.). (1993). *Arab women: Old boundaries, new frontiers.* Bloomington & Indianapolis: Indiana University Press.

Tucker-Ladd, C. (1996, 2000). *Psychological self-help.* Retrieved May 10, 2005, from http://mentalhelp.net/psyhelp/

UNESCO Institute for Statistics. (2005). *Gross enrolment ratio in tertiary education— definition, gender parity index—definition, gross enrolment ratios tertiary education, world all countries.* Retrieved May 12, 2004, from http://www.business. nsw.gov.au/aboutnsw/labour/C12_gross_enrolment_tertiary.htm

Vidyasagar, G. & Rea, D. (2004). Saudi women doctors: Gender and careers within Wahhabic Islam and a "Westernised' work culture. *Women's Studies International Forum, 27,* 261–280.

Viswanathan, G. (Ed). (2001). *Power, politics, and culture: Interviews with Edward Said.* New York: Pantheon Books.

Wadud, A. (1992). *Quran and women.* Kuala Lumpur: Pernerbit Fajar Bakti Sdn. Bhd.

Wadud, A. (1999). *Qur'an and woman: Re-reading the sacred text from a woman's perspective.* New York: Oxford University Press.

Walbridge, L. (1997). *Without forgetting the imam: Lebanese Shi'ism in an American community.* Detroit: Wayne Sate University Press.

Walther, W. (1993). *Women in Islam: From medieval to modern times.* Princeton: M. Wiener Publishing.

Weiler, K. (2001). Reading Paulo Freire. In K. Weiler (Ed.), *Feminist engagements: Reading, resisting, and revisioning male theorists in education and cultural studies* (pp. 67–88). New York: Routledge.

Weitzman, L. (1985). Sex-role socialization: A focus on women. In J. Freeman (Ed.), *Women: A feminist perspective* (pp. 153–216). Mountain View: Mayfield Publishing Co.

Wesley, I. (2000). Multiple masculinities and schooling of boys. *Canadian Journal of Education, 25*(2), 152–162.

Whyte, J., Deem, R., Kant, L. & Cruickshank, M. (Eds.). (1985). *Girl-friendly schooling.* London: Methuen.

Williams, D. (1985). Gender difference in interpersonal relationships and well-being. In A. Kerckhoff (Ed.), *Research in sociology of education and socialization: A research annual* (pp. 234–267). Greenwich: JAI Press.

Winter, D. (1973). *The power motive.* New York: The Free Press.

Winter, D. & McClelland, D. (1978). Thematic analysis: An empirically derived measure of the effects of liberal arts education. *Journal of Educational Psychology, 70,* 8–16.

Winterson, J. (1997). *Oranges are not the only fruit.* New York: Grove Press.

Yahmed, H. (2006, April 2). *French commission recommends hijab ban*. Retrieved April 12, 2006, from www.islamonline.com

Yamani, M. (1996). Some observations on women in Saudi Arabia. In M. Yamani (Ed.), *Feminism and Islam: Legal and literary perspectives* (pp. 263–282). New York: New York University Press.

Youssef, N. (1977). Education and female modernism in the Muslim world. *Journal of International Affairs, 30*(2), 191–209.

Yuval-Davis, N. (1993). Beyond difference: Women and coalition politics. In M. Kennedy, C. Lubelska & V. Walsh (Eds.), *Making connections: Women's studies, women's movements, women's lives* (pp. 3–10). London: Taylor & Francis.

Zine, J. (2001). Negotiating equity: The dynamics of minority community engagement in constructing inclusive educational policy. *Cambridge Journal of Education, 31*(2).

Zine, J. (2003). *Staying on the "straight path": A critical ethnography of Islamic schooling in Ontario*. Unpublished PhD dissertation, University of Toronto.

Zuhur, S. (1992). *Revealing reveiling: Islamist gender ideology in contemporary Egypt*. Albany: State University of New York Press.